Praise for *The Once & *

"A scholarly and magical interweaving of and two women's sensibilities. ... Markham-Cantor brings to vivid life a sharp and independent woman, and ... in detailing her own research journey, she sets the destructive misogyny of that time in the wider context of witch trials before and since, in the United States and elsewhere. A compelling, eye-opening, and chilling read."

—SYLVIA BROWNRIGG, author of *The Whole Staggering Mystery*

"Through lively characters and fast-paced storytelling, Markham-Cantor transports us directly into the world of the Salem witch trials. *The Once & Future Witch Hunt* clearly shows that there is nothing exceptional about the conditions in which witch hunts arise."

—MIRANDA FORSYTH, director of the International Network Against Accusations of Witchcraft and Associated Harmful Practices

"The most vivid and accessible introduction to the world's most notorious witch trials that a newcomer is likely to find, and also a very timely warning for the present."

—RONALD HUTTON, author of *The Witch: A History of Fear, from Ancient Times to the Present*

"I could not put this book down. The author's remote ancestor becomes a real person, whose death by hanging was provoked by neighbors' claims of her witchcraft, encouraged by religious leaders. The modern cases listed show such beliefs occurring worldwide and generating similar responses."

—JEAN LA FONTAINE, author of *Witches and Demons: A Comparative Perspective on Witchcraft and Satanism*

"Alice Markham-Cantor has done a remarkable thing here. From the sparest bones of ancestor's story, she has fashioned a thoroughly engaging work of scholarship that is equal parts historical fiction, personal narrative, feminist theory, and a good old-fashioned detective yarn. In *The Once & Future Witch Hunt*, Markham-Cantor rescues Martha Carrier from one of the darkest corners of our nation's past. Her voice, and Markham-Cantor's too, will linger in your memory long after you've turned the final page."

—ALEXANDRA STYRON, author of *Reading My Father*

"In this fascinating and powerful look at the story of one family caught up in the Salem witch trials, Alice Markham-Cantor performs a kind of literary magic, blending fact and fiction into a form perfectly suited to the troubling subject matter and the limits of the historical record. ... Thanks to this indelible book, readers can imagine Martha's life and, alas, her death."

—ANN PACKER, author of *The Children's Crusade*

The ONCE & FUTURE WITCH HUNT

The ONCE &
FUTURE
WITCH
HUNT

A Descendant's Reckoning
from Salem *to the* Present

Llewellyn Publications
Woodbury, Minnesota

FIRST EDITION
First Printing, 2024

Book design by Christine Ha
Cover design by Kevin R. Brown
Interior illustrations
   Andover and Salem Village maps by the Llewellyn Art Department
   Martha Capo gravestone photo from Alamy (image ID JFMDN6)
   Murder wall photo provided by Alice Markham-Cantor
   The author with Thomas's grave, credit to Brackets Kaplan

Photography is used for illustrative purposes only. The persons depicted may not endorse or
   represent the book's subject.

Llewellyn Publications is a registered trademark of Llewellyn Worldwide Ltd.

Library of Congress Cataloging-in-Publication Data (Pending)
ISBN: 978-0-7387-7627-9

Llewellyn Worldwide Ltd. does not participate in, endorse, or have any authority or responsibility concerning private business transactions between our authors and the public.
   All mail addressed to the author is forwarded but the publisher cannot, unless specifically instructed by the author, give out an address or phone number.
   Any internet references contained in this work are current at publication time, but the publisher cannot guarantee that a specific location will continue to be maintained. Please refer to the publisher's website for links to authors' websites and other sources.

Llewellyn Publications
A Division of Llewellyn Worldwide Ltd.
2143 Wooddale Drive
Woodbury, MN 55125-2989
www.llewellyn.com

Printed in the United States of America

For Martha

"...less a history than a moral detective story."
—Victor S. Navasky, *Naming Names*

"Ghosts don't want to destroy the living. They only want to be seen."
—Jude Doyle, *Dead Blondes and Bad Mothers*

Contents

Foreword

It was in the middle of a plague that I discovered that I, like Alice Markham-Cantor, am descended from an accused Salem witch.

I was amongst those privileged enough to be locked down during COVID. After months with two adults, two kids, and two cats in a 700-square-foot Brooklyn apartment, my family had decamped for northern rural Maine, to the potato farm where my mother had grown up. It was there, curious about the half of my family that hailed from such remote rural climes—such a contrast from the Bronx Jews of my father's side—that I took a dive into my own family's history.

Several years earlier, a genealogically intrepid uncle had told me he'd discovered that we came from witches; I'd waved him off as a fantasist. But in those long, isolated evenings of autumn 2020, I would stare into the light of the ancestry.com website and watch as the marriage licenses, census records, birth certificates, and family trees confirmed my uncle's claim: I could trace my roots back to Salem in 1692.

As it turned out, so could the tiny Canadian border town in which I was living. It had been founded as an outpost of New Salem by Joseph Houlton, the great-great-grandson of Salem's Joseph Houlton, who defended the accused Rebecca Nurse and whose son John accused ten others, including Markham-Cantor's forebear Martha Carrier, of witchcraft. Even today, the small Maine town Houlton founded, and where I discovered my own familial ties to the mass murder that took place in seventeenth-century Massachusetts, is littered with the names of Salem: Putnams, Olivers, Bradburys, Goods, and Carys.

As a child, I had gobbled up the stories of the trials, read every novel I could lay my hands on about witches. My mother, a Shakespeare professor, had focused much of her scholarship on Renaissance ideas of the occult; her first book had been called *Heavenly Necromancers*; she had embarrassed me in junior high by coming in for a lecture on *Macbeth* and explaining what a "witch's tit" was. My own daughters skitter through the house casting spells and speaking in tongues, immersed in imaginative worlds of witches and wizards that contemporary children's literature has delivered directly into their bloodstreams.

In my professional life, in which I write about power and politics from a feminist perspective, covering #MeToo and progressive activist agitation and several presidential administrations, I found myself regularly writing about public figures eager to brand themselves victims of "witch hunts." Conversely, in feminist circles, there was a different desire to lay claim to this world: the writer Lindy West in 2017 promised in the *New York Times*, "Yes, this is a witch hunt. I'm a witch and I'm hunting you." In 2015, I attended a gathering of female-identifying political candidates, at which groups posed under a kitschy banner: *We are the granddaughters of the witches you tried to burn.*

Why are so many people driven to stake their claims to witchcraft? Why did I inhale those stories of Salem, what drew my mother to witchcraft in her studies, why do beleaguered abusers work to summon sympathy by calling back to grievous periods of injustice, and why did I get such a satisfying frisson in drawing a direct line between myself and some ancestors nine generations back? Why would any of us want a personal stake in history so gruesome?

Perhaps it is that question of magic itself, the alleged violation of the civil and religious and moral codes, the enticing suggestion that maybe someone, somewhere in our bloodline, *did* have the means to channel an inexplicable force. I supposed that many of us are drawn to magic, as some are drawn to religion itself, because of its ability to fill in yawning blanks in understanding, to help us make sense of the insensible.

We can blame terrible occurrences—plagues, sudden deaths, or tragedies—on something besides bad luck or happenstance or the human failures and malevolence from which we reflexively turn away. Similarly, many of us—perhaps especially women or gender-nonconforming people—linger with curiosity or longing on the idea of magic and the *power* it would offer...the promise of subversion, an authority not offered on the terrestrial plane.

"People are always looking for magic in Salem, even me," Markham-Cantor writes in this volume, describing the hunger her friends and family and strangers and, yes, she herself felt—while staring straight at a story of American brutality and injustice. It is perplexing, the animal, visceral yearning to believe in enchantment, in the supernatural.

Perhaps we seek the magic because we want it not to have been as ugly and base and despicably human as it was. Or maybe we want there to be magic—in some despicable part of our own human souls—because we want it to have been on some level justified. Or both. Because another way the figure of the witch entices is by so neatly embodying dualities. The witch figure is human and inhuman. We want accused witches to have been magic and know that they were mortal. The power we imagine we want them to have possessed compels and terrifies in equal measure.

It's all so knotty, so combustible and fraught. In this remarkable volume, Markham-Cantor cites the venerable socialist feminist Silvia Federici, who has herself written about historical and contemporary witch hunts, noting that capitalism—the force that provokes these panics—rests on exclusion. I could not help but consider that while capitalism and its discontents are a global plague, there is something particularly *American* about the way that capitalism, then stretching its roots deep into the very soil of the colonies in the seventeenth century, bloomed as a witch panic and mass murder in Salem.

Federici's point—that the exclusions of profit and production are the hallmark of this system—twins so neatly with the fetal nation's very character, the way that in centuries to come, American identity itself would be forged by the excluded, whose paths to inclusion so often rested on the act of identifying and excluding others. We are exploited and oppressed and then make our way by exploiting and oppressing others. This is America.

Perhaps some of this is why the story of Salem has such resonance, hits so many buttons for so many generations of Americans, perhaps especially for white women, including me and Markham-Cantor, people trying to make sense not just of our ancestry but of our place in the power structure. Is there any more ur-white women story than those young girls whose every cry and convulsion and allegation was taken seriously by a punitive state that otherwise took nothing about them seriously? The predominantly white women and girls of Salem were the violent perpetrators and also the victims of this tragedy; they were the afflicters and also afflicted by the same systems—church and state and their rigidly hierarchical community—that they made strenuous and often malevolent efforts to uphold and strengthen by pointing quaking fingers at those they could gesture toward as outsiders.

Late in this book, Markham-Cantor writes about the cognitive dissonance experienced by those descended from both witch and witch hunter. To me there could be no more perfect encapsulation of what it means to be American, for the vast majority of us are born of lineages stitched together of exactly these contradictions: descended from the oppressed and the oppressors, from enslaved people and those who enslaved them, from the poor and also those who profited on their backs, from the victims and the brutes.

For me, the dissonances of my own witch-related ancestry were clear from the second I discovered who my forebears were. Before I knew that Alice was writing this book about Martha Carrier, I discovered that I was descended from Martha's sister Mary Toothaker and her husband, Roger, each of them figures who were *both*, all the contradictions held in single bodies: victims and villains, accusers and accused.

Alice and I are distant cousins in calumny and convulsions, her story beginning with my eighth great-grandmother rushing to witness the birth of her ninth great-grandmother. Whatever it may augur, however meaningless the claim, it's true: *we are the granddaughters of the witches you tried to burn.*

—*Rebecca Traister, 2023*

Cast of Historical Figures

In Andover:
Martha Allen Carrier, a farmwife
Thomas Carrier, her husband
Their children by age at the start of the trials:
Richard, 17
Andrew, 15
Thomas Jr., 9
Sarah, 7
Hannah, 2

Faith Allen, Martha's mother
Andrew Allen, her father
Hannah and Sarah Allen, two of her sisters
Andrew Jr. and John Allen, her brothers

Ann Foster, a neighbor of Martha's parents, accused of witchcraft
Andrew Foster, her husband, deceased
Goody Lacey, her daughter, accused of witchcraft
Mary Lacey Jr., her granddaughter, accused of witchcraft

Deliverance Dane, goodwife

In Billerica:
Mary Allen Toothaker, Martha's eldest sister
Roger Toothaker, Mary's husband
Allen Toothaker, Mary's son
Margaret Toothaker, Mary's daughter

In Salem Village:
Samuel Parris, the minister
Elizabeth Parris, his wife
Betty Parris, his daughter, an afflicted girl
Abigail Williams, his niece, an afflicted girl
Tituba, an enslaved woman in his household, accused of witchcraft
John Indian, an enslaved man in his household
Mary Sibley, the minister's neighbor

Thomas Putnam Jr., a villager
Joseph Putnam, his estranged half brother
Ann Putnam Sr., Thomas's wife, an afflicted woman
Ann Putnam Jr., their daughter and a leader of the afflicted girls
Mercy Lewis, their maid, an afflicted girl

Doctor William Griggs, a doctor
Elizabeth (Betty) Hubbard, his great-niece, an afflicted girl

Susannah Sheldon, an afflicted girl
Mary Walcott, an afflicted girl
Sarah Bibber, an afflicted woman
Sarah Good, a beggar, accused of witchcraft
Sarah Osborne, accused of witchcraft
Susannah Martin, a widow, accused of witchcraft
George Jacobs, an elderly farmer, accused of witchcraft
Rebecca Nurse, a pious matriarch, accused of witchcraft
Francis Nurse, her husband
Sarah Nurse, her daughter
Mary Easty, her sister, accused of witchcraft
Martha Corey, accused of witchcraft
John Willard, a constable, accused of witchcraft
Joseph Herrick, a constable

In Salem Town:

John Hathorne, a magistrate

Jonathan Corwin, a magistrate

George Corwin, his nephew, a sheriff

Bridget Bishop, a tavern-keeper, accused of witchcraft

John Procter, a farmer and tavern-keeper, accused of witchcraft

Elizabeth Procter, his wife, accused of witchcraft

Mary Warren, the Procters' maid, an afflicted girl, later accused of witchcraft

Philip English, also known as Philippe L'Anglais, a merchant, accused of
    witchcraft

Alice Parker, a fisherman's wife, accused of witchcraft

In Boston:

Cotton Mather, a young minister

Increase Mather, his father, president of Harvard

William Stoughton, lieutenant governor of the colony and chief justice of
    the witchcraft court

Sir William Phips, newly appointed governor of the colony

Elsewhere:

George Burroughs, minister of Wells, Maine, formerly of Salem Village;
    accused of witchcraft

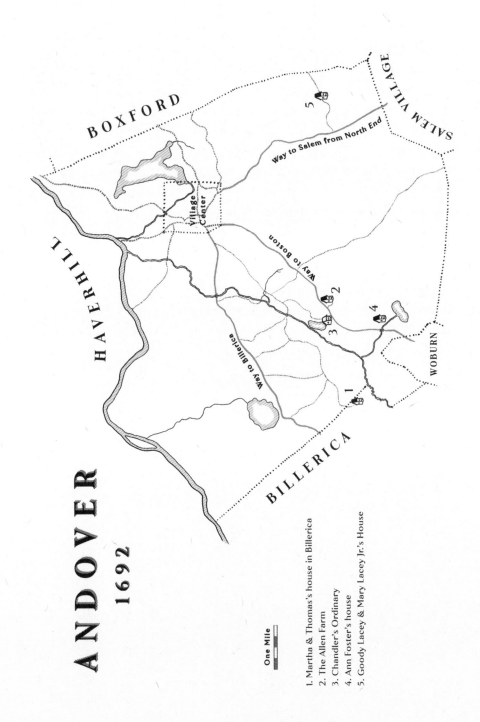

ANDOVER
1692

One Mile

1. Martha & Thomas's house in Billerica
2. The Allen Farm
3. Chandler's Ordinary
4. Ann Foster's house
5. Goody Lacey & Mary Lacey Jr.'s House

BOXFORD

HAVERHILL

BILLERICA

WOBURN

SALEM VILLAGE

Way to Salem from North End

Village Center

Way to Boston

Way to Billerica

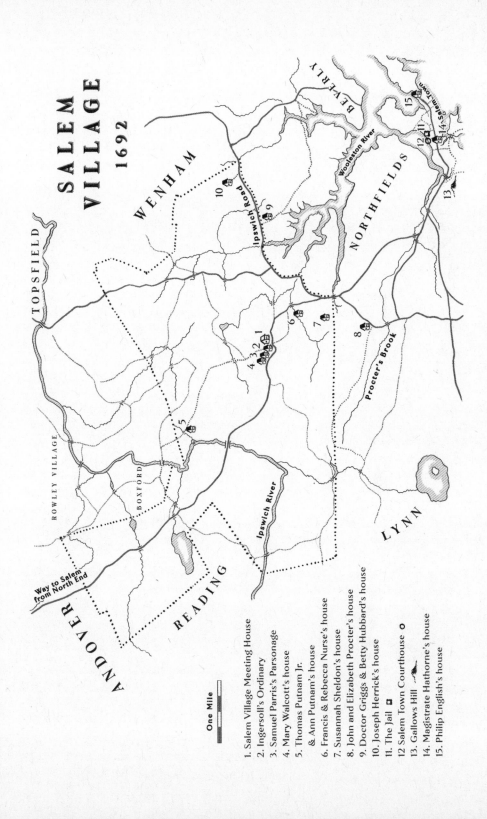

SALEM VILLAGE 1692

TOPSFIELD

WENHAM

BEVERLY

NORTHFIELDS

Salem Town

Woolleston River

Ipswich Road

Procter's Brook

Ipswich River

ROWLEY VILLAGE

BOXFORD

Way to Salem from North End

ANDOVER

READING

LYNN

One Mile

10   9   6   7   8   5   4   3   2   1   12   11   14   13   15

1. Salem Village Meeting House
2. Ingersoll's Ordinary
3. Samuel Parris's Parsonage
4. Mary Walcott's house
5. Thomas Putnam Jr. & Ann Putnam's house
6. Francis & Rebecca Nurse's house
7. Susannah Sheldon's house
8. John and Elizabeth Procter's house
9. Doctor Griggs & Betty Hubbard's house
10. Joseph Herrick's house
11. The Jail
12. Salem Town Courthouse
13. Gallows Hill
14. Magistrate Hathorne's house
15. Philip English's house

Introduction
Truth and Fiction

Salem is a story about stories—how they're created, whose are believed, how a good one can peel itself off the page or the tongue and float up into the world and, if caught by the right wind, travel great distances. In time a good story can become so diffuse that it no longer rides the air but becomes it. Stories are what we breathe, and they bring color into the world the same way that air pollution creates the most spectacular sunsets. And just like air pollution, they can kill.

To tell this story of stories I've written down two, alternating like the rungs of a ladder. Even-numbered chapters follow the life of Martha Carrier, my ninth-great-grandmother, and her death by hanging in the Salem witch trials. Odd-numbered chapters follow my own story as I grappled with Salem and what came after.

I wrote it this way because a fundamental issue of writing about witch hunts is that people tend to regard them as the province of the past. As the last major North American witch hunt, Salem exists in the popular imagination as the last witch hunt, period. But witch hunts—real, nonmetaphorical witch hunts, where people are harmed or killed after others accuse them of having magical powers—continue to take place weekly in our world. Understanding Salem's story as a single, if high profile, link in a chain changes how we understand what happened in the Massachusetts Bay Colony in 1692. And, perhaps, the awareness that Salem is one witch hunt of many can reframe our understanding of witch hunts taking place today.

The other reason I wrote it this way is that much of Martha's story can't be known or proved. Salem is like a run-down house: the foundation is intact, but the walls and roof are half-gone. Some damage is natural, accumulated over the centuries, and some is more purposeful, done by those who wanted Salem and her ghosts to be forgotten.

Still, the house stands. In many places the walls have been patched, either with serious scholarship or popular theories, and there's a fair amount of primary source material from the trials itself. Residents of Puritan Massachusetts kept diaries, wrote down their sermons, and maintained detailed logbooks for whole villages the way captains did on ship-crossings, as if whole towns never quite believed they'd made port. There are personal letters and legal documents, transcripts of some of the witchcraft court's proceedings, and descriptions of trials and executions by contemporary ministers and observers.

But this is a fraction of the source material that should exist. The witchcraft court in Salem kept an official record book, which would have recorded the trials in detail. It hasn't been seen in centuries. The minister of Salem Village kept a notebook on the conditions of those who claimed to be afflicted by witches. Only one page of that notebook survives. Most damning, the entire year of the trials is missing from the Salem Village Book of Transactions, the book that tracked all activity in the village. The book jumps from January of 1692 to the following December, neatly leapfrogging over the witch trials.

Those missing pages could be the result of a contemporaneous failure to keep records. Or it could be that the book was rewritten afterward by someone who didn't want whatever story it told to endure.

Either way, we're left with blank spaces in the record, holes knocked in the walls. We fill them in as best we can. We tell the story. "Our past is sedimented in our present," the philosopher Charles Taylor writes in *A Secular Age,* "and we are doomed to misidentify ourselves, as long as we can't do justice to where we come from. This is why the narrative is not an optional extra, why I believe that I have to tell a story here."[1]

Martha's story, as much as I can make it, is hers. At the beginning of each of her chapters, I note major influences and sources. All events in the trials (accusations, hearings, confessions, torture, executions) are drawn from the historical record, as are all births, deaths, marriages, and other major events in Martha's life.

In her chapters, too, I've attempted to stick to language that she and other Puritans would have used (e.g., *slave* instead of *enslaved person* and *Indian* rather than *Native American, Indigenous,* or the names of individual communities). I have also elected not to use the word *Puritan* in those chapters, as the Puritans did not call themselves Puritans. They understood themselves as Christians and tended to refer to themselves as "the faithful" or "the godly."

I have made only one willful change to Martha's story. In writing about her time under arrest, I placed her and everyone else in the Salem Town jail rather than in the Boston jail, Nathaniel Ingersoll's tavern (occasionally used as a prison), or various other holding locations. I did this in order to gather the players in one place and avoid switching perspectives too often. Forgive me. This is a true story, but it is still a story.

This is a story, but it's still true.

1
The Red Book

It started when I found what was left of Martha in the underground library. Most mysteries begin with the discovery of a corpse in some degree of decomposition. I didn't come upon a body, just a name. But in a case like hers, where the body was never found, a name is all we have.

The library was only in the basement but it felt deeper, the kind of place where the floor is perfectly level and you still think you're walking downhill. The skylights, reinforced glass set flush into the courtyard above, let down pillars of mellow autumn light that flickered whenever somebody walked overhead. If you looked up at just the right moment you could see a blurry outline through the glass, the shape of a person there and then gone.

I was fourteen years old, edging through the stacks, trying to muffle my sneakers. The soles were coming loose, and they had a habit of slapping on any smooth surface. My mother, who kept trying to take me to the shoe store, was somewhere nearby with my brother—we were all supposed to be touring Eli's favorite study spots—but I'd wandered off, so when it happened I was alone.

I still couldn't tell you what drew me to that particular shelf. The book itself was nothing special, a small red hardcover, the corners grayed and fraying, a laminated Dewey decimal code sticker peeling at the base of the spine. I have no memory of a title or an author, only its color, like oxblood, and the way it was so light in my hands that it barely seemed there. The pages were flimsy, the spine crackling as I smoothed them over. And then I saw her name on a page.

I didn't grow up knowing we had a witch in the family. None of my relatives did, and in retrospect this isn't a surprise: after the Salem witch trials were over, plenty of the affected families left the area and didn't necessarily talk about what had happened. Many descendants never even knew. When my grandfather found out, in his seventies, that he was descended from a woman who had been killed for witchcraft, he said, "Oh. Well, I hope she didn't hurt anyone."

"Dad," my mom told him over the phone, half laughing and half annoyed. "Witches aren't real."

"Oh," he repeated. "Right."

That conversation took place a year before I found the red book in the underground library. An uncle had been doing some genealogy research and discovered that one of our ancestors had died in the Salem witch trials. I remember bragging about it at school—to have a witch in the family was enough to be briefly cool in eighth grade—but aside from that, and my grandfather on the telephone, I have no memory of how anyone else reacted. I don't think we really reacted at all. It was as if the story flitted into the room, preened under our gazes, and then, without ever touching down, it darted back out the window and disappeared.

The first lesson: if you want the story to stay, you have to pay attention.

It was luck, I think, that she ever came my way again. Though there are those who say that *luck* is different than *coincidence*.

That day in the library, I hurtled through the stacks, sneakers slapping on the floor, and skidded to a halt in front of my family, clutching the little red book. "Look! I found her. *Martha Carrier.*"

"You can't run in here." My brother, Eli, plucked the book from my hands. "What's this?"

I grabbed it back, flipping to the right page and stabbing a finger into her name. "It's about Salem, and that's her, isn't it? Martha Carrier? That's the witch we're related to."

Eli frowned, scanning the page, and then shook his head. "I don't think so."

I stared at him. "No, but—I remember her name." I appealed to my mother, arbiter of all things. "It *was* Martha Carrier, wasn't it?"

She agreed that it sounded familiar, but she didn't remember the name for sure; we'd have to check when we got home.

It was too late. I knew that name. I *knew* I knew it. "I wonder who killed her?"

"The other villagers," Eli said, with the easy assurance of the older sibling. "Put the book back."

The Puritans in Salem believed that witchcraft could be passed down through the mother's line. If a mother or grandmother was believed to be a witch, a daughter or granddaughter was suspected to have a predisposition for witchcraft. But being a witch wasn't only about bloodlines. The potential for witchcraft might be inherited, but the practice of it, the becoming, was a choice.

According to testimony from the Salem witch trials, a person made that choice and became a witch when she signed her name in what they called *the devil's book*. What a witch was supposed to receive from the devil in exchange for her signature in his book varied. People said they'd been promised power, riches, or safety. A few said they'd signed in the throes of boredom. Whatever the individual enticement, the idea of signing one's name in the book persists, and some of the Salem records describe the devil's book itself. It was said to be small and red and full of power, full of dangerous names.

If I'm pulling too hard at the thin thread of coincidence, I'm hardly the first to fall prey to Salem's particular charms. "It's bad business meddling with the devil," Marion L. Starkey wrote in *The Devil in Massachusetts* in 1949. "It makes you superstitious."[1]

* * *

Everyone knows Salem's story, or thinks they do. Here is the skeleton: In January of 1692, two young girls in Salem Village began having fits, convulsing in ways that local physicians couldn't explain. After about six weeks of these fits, the girls—who happened to be the daughter and niece of the village minister—accused a handful of local women of witchcraft. Other girls in the village began to show symptoms and leveled accusations of their own.

Eventually the accusations spilled into surrounding towns. Over the course of that year, some 150 people were arrested for the crime of witchcraft in the Massachusetts Bay Colony. More than fifty of the accused ultimately confessed that they were, indeed, witches. Nineteen people refused to confess, were convicted of witchcraft by the court, and were hanged. Five more people died in prison, and one was tortured to death.

And then, at the end of 1692, Massachusetts Governor William Phips dissolved the witchcraft court. The entire affair, from the very first accusation to the order to discharge all remaining prisoners, lasted only fourteen months, but the Salem witch trials remain lodged in the national psyche. For the last three centuries, people have debated how and why Salem's witch hunt could have happened. Why so many were accused of witchcraft, why so many *confessed*, and how the accusers could have been so readily believed.

The answers to these questions shift with the times. Only a few years after the trials, clergymen in Boston attempted to explain what had happened in Salem as divine retribution: God had let the devil deceive the Puritans into bloodshed as punishment for their sins. In the nineteenth century, those who had been executed came to be regarded as Christian martyrs, people who had taken their faith so seriously that they would rather die than tell a lie. In the twentieth and twenty-first centuries, Salem has been variously explained as class conflict, geographic factionalism, the work of patriarchy, cultural provincialism, mental illness, encephalitis, hysteria, a bad acid trip, fear of Indigenous people, a reaction to capitalism, and the possibility that people actually *were* attempting to practice witchcraft.

A hundred explanations, all circling that single, irrepressible question: *How could this have happened?* With each answer, Salem becomes a different story, one that reveals as much about the author as about the witch hunt. Salem is less a history than a Rorschach test. When we tell it we reveal what we value, what we long for, what we fear.

* * *

When I found the red book that day in the library, I knew only two things about Martha: she was related to me and she was dead. I didn't have the words yet for why her name was in me like a fishhook, but here is what I suspected: that Salem, at its core, was a story about women and power. I'd been calling myself a feminist since middle school, read plenty of books about "strong women," but this felt different. Martha was real. And Martha was mine.

I found myself thinking of her whenever I pushed up against the walls built around girlhood. Found myself wondering if Salem's story was less a cautionary tale than an instruction manual. Somehow, Martha Carrier had become so frightening to the men around her that they regarded her as dangerous enough to kill. It was a terrible kind of compliment, but I was fourteen years old. I wanted to know how she'd done it.

Over the next few years, I did flurries of research, accumulating details and putting together the rough shape of Salem's story, but it wasn't until college that I took a real stab at understanding her. I pitched Salem as my senior the-sis, the capstone project required to graduate. A long paper would give me the chance to immerse myself in the trials, to answer Salem's irrepressible question: *How could this have happened?*

That question is actually the first strike of a one-two punch. *How could this have happened? What's to keep this from happening again?*

The second question is the real reason we tell Salem's story over and over. Each time we retell it, we can distance ourselves from the witch hunters. We tell the story as if we would stand up against them—though of course we don't need to, because Salem is a fragment of a world left far behind. The world has changed. We've changed. The monster under the bed died three centuries ago.

It would be comforting if it were true.

* * *

I wasn't thinking about this second question at the beginning. My focus was on finding out what had happened to Martha, because there were Salem's questions and then there was mine, the one I'd asked all those years ago in the underground library, holding the red book: *I wonder who killed her?* Embarking on the thesis felt less like beginning an academic project than being cast in a murder mystery, loosed with a hound on some dark cobbled street.

There wasn't any way to know how right that feeling was until much later. Not the grandiose hunting-dog whiff of it all—the part where I'd been cast. Where I had a role to play, and I was following the script like everyone else.

No matter how noble it felt, it started like any other research project: with a metric ton of reading. The university gave me a cubicle on the top floor of the old library with room for a desk, a spinny chair, a shelf, and a corkboard. I added a bag of salt and pepper kettle chips and a bottle of cheap whiskey for emergencies and got to work dragging books to the front desk, where the checkout girl did a double take at the titles: *The Devil in the Shape of a Woman, The Devil in Massachusetts, Day of Doom, Malleus Maleficarum* (a fifteenth-century witch-hunting manual with a number of unpleasant woodcuts on the cover).

When she got to *Entertaining Satan,* the checkout girl said, "This is for a paper, right?"

I got back to my desk and unloaded the books. There, the tower of musty paper and old glue—the sheer volume of what I didn't know and had shoveled onto my plate—was a little daunting. I took a sip of whiskey for luck, held it in my mouth until it turned to water.

But under the nervousness there was a kind of elation. The sense of a door cracking open, an unfamiliar wind washing through the jamb. The joy of arrival. It felt like I'd been circling this moment for years. And if there were only crumbs by which to track her, a trail of records twisting through the towns and forests of Massachusetts, I was optimistic. If fairy tales had taught me anything, it was that breadcrumbs in the dark forest nearly always led to a witch.

2
Traps and Rabbits

Puritan cultural ideologies and value frameworks are drawn from primary source documents and theological texts of the time period, including Cotton Mather's Magnalia Christi Americana *(1702).*

Mary Allen was on her knees by the kitchen hearth when she heard the screaming start. All her concentration had been on coaxing the tinder to catch, for the fire was her responsibility and she had let it go to ash in the night, having misjudged what it would need to stay alive.

When the scream ripped through the autumn dawn, Mary jolted, dropping the tinder. She leapt to her feet and ran, past the rough-hewn table and the pantry with its barrels of half-drunk cider, forgetting everything except the need to be near her mother. Behind her in the fireplace, the spark, ignored, caught.

Her father stood at the door to the bedroom, twisting his hands the way he did when the rain pained them. Mary went past him. Her aunts ringed the bed, speaking to her mother, their words merging under the sound of howling. Mary slipped through their ranks and tried to take her mother's hand, but it was clenched in the coverlet, her swollen body arching backward like a bow. One of the aunts pulled Mary away, toward the window, where the heavy shutters had been thrown open to let in the morning air.

The last time her mother had given birth, Mary had been too young to remember it, confined to her crib like her sister Sarah was now. This time, she was old enough not only to remember but to be afraid, as frightened as she'd ever been in her short life. Mary would, in fact, remember that morning until she died: her mother in the bed and the red dawn coming in through the window, the last bright leaves of autumn trembling on the maple trees outside. All that red, and the baby coming.

The infant was born wailing and didn't stop. Her mother, sweaty and tired, held her close as the women marveled at the power and volume of the cries. "Lungs to wake the dead," her aunt said, as Mary's father came in to touch the squalling, red-faced bundle with his fingertips. Mary followed him, creeping forward until she could touch her sister's wispy head with a careful hand.

It was impossible to imagine she had ever been so little, or so loud. She felt possessive, and the stirrings of pride, though pride was a sin. In addition to keeping the hearth, Mary was often responsible for her sister Sarah, and now she would be the keeper of both little girls. *My sister,* she thought, touching the red cheek with one nail-bitten finger, marveling. *Lungs to wake the dead.*

The novelty of those lungs wore off rather fast. The baby was baptized in the Andover meeting house, Mary and Sarah and their parents in stiff Sunday garb. The first frost of the season had crept in the night before and formed a thin layer of ice in the christening bowl, and the minister had to smash it with his fist before dunking the baby. When he lifted her out she was quiet, momentarily shocked into silence by the cold.

But she didn't stay silent for long. Never for long, and when she cried in the night more often than not it was Mary, never a good sleeper (too many nightmares), who rose from her straw tick to rock the baby back to sleep. And so, over the coming months, Mary Allen learned that noise had a human shape and a voice and a name, which was Martha.

Martha was small through her childhood, with dark hair that rose in the heat and eyes the color of freshly turned soil. She was aggressive from the start, either by nature or in reaction to her size, and had no sense of commensurate force; if one of her older sisters pinched her, she was likely to strike back with her teeth. Revenge for any slight was immediate, straightforward, and out of proportion.

It was trying for the rest of her family, but aggressive wasn't the absolute *worst* thing a child could be, her mother, Faith, supposed. The worst thing a child could be was dead. The second worst thing a child could be was impious, and Martha was nothing of the sort.

Like all the women of the colony, Faith was in charge of her children's religious education as well as their literacy, and she wove her teachings in and out of daily life. *You must not sin,* she told them as they carefully measured water and rye flour on baking days, as they helped her wring out the washing and milk the cows. *You must not fall prey to pride, nor arrogance, nor untoward pleasure. You must hold the Lord Christ Jesus in your mind and pledge to serve him.*

Martha took to her mother's lessons like the gulls in Salem harbor took to a strong wind, shrieking but with undeniable mastery. She learned scripture before she learned to speak in full sentences and read the Bible for as long as was allowed. And as soon as she was old enough to conceptualize the sin of lying, she could be counted on, if one of her sisters attempted to disown something they'd done, to tattle to their mother immediately.

Faith Allen appreciated this. Lying was not acceptable. No impiety was, for as followers of Christ, this was their covenant: they were sworn to God, and God was sworn to them. And if they broke faith, even for an instant, God would forsake them to the tender ministrations of the devil.

The devil was a real and constant threat, particularly in the New World, which was, as all the godly knew, his natural domain. He waited everywhere, Faith told her daughters—in the woods and in the fire, in the temptation for little girls to disobey their parents.

As a child, Martha was not, in fact, particularly inclined to disobey her parents. (Not yet.) She especially adored her father. When she was around seven years old, she began clamoring to follow him into the fields, and Andrew Allen, who had no sons until Martha was well into girlhood, acquiesced. He let her follow his plow, sowing the squash and nightshades behind him, and Martha came to field work in the same way she came to her sisters' skipping games and her mother's lessons: doggedly, loudly, and with a lot of blind faith.

When Martha was seven years old and a muddy whip of a girl, her father taught her how to kill rabbits. She was in the kitchen, pinching the bread dough—there was nothing more she could do to it until Mary returned with fresh water from the well—when she saw her father's silhouette pass by the window, and then his hat dipped, like he was sitting on the pine bench shoved against the outside wall where her mother sat to catch the last of the light for her sewing. Martha heard a long sigh and then a hush.

She was too small to see over the sill, so she dragged a three-legged stool over to the window and clambered onto it, holding her breath. Her father was right where she thought he'd be, his hat on the bench beside him. He was beginning to lose his hair, making a smooth circle at the back of his head that Martha resisted the urge to poke, and there was something in his hands, a bit of twine. As she watched, he fashioned it into a loop, fastening one end to a hooked bit of wood.

Then, head bent, her father said, "You may as well come out, girl. I expect you'll see little enough from up there."

She managed not to gasp or fall from the window. Before he could change his mind, Martha was leaping off the stool and scampering out the door, around the stacks of firewood tucked under the eaves, dodging the edge of the vegetable garden, bare feet slipping in the dirt.

She careened to a halt. Her father raised his eyes slowly, taking in the panting child with bits of hair coming loose from her dark braids and one sleeve pushed up higher than the other. He waited long enough to speak that Martha began to bristle at the possibility of a scolding—an unfair one, when he himself had told her to come out—but all he said was "Don't let your mother see you running."

Hardly a reproof at all; practically an invitation. Martha threw herself onto the bench beside him and looked expectantly at his bit of twine.

He held it up. "This is the noose," he said. "Do you know what the noose does?"

She nodded. It wasn't her first time watching. "Kills the rabbit."

"Aye. This end fastens to the hook—" He held up a piece of wood like a crooked finger. "Which sits itself right here." He held out another stick for her inspection, this one sturdier, with a pointed tip, and demonstrated how the two fit into each other. "The base goes into the ground. You've got to do it close to a young sapling, one that's not too fragile. As soon as a rabbit sticks his head through and knocks the hook away, the noose will pull tight. Give me your hand."

Martha frowned but did as she was told, sticking out her fist. Her father looped the twine around it and pulled slowly at one end, showing her how the string slid closed. Just before it drew tight, she yanked her hand back, letting the circle shut on empty air. "Can't the rabbit turn round?" she asked doubt-fully. "What if he's only looking?"

"He can't go anywhere if the tree's got him," her father said. "Once the sapling springs upright, he's done for." She frowned, and he demonstrated again. "The tree moves quick. If he so much as puts his head inside, he'll be caught."

"*I* see," Martha said, and mostly did. "You have to find the right tree."

"The right tree, the right earth, the right hook. Each piece of the trap must hold."

"What if one breaks?"

"Then," he said gravely, "we go hungry."

A voice snapped through the window. "Martha? Where *is* she; you take your eyes off that girl for a moment—"

Martha turned to her father, ready to plead, but he ruffled her hair. "Go on, then."

"Can't I stay?"

"No. And don't whine."

Martha slunk back along the side of the house, brushing off her feet. Mary was in the kitchen with the bucket of fresh-drawn water, her hands already in the bread dough, scowling. "It's sinful to shirk, Martha."

"I wasn't shirking, I was waiting for you. You took so long—"

"Where'd you get to?"

"I was with Father."

"Don't you go bothering Father."

"I wasn't *bothering* him. He was teaching me to trap rabbits."

"Martha Allen," Mary shrilled, "don't you even *think* of going into the woods to trap rabbits."

"I wasn't," Martha protested, and then frowned, distracted. "Why shan't I?"

"Don't you know?" Mary said archly. "There are Indians with big teeth in the woods, and they like to *eat* little girls. They'd find you tasty."

"They would not!"

"They would. And if they're not hungry when they catch you, they'll bring you to their master the devil, and he'll tear the tongue right out of your mouth."

"They'll do nothing of the sort," their father said through the window. Martha had forgotten about him. He was standing now, looking gravely in at them, a dark figure against the overcast white sky. "Mary, don't frighten your sister."

"But she has to mind!"

"She'll mind. Won't you, Martha?"

She nodded vigorously. Meant it, at the time. And then her father informed her that Mary had been lying, the Indians in their woods ate corn cakes like anyone else, and Martha screeched and splashed the newly-drawn bucket of water all over her sister's skirts.

"A lie," Martha's mother was fond of saying, "is a door for the devil to walk through."

Faith Allen was something of a poet, though she would have bridled at the suggestion, considering poetry a frivolous thing. But the floweriness of her language did nothing to temper its effect on her children; if anything, it lent power to her warnings. When Martha was quite young, she developed a mental picture of a little devil lurking outside the locked door of the farmhouse, slipping from window to window, whispering, wheedling, his voice twisting through the chinks in the planking. *Just turn the key,* he'd murmur. *I won't tell anyone if you don't, if you let me in to play.*

Martha told no one about these imaginings. It was a horrible omen to be plagued by the devil at such a young age, and from what she understood of scripture, such thoughts probably meant that she'd sinned in some inescapable way—by living, most likely, by having been born. She tried ignoring the devil in her mind, tried humming hymns or reciting verses. It increased her piety, certainly, but ignoring the devil proved useless. His whispers always crept through.

But there was one thing, Martha discovered, as she lay shivering in bed next to her sisters, that shut the devil up. It wasn't turning her back or plugging her ears. She had to keep an eye on him, point a finger wherever he tried to appear, and talk back.

I see you, she told him. Whispered the words at night, too softly for anyone else to hear. *I see you, and you are not so frightening. You can't get in unless I open the door.*

3
The Witch Question

As soon as I started researching Martha, young women at my university began to ask if I could do witchcraft. Just a little witchcraft, as a favor. A friend of a friend asked me to send her luck for an exam. A different girl wanted me to teach her to read tarot, and a third requested a recommendation for a reliable witch supplies store.

At first I was flattered. There was an undertone of female solidarity in the way they asked, and I liked the idea of being the campus wisewoman, the one you go to in the night for aid. It wasn't exactly a mystery why they were asking: I was talking about Salem all the time, and when people think of witch hunts, they think of witch*craft,* regardless of whether the two are related in a given instance. Plus—a subtler component, but one I couldn't dismiss—I was stumping around campus leaning on a copper cane, the aftereffect of an unfortunate encounter with a dengue mosquito the year before. Certain kinds of illness can lend authority, or at least help you look the part. I had apparently aged fifty years over the course of a summer; of course they saw the crone.

I wished I could tell them they saw true. It was with some regret that I admitted I didn't know any good witchcraft stores, my knowledge of tarot was limited to the googleable, and I could send out good vibes during the exam but that was really all I could offer.

Then came the fourth girl, and her ask was different. As I listened—her kitchen, after dark, the lingering scent of exhaustion and chamomile tea— I felt a growing unease. The fourth girl wanted to know if I could hex her ex-housemate, who had recently departed the apartment without suffering for the pain she'd caused. The fourth girl wanted revenge.

"Oh," I said, "um, no. Sorry. Out of curiosity, why did you think I'd be able to hex someone?"

"I don't know," she said. "You just sort of seem like you would know that kind of thing."

Walking home, I decided that being told I seemed like someone who knew how to cast a hex wasn't, on its own, so bothersome. (The wisewoman role always comes with the possibility of being seen as dangerous; in a culture that isolates women to control them, every woman who helps other women in the night is a threat to someone.) Nor was the girl's desire to get her revenge from a distance giving me pause, although my own preference has always been for close combat.

What bothered me was the simplest part: how easily she'd accepted I might have real power. How easily the role on offer had turned from *wise-woman* to *witch*.

This is a good moment to clarify how I define a witch. A witch, in this story, is someone who is believed to have access to systems of power that the bulk of the community does not have, and who uses this power to cause harm. Many cultures, including modern subcultures, also have a belief in people who use such power beneficially for the community. But the witch that I'm talking about is associated with threat. This kind of witch is a cultural role: a repository for fear.[1]

The witch role cannot be assumed by choice. It is inherently relational, because the witch is identified by—created by—those who define themselves as *not* being witches. The witch does not actually exist until an accusation has been made. Before she's accused, the witch is only a person.

But once she's accused, the individual disappears, her humanity stripped away. Accusing someone of being a witch is to redraw the boundaries of society with her on the other side. An accused witch is assigned the role of a person who has betrayed the social contract and is, therefore, no longer covered by it.

I wanted to know who Martha had been before she was a witch, back when she was a person. Plenty of people—including the girls asking me for magic—seemed to assume that Martha was, or could have been, someone who had the kind of power she was accused of having. A real witch, if you will. I wanted to get my hands on the woman underneath.

The problem was that all the information about her came from the trials, and the trial records were made up almost entirely of what other people had said. Martha Carrier left behind no letters, no diaries, nothing that she herself wrote down. She made it to the twenty-first century filtered through a sieve of other people's words—a neighbor who complained she cursed him out, a girl from church who said Martha scared her. But these weren't unbiased observers: these were the people who took part in her trial. Anything they said had to be considered for flaws, motives, lies.

Those early days of research saw me sleepless in the library, grubbing through accusation and rumor and trying to find the fire under all that smoke. I kept thinking about Orpheus. He'd never been my favorite myth, but I could almost see him, climbing out of Hades with a ghost at his shoulder. I felt an affinity. I felt like I was standing at the mouth of the underworld, trying to kick down the door, shouting, *I know you're in there! I just want to talk!*

The hardest part was the beginning of her life. Even if I could trust the trial records, none of them recounted her childhood. I had to take where she had ended up and extrapolate backward, which was like trying to figure out how someone had gotten from Brooklyn to the Bronx with only the hint that they'd transferred in Times Square—170 starting points, twelve possible subway lines, crossing in a hub where anything could have happened. I wanted some signposts. I needed a map.

What I had instead was Puritanism. The defining story of Martha's community, the air that she and everyone around her breathed. The Puritans arrived on the shores of Massachusetts in the early 1600s as a breakaway group of Christian fundamentalists from the Church of England. They believed in stripping away what they saw as the excesses of Catholicism, purifying the religion to the teachings of scripture. They hoped to make Massachusetts not only their new home but a new holy land. The Puritan project in the New World was to carve out a Christian society whose citizens would be guided by and responsible to the Bible, without the distractions that had plagued the Old World—dancing on Christmas, going to the theater, the usual frivolities.

The first Puritan colonizers were self-conscious of this project. John Winthrop, the first governor of the Massachusetts Bay Colony, famously said they were building a "city upon a hill,"[2] by which he meant that the rest of the world was watching. Whether or not the rest of the world cared at all is a matter of some debate. But Winthrop believed that if the Puritans succeeded in their project, they would stand as a model for other communities, a light for other nations to follow when things went dark.

And they expected things to go dark: the Puritans took it for granted that someday, probably not too far in the future, Armageddon would come. Sinners would be cast into Hell while a select few would be resurrected and elevated to Heaven.

But while they waited for the end of the world, the Puritans created a fairly modern society. They had a charter from the king of England—a document that granted them dispensation in the eyes of the British Empire to make their own laws, form their own courts, and otherwise govern themselves and colonize the land. The colony they built was bureaucratic, literate, and status obsessed. Only upper-class men were called "Mister," for example; lower status men were referred to as "Goodman" and their wives as "Goodwife," shortened to the ubiquitous "Goody." They were wary of outsiders, warlike toward the surrounding Indigenous nations, and oppressive to other Christian sects, punishing Baptists and Quakers for preaching.

They were also remarkably litigious, and inside their enclave-like towns, they commonly sued each other to resolve disputes. So it shouldn't be a surprise that Salem's witch hunt took the form of a series of *trials*. For a culture that saw theater as a sinful distraction from God, the Puritans absolutely loved courtroom drama.

Perhaps no one in Puritan Massachusetts saw the drama of the courtroom as clearly as a man named Cotton Mather. Mather was an up-and-coming young minister, son of the president of the new Harvard University and the kind of overachiever who would have been on every 30 Under 30 list in colonial Boston. He was, in many ways, Puritanism incarnate: a hardworking, self-obsessed, ethnocentric overthinker.

Mather lived in Boston, not Salem, and was only twenty-nine during the trials, but he has gone down in history as a major player. Some twentieth-century historians went so far as to blame him for the trials outright. He doesn't deserve that, but Mather did play a pivotal role in five deaths in Salem, and Martha Carrier's was one of them.

In 1692, in the midst of the trials, Mather wrote a book—a propaganda piece, really—called *The Wonders of the Invisible World*, which purported to explain what was happening in Salem. At one point, between the descriptions of accused witches and an extensive theological analysis, Mather described all of existence as a courtroom.

"There is a Court somewhere kept," he wrote, "a Court of Spirits, where the Devil enters all sorts of Complaints against us; he charges us with manifold sins against the Lord our God... whereupon he urges, Lord, let'em now have the death which is wages. ... Having first been an Attorney, to bespeak that the Judgments of Heaven may be ordered for us, he then also pleads, that he may be the Executioner."[3]

In Mather's view, humanity was on trial, God was the judge, and Satan was both prosecution and executioner. The devil was not only God's adversary but his tool, playing his part in spurring humanity along the road to godliness, afflicting them whenever they strayed from the right path. He needed permission from God to act, but often got it because humans were so fallible, so prone to sin. The cosmic struggle between God and the devil was between Good and Evil, but for humanity this manifested as crime and punishment.

Each time the Puritans broke faith with God, failing to live up to religious standards, Satan won his case and was permitted to send another misfortune upon them. And Cotton Mather thought that Satan was targeting New England in particular. It was widely believed that the Americas were one of the devil's last strongholds on earth; thus, irate that the Puritans were attempting to make it their holy land, Satan had reason to argue viciously against them in the Court of Spirits.

These otherworldly beliefs were reinforced by real-world "hardships," most prominently battles with Indigenous Americans.[4] Indigenous violence toward English settlements was, of course, often provoked by the actions of the British crown and the settlers themselves. The war with the Pequot in Massachusetts the 1630s—which left a mark on the Puritan consciousness to the point that Cotton Mather was still writing about it sixty years later—was precipitated by competition over the fur and wampum trades and a violent attack on a Niantic community by English settlers. King William's War, a war between the Puritans and the Wabanaki Confederacy (an alliance of four Indigenous nations in Maine and Eastern Canada) that started a few years before the Salem witch trials, was spurred by English expansion into Maine.

But the Puritans did not, by and large, understand the Wabanaki Confederacy or the Pequot to be actors in their own right, fighting for their political and economic interests. Instead, they tended to transpose the clashes of colonization onto their own cosmology, casting the settlers as servants of God and Indigenous people as servants of the devil.[5] In other words, the Puritans thought it reasonable that Satan might be angry that they were occupying his land but hesitated to extend the same understanding to Indigenous people. We see the enemies we look for.

Theologians long before Cotton Mather had identified the New World as the devil's home turf, or at least a place where Satan held significant sway. One such man was Pierre de Lancre, a judge in Bordeaux who led a witch hunt in 1609 in the Basque region of France. He burned seventy people at the stake in the span of a few months. De Lancre later wrote that he'd actually hoped to burn three thousand people, but he hadn't quite managed to pull that off. Still, seventy pyres were a lot for one witch hunt, made more striking by the fact that in the medieval era, witch hunts in Europe were exceedingly rare. Not to worry: de Lancre had an explanation for why there were so many witches who needed killing in France these days. It was because of colonization. European expansion and missionaries had driven all the "demons and evil angels" out of foreign lands like the West Indies and Japan and had "unleashed [them] on Christendom in large numbers" instead.[6] Those demons had recruited unprecedented numbers of witches in Europe, and now it was de Lancre's charge to eradicate them, a holy exterminator in an infested cathedral.

De Lancre wanted to be a witch hunter. I don't believe that Cotton Mather, working eighty years later and an ocean away, ever expected that he would become a more famous one, nor did he expect his name to become synonymous with the Salem witch trials. Mather wasn't overwhelmed with bloodlust. He didn't see witches everywhere he looked. His problem was different. He was a writer. He wrote himself into Salem's story until he was too deep to dig his way out.

Cotton Mather did this in part because he wanted to understand. His 1692 account of the trials is an attempt to detail how witches worked, how they made deals with the devil, how they called down ruin. He was sure that the whole cosmos could be explained in neat cause and effect, and he wanted to be the one to do it. As if he could control the narrative if he only understood it, if he wrote it down.

He failed, of course. The witch cannot be known with any certainty. It is one of the role's fundamental qualities. The witch's mechanisms—how she operates, where she draws succor—can be hypothesized, theorized, argued over, with different answers produced in different cultures, but the witch needs to be fundamentally unknowable in order to maintain the illusion that she was not created by society. She has to stay unknowable to stay dangerous.

To know a witch means one of two things: either she is not a witch, just a person, or you acquired your information through occult means. Either she is not a witch, or you are one.

It was my job to make Martha knowable. The most precious clue I had was a short file in the trial records, the transcript of Martha's "preliminary hearing" for witchcraft.

The Massachusetts Bay Colony had a multistep legal process. After an accusation, the accused would appear before a magistrate for a preliminary hearing. If the accused pled innocent but the magistrate nevertheless determined there was sufficient evidence to proceed, the next step was the grand jury. If the grand jury concurred that there was enough evidence, the final step was a full trial.

Much of Martha's court record no longer exists, but what does has been digitized by Benjamin Ray and the University of Virginia for the Salem Witch Trials Documentary Archive. In that archive is the transcript of Martha's preliminary hearing, a line-by-line record of her conversation with the magistrates. It is the only place where her words come through without interference, where the signal is perfectly clear.

I sat in the library and read that transcript over and over, the language crackling off the page. She said:

It is false.

The devil is a liar.

I am wronged.

It is a shameful thing that you should mind these folk that are out of their wits.[7]

For the first time, I could see her, a woman of little fear and less tact. She was of her time, certainly—she spoke about the devil in the hearing—but that didn't stop her from being dismissive and brash and angry, calling her accusers crazy, trying to shame the court. This was a woman who would curse out her neighbors, who would scare a girl for being disruptive in church.

Maybe the trial records would be enough to get to know her after all. If accusations of witchcraft are inherently relational—if two parties, accuser and accused, are required to create a witch—then I needed to know how Martha had related to her accusers. I needed to know what they had said about her, what they believed she had done. The witch has always existed in the eye of the beholder. But the woman underneath—her, I'd find by following her voice.

I went back to her upbringing. When Martha was in her late teens or early twenties, she ended up in the nearby town of Billerica, and I couldn't figure out why until I read about the practice of hiring out: sending children to the homes of relatives or friends to learn trades and discipline. Girls in particular often spent their teenage years living with another family, acting as their servant in exchange for room and board. Martha was older than most, but it would still have been acceptable, and her oldest sister Mary was living in Billerica by then with her husband, a man named Roger Toothaker, who had a side hustle as a folk healer.

My hunch is that Martha's parents sent her there in her late teens to live with her sister Mary *because* of the same voice that appears in her preliminary hearing. A tongue that sharp, that derisive, takes years to hone, meaning Martha would have been that way as a teenager, as a young adult, and she would have been guaranteed to loose it on neighbors and relatives alike.

So her parents sent her away. Maybe her mother hoped that Martha would learn to quiet down.

They should have known better. In Billerica, relatively unsupervised, Martha managed to get into more trouble than she ever had in Andover, for it was in Billerica that Martha set out on the path that led, twisting like a snake in a garden, to Salem.

4
The King's Guard

The information on Thomas Carrier's past comes from Rever-
end Henry Hazen's History of Billerica, Massachusetts, *with*
a Genealogical Register *(1883); see the next chapter for more*
information. The dates of Martha's marriage and the birth dates
of her children are attributed according to the records noted by
Hazen, Sarah Loring Bailey's Historical Sketches of Andover,
Massachusetts *(1880), and the New England Historic Genealog-*
ical Society's "Middlesex County, MA: Abstracts of Court Files,
1649–1675" online database (2003).

Billerica, Massachusetts Bay Colony
April 1672

Martha was of two minds about her sister Mary's house. It was newly built and set into a lovely meadow, but still drafty without caulking, and—most pressing—it contained Mary's insufferable husband.

"I don't mean to *criticize*," Martha told her sister early one morning as they headed into the barn for the milking. They'd left the older two of Mary's three young children in the house, and Martha had the toddler, Allen, hoisted up on her hip, as Mary was pregnant again and didn't want to carry him. Allen was babbling something about cows, pulling at Martha's ear. She flicked him away and added, "It's only that I've been thinking about it all night."

"You always mean to criticize," Mary said dryly. "Go on, then."

Martha snagged the milking pails in one hand, managing Allen with the other. "Roger wants his supper at sunset—very well. He's entitled to that."

"Indeed?"

"Of course. He's even entitled to scold you if supper isn't ready at the proper time."

"Mm."

"But it's absurd to demand such a thing when he doesn't even come *home*," Martha finished. "He's always off—practicing his healing, I *know*, neither of you will let me forget—but it isn't fair to scold you if you don't even know when he'll be there."

"It isn't about fairness." Mary eased onto the stool with a hand on her back. "It's about duty."

"He doesn't do *his* duty. The way he runs this farm—"

"And I suppose you think you'd do better?"

"I might. Father taught me—"

"Not much, in the scheme of things," Mary cut in. "You know how to plant a few seeds, and you think you could take on the running of a farm. What makes you think you have any kind of right to pass judgment upon others? Upon my husband?"

"Well," Martha snapped, *"someone* has to."

She stepped back as Mary wet the cow's udders and began to coax the milk free. "Mind your own household, Martha, won't you? Oh, I'd forgotten. You haven't got one."

Martha made a face at her sister and plopped her little nephew down on the ground. Allen immediately crawled over to a pile of hay with the clear intent of burying his head inside it.

"Martha," Mary snapped, "get the child."

"I thought you wanted me to mind my own household," Martha said, as Allen gleefully dug his face into the haystack.

They had variations on the same argument for weeks. Mary called Martha childish; Martha told Mary that allowing anyone to shirk their duty in the home, even her husband, was neglect of a woman's responsibility. Mary offered that they could agree to disagree; Martha declined.

Eventually Mary decided it would be better for everyone if Martha spent more time away from the farmhouse. If she couldn't see her brother-in-law's shortcomings, she wouldn't argue about them. She had Martha take on the vegetable garden instead. "Since you're good in the fields," Mary told her.

Martha brushed off the jab. Instead, she decided, on her first day of weeding, she would use the opportunity to prove to her sister that she *had* learned from her father well enough, that she *did* know what she was talking about when she critiqued the way that Mary's husband ran his farm. She would show them both.

She took to walking the nearby fields whenever she had a free moment, trying to watch the other farmers work. She weeded and watered and weeded some more. Some of her squash rotted, and her cucumbers were small and knobby, but when the first tomatoes ripened, blood-warm from the sun, she felt such a wave of pride that she went to her knees in the dirt to repent.

Then she brought them in, cradled in her apron, and placed them carefully on the table before Mary in a glorious pile of red. "There," she said, the word sweet as anything she'd grown.

She was still buzzing with success two days later when she and Mary were kneading bread in the kitchen, and Roger came in to announce that someone had bewitched his best ram.

The ram had gone suddenly lame. Roger's theory was that one of the old women who plied their trades as healers had been jealous of his success—he was the best folk physicker in town, and everyone knew it—and cast the evil eye upon him.

Before Mary could say a word, Martha interrupted. Witchcraft was certainly a possibility, though privately she didn't think any of the old healers would be jealous of Roger, who was hardly as well regarded as he made out. More to the point, she was flush with farm-knowledge and suspected the ram was hobbling for a simpler reason: with all the healing work that Roger been doing away from home, it had been too long since he had properly trimmed the animal's hooves. She turned to her sister. "Isn't that possible?"

Mary pressed her lips together and said nothing. Roger flushed red. "Hold your tongue."

"I'll do no such thing," Martha snapped back, needled by Mary's silence as much as Roger's words. "How would you know if something had happened? You've been away. It could've caught its leg. It—"

Martha's mother had told her daughters stories of the brank, a tool used in England to muzzle a loud or disobedient woman. It was a metal cage about the head, with an iron tongue that sat upon a woman's tongue with a nail, pointing downward, that would pin the tongue and tear it if she tried to speak. They didn't have branks in Massachusetts. Roger hit her across the face instead.

Martha went out into the fields, her jaw aching. She found the ram and trimmed his hoof with her own dull knife, though as it turned out it didn't need much trimming. That only made her angrier, and she sent the indignant animal off into the pasture.

The idea of going back to the farmhouse was still intolerable, so she let her feet pick their own path through the fields. It was late afternoon, the air thick as honey. Brown and black-spotted finches cheeped and darted from the nearby trees. Martha walked until she caught sight of some stalks of wild garlic and began gathering their bulbs into her apron pockets, letting the hot press of sunlight on her neck melt the edges of her anger.

She gathered the last of the garlic and stretched as the sun sank toward the horizon, a glowing coin dropped into cloudy water. The Toothaker farm stood at the edge of Billerica, its fields hacked out of forest and brush, only a few miles from an Indian settlement that traded pleasantly enough with the town but gave Mary perpetual nightmares. It was not wise for a young woman to linger in the fields at dusk—at least, that was what Mary would have said—but Martha closed her eyes and breathed deeply. If Mary wanted her, she could come and get her.

"Miss?"

Martha's eyes snapped open. She took a step back, nearly stumbling over a rut in the field. A man was approaching—a man, but he seemed a mountain. He was enormous, so tall she had to crane her neck back to see his face, shoulders and chest absurdly broad under brown homespun. He carried an ax in one hand as easily as another man might carry a hammer.

He slowed, then stopped as she found her footing. "Forgive me if I startled you." He spoke with an accent, something craggy and lilting. A foreigner, recent come. Under a thatch of black hair, his face was unremarkable, mouth half buried in a thick beard. "Are you well?"

"I've seen you in meeting," she told him. Announced it, rather, to cover the surprise of his sudden appearance. She had seen him in the weekly church meeting more than once, sitting quietly with one of the Billerica households, though she'd never heard him speak.

He inclined his head. "Indeed, I've been there."

"What's your name?"

"Thomas Carrier, miss. Brush cutter for Master William Chamberlain."

"And what are you doing here, Thomas Carrier, brush cutter for William Chamberlain?"

"Why, cutting brush, miss."

"I see no brush."

"Left it in the forest," he said, not seeming at all put out by her interrogation. "But I saw you out here alone and hoped nothing was amiss."

"I'm quite well."

He hoisted the ax up over his shoulder. "Very good. If you'll excuse me, then, I'm to get that brush in afore dark."

Martha blinked as he turned to go. "You aren't going to ask what *I'm* doing here?"

He glanced back. "Should I?"

"If you're William Chamberlain's man, *shouldn't* you?" she challenged. Any self-respecting godly man would be curious as to what she was doing wandering about. "What if I was here to"—she cast around—"steal Master Chamberlain's brush?"

Thomas Carrier grinned, a startling, unashamed flash of teeth behind the beard. "At that size, I don't think you could carry much of it," he said. "I would hardly begrudge you a few sticks."

"I could carry more than a few *sticks*."

He looked her up and down. "Could you?"

Which was how she found herself helping him to haul his load of brush back to Chamberlain's homestead, knowing she'd been tricked into it but too stubborn to back down.

"Tell you the truth," Carrier was saying as he kept pace beside her, despite the fact that his bushel was roughly four times larger, "I had thought you were out there for some peace and quiet." She shot him a look, which he met without judgment. "You're the Allen girl, are you not? Goodwife Toothaker's sister?"

"And that means I'd need peace and quiet?"

"I heard Goody Toothaker was recently blessed with another baby."

"I would not have thought you to be such a gossip, Mister Carrier."

"Carrier," he grunted. "I'm no Mister."

Dusk was drawing over the woods, making it hard to tell his expression. Mary would be angry that she wasn't home already, but Martha, examining the feeling, found that she didn't care. Fancy that. "The baby's not so difficult. I've been reading him the Bible."

"He likes that?"

"He can't understand it at all. But it helps him to sleep, and it passes the time."

"Aye, I've heard it does."

"Don't you like reading?"

"Never learned, miss."

"Never?" All children in the colony learned to read, unless they proved incapable. "Why not?"

"No one taught me, I suppose. Do you read the baby any other books?"

"Mary hasn't any others."

"At least the child'll have a head start on living here."

Something about the way he said it made her eye him. "Do you dislike the attention we pay to Christ here?"

"It's only that I'm unaccustomed to it."

"Do you come from such a godless place?"

"Aye. Heard of Wales?"

She laughed, couldn't help it. "Mister Carrier—"

"I told you, I'm no—"

"I heard you," she said, "but it felt rather unmannerly to only call you Carrier."

"Thomas, then."

"Thomas," she repeated. It was brazen of him, but she wasn't about to be outdone. "My name is Martha. You should learn to read."

They had reached the road, turning toward town. It was full night, now, but Martha had never been as frightened of the dark as Mary. A flight of bats whipped overhead and away.

"I'm old for it," Thomas Carrier said, and Martha shook her head.

"I don't believe that's inhibitory. I'll teach you."

"Miss," he said, stopping before a well-appointed house that Martha vaguely recognized as William Chamberlain's. "I cannot—"

"Everyone should be able to read the word of God," Martha told him. "Welshmen included."

"Miss Allen—"

"You were right," she told him. "I *did* need peace and quiet. What better way to find some than to spend time with the Good Book?"

Martha wasn't entirely sure why she wanted him to say yes, but she decided that it was the promise of not being bored for a long while, the promise of having something to do apart from waiting in Mary's house, trying to control her temper.

"There's a shed behind Captain Danforth's barn," she said. "He doesn't use it. If you'd like to learn, meet me there tomorrow two hours afore sunset. And if you wouldn't like to"—she heaved the load of firewood off her shoulders and dropped it in the road with a *thunk*—"well, the Lord knows I'll have done my best."

Thomas learned slowly. In the shed behind Danforth's barn, Martha showed him the letters and how to sound out the words, and for a while at the end of each session she read aloud to him. Mary allowed Martha to carry the Bible day-to-day with her—her love for it was neither feigned nor secret—and Martha discovered that she liked reading aloud. She enjoyed the physical pleasure of speaking, of shaping language with tongue and teeth, and hearing her own voice slide out into the quiet of the shed and coil around itself until there was something shimmering and half-seen in the air. Wind came through the cracks in the shed walls and light moved around the edges of the door and time didn't seem to pass at all. Thomas would lie back with a straw in his mouth, his eyes on her face or fixed on a distant point, and listen, and sometimes she found herself so animated in the reading that he had to hush her when footsteps came near. It was the only time she didn't mind being silenced.

When they passed each other in the street, they nodded politely and continued without speaking, Martha's stomach fluttering with the sweet-bad risk of discovery long before they ever did anything illicit. He didn't steal his first kiss until the story of Daniel, and they did not lie together. Thomas wasn't established in Massachusetts, and she knew her parents would never agree to a match between their daughter and a Welsh laborer. He was a foreigner, barely more than an indentured servant, hardly one of God's children, and twice her age.

Martha didn't care. He made her laugh, which was something she'd never done much of, and he was gentle with her, with the world, in a way that only people who have been grooved by violence can be.

She was aware from the beginning that there were stories told about Thomas. He was simply too tall to ignore, like a giant from a folktale come to life, and while his scars weren't unusual—to be unscarred was the province of young men and unmarried women—he had deep gouges in his arms and across the backs of his hands that could only have come from a knife. Another along his scalp looked as if it had come close to slicing his ear clean off. And he handled his ax like a tree handled its branches.

She was aware that there were stories told, but she didn't seek them out, which would have been suspicious. She assumed that gossip about Thomas Carrier had bought many a pint at the ordinary when he'd first come to town, but the chatter had quieted by the time she herself arrived. The colony had no shortage of those who hoped to leave behind their reasons for making the journey to the New World, after all. There was an ocean between the present and the past, and without much difficulty a man could persuade himself that what was on the far shore didn't matter.

Unless, of course, he was repeatedly pestered by a young woman who took silence as a personal affront. Martha didn't seek out Thomas's story's story from *other* people. She asked the man himself, coaxing out fragments over the course of that autumn and winter in fits and starts, like a rusty gate creaking open on a disused path. Yes, he had been in the army—yes, he had seen battle— yes, he had been in the great war.

By spring, Martha wanted the whole story. "Thomas," she commanded. "Tell me why you came to Massachusetts. If I'm going to marry you I need to know."

She hadn't warned him, but he took it well enough in stride: His eyebrows rose, and for a long moment he was quiet. And then Thomas said, "Fair enough."

And he began to tell her quietly what had happened, and Martha realized that she, in fact, was the one who had been unprepared.

He had been born in a village in Wales. His name back then was Thomas Morgan, he informed her. There was an obvious career for a boy built like him, so as a young man, he went north and joined the Royal Army of King Charles I.

When he was twenty, he was placed in the king's personal guard. It wasn't anything he'd earned, he was careful to say, only the captain had wanted a man whom he could plant behind the king like a tree, and he'd been the right size.

The king wasn't particularly easy to guard. He was blunt and arrogant and didn't know how to back away from a fight. He'd dissolved Parliament before Thomas was born, making himself the target of more than a few furious noblemen and most of the merchant class. But he was the king, by divine right, God's holy and anointed ruler, and Thomas had the honor of protecting him. It was more than an honor. It was a life's purpose. How many men of twenty could claim to have one?

Thomas was no one special, a Welsh soldier, unusually tall but not particularly ambitious and certainly not meant for the annals of history. If his king had been a little more conciliatory, he would have guarded him until one of them died of old age or dysentery.

But the king pushed too far. The English Civil War broke the kingdom into pieces. By the time it was over, there were horses rotting in the streets, flies swarming in the gutters and the fields, and Thomas's king had lost.

The Parliamentary Army sentenced King Charles I to death by beheading. It was 1649. Thomas was twenty-three years old.

On a freezing afternoon in January, the stench of the sewage-filled Thames dulled by cold, the ax swung in front of the Palace of Whitehall. The king's head rolled, his blood spurting over two layered shirts. Thomas could see the blood on those shirts if he closed his eyes. He could hear the crowd cheering.

"He asked me to," Thomas said, low and rough, as Martha sat in the shed with her heart thudding in her throat. "Understand? And when I refused he ordered me."

He stopped. There was silence, and the wind outside.

"It is difficult to kill a man that way," Thomas said finally. "But he had seen me do it afore, and he knew I would do it clean."

For possibly the first time in her life, Martha found herself entirely lost for words. She had not been taught to love the dead king, the man Thomas had served, but she'd also never quite understood him to be real. He was a part of history, and now history was sitting in front of her in Danforth's shed and telling her he had wielded the ax.

Of course he hadn't told her details, she realized. It was horribly dangerous that he was telling her now.

Thomas waited. When Martha could speak, she said, "What did you do then?"

"Stayed for a while. Took a ship for the colonies."

"To Massachusetts."

"Nova Scotia."

"Nova Scotia? Why?"

"That's where the ship was bound."

"But," she said, "how did you—"

"Word came that Charles's son had clambered his way back onto the throne. England was whole again." He looked at his hands, loose in his lap. "I knew that boy, see. He wasn't a boy, we're of an age, but he'd been rather droopy-faced, and I always thought of him as younger. But—if I remembered him, there was a chance—I thought—he'd remember me."

When she said nothing, he glanced up with a flash of dark humor. "Conceited, I know."

"Wise," she corrected. "And then?"

"I walked."

She stared at him. "From Nova Scotia."

"Aye. And when I came out of the woods I gave my name as Carrier."

Why? Martha wanted to ask. *What is it that you carry?* But she could imagine. A lost kingdom, the memory of its lost king, small and fierce and arrogant, and loved, and dying.

Hoping to comfort him, she said, as she'd been taught, "He was no rightful king."

As soon as the words were spoken, she wished she could take them back. She fought the urge to look away from the expression on Thomas's face.

"He was God's king," Thomas said quietly. "And he was mine."

There was a long silence. Finally Martha asked, hesitantly, "If you had not agreed, would you not have been killed as well?"

"Does it matter? I would have died for him."

She'd thought Thomas hadn't told her because it was dangerous for any-one to know, but it occurred to her that the truth was something simpler and far more jagged. He was ashamed. What he had done to his king had broken him, in some bone-deep fashion, and he had healed crooked. She couldn't imagine it—being ready to die for someone, and being made to kill them instead. What would that do to a person?

He was showing her what it had done to him. The trust made her knees weak.

Well, Martha thought, overwhelmed. I've got to marry him now, haven't I?

After that it was all strategy. She said nothing of marriage that next spring and summer as she helped Mary with the house and the children, but by the time autumn came around, and her twenty-first birthday, Martha knew that her mother was beginning to sniff out a husband.

She went home to the old farmhouse in Andover to make her appeal. She bowed her head, aware of her parents only at the edges of her vision. Her mother, slender and white-haired and shrewd; her father, stocky and balding and utterly unreadable. He confided in her younger brothers now, not her. "Mother, Father. I have tidings."

"What tidings?" Faith put aside her knitting. "Mary hasn't told us."

"Mary, ah, does not know." She cleared her throat.

"Go ahead, child," her father said.

She told them she wanted to marry.

She told them whom she wanted to marry.

Martha rode back to Billerica the next day with her throat closed and her stomach churning. Her mother's voice, low and sharp, still throbbing in her ears. *A shameful thing, that you would consider this!*

It was over; it would have to be over. She could not marry without her father's permission—he had both the legal responsibility and the right to approve any suitors—and he wouldn't give it.

Which *enraged* her. They hadn't even listened to what she had to say. Hadn't considered her arguments, her thoughts. Her mother had simply kept repeating herself—*a shameful thing.*

It came to Martha slowly, through the thudding of blood in her skull. Her horse snorted, tossing its head, and she realized she'd been gripping the reins too tightly.

She let go, thinking swiftly. Her father might confide in her brothers now, but she still knew who he was at his core—a private man, not prone to exposing himself to undue embarrassment. He feared shame. If she could trap him and make him see the trap had already closed, like the rabbits he'd taught her to catch so long ago, he would not thrash. He would submit.

Her father had denied her under the impression that his choice was between her marriage to Thomas and her marriage to someone else. Martha couldn't force him to approve of Thomas over another suitor, but she could change his choice.

Nearly as soon as she'd considered the idea, she dismissed it. Her father might submit, but her mother would flay her alive. Would agitate for Andrew to sue Thomas for improper conduct, as was proper if a girl was courted without her father's permission. And then there was the matter of Martha's own soul. She wasn't *supposed* to be considering how to trap her father for her own ends, for to defy her father was to defy God. She was considering sin, in both aim and method.

She could not, should not. Should walk away, take some suitor of whom her father approved, swear to honor and obey and love him.

Only, Martha thought mulishly, riding through the woods, to swear such a thing to anyone but Thomas would be a *lie*.

Some things were not permitted in the world, she knew, particularly for women, and one lived as one was required to live in God's faith and in good conscience, but God had given his children the world to live in for a reason. He had given them the world because it was full of tests.

This was a test. To swear that she loved someone she did not, that she felt something she did not—she understood that women did this, all the time, and it was all very well if you had a nature that allowed for subtleness or patience. Her sister Mary's nature allowed for those things. Her own did not, and God must have seen some value in it, for he was the one who had made her that way.

Her choice, as Martha saw it, was this: she could bring shame upon her family, or upon herself, by dissembling to feel something she did not.

Martha was not her father; she was not a private person, did not care what people thought of her nor what they said. There were many things that frightened her—illness, childbirth, centipedes—but shame wasn't one of them. And a lie was a door for the devil to walk through.

Martha fasted for three days, praying to God for a sign that the path she was considering was the right one.

When no guidance came, she made the decision herself.

Late afternoon, autumn again, leaves shaking on the chestnut trees. They had been meeting for a year. Before she could lose her nerve, Martha went to Thomas in the shed behind the Danforth's barn and told him what she intended.

He did not try to order her away. He trusted her. She loved him for it.

She waited until the first crocuses and daffodils of spring poked their merry heads aboveground before telling her parents. In her haste to stand and confirm the swell of Martha's belly, Faith nearly stabbed herself with a knitting needle, and then she beat Martha about the head and shoulders, crying out. Andrew looked at his daughter like he didn't know who she was. He did not raise a hand to her. He simply turned away. Facing the wall, he gave his daughter permission to marry before the child was born a bastard.

When she arrived back in Billerica, Martha ran at Thomas heedless of who might see them. He lifted her up and swung her around. They were married on the seventh of May 1674, a blooming day when the fields rippled bright and green. Under her gray wedding gown, Martha was seven months pregnant.

5
The Surveillance Age

Full disclosure: Thomas Carrier's past is more legend than hard evidence. It comes mostly from a book on Billerica written in 1883 by the Reverend Henry Hazen. His entry for Thomas Carrier—who he notes was sometimes called Morgan—quotes from the town records of Colchester, Connecticut, where Thomas lived out the last years of his life. The relevant passage reads:

> *Carrier had belonged to the body-guard of Charles Ist. of Great Britain, and was notorious for fleetness of foot, even after he was more than 100 years old. It is said that he killed the King of England.*[1]

It is said. Not much to base an accusation of regicide on, not exactly a reliable source, but it is possible. No one knows for sure who swung the ax to behead Charles I. Thomas would have been young when Charles I was killed, but not prohibitively so. The executioner was hooded, and the "Common Hangman" of London—who normally would have performed the deed—denied killing the king for the rest of his life. A confession was published after the Hangman died but is regarded as a forgery. A soldier named William Hulet was later tried as the executioner and sentenced—but his sentence was overturned. Hulet, it seems, proved his innocence.

Perhaps because it wasn't him. Perhaps because the job fell to Thomas Morgan, as the Colchester records suggest, if he was indeed in the king's guard and they needed a strong man at the last minute. When the king's son, Charles II, retook the throne a decade after his father's death, he agreed to pardon most of those who had been involved in the civil war. But he was inflexible on the matter of the regicides themselves. The men who had taken part directly in his father's execution were to be imprisoned in the Tower of London.

A man named Major General William Goffe, who had been involved in the coup, fled to the British colony of Connecticut. There, he allegedly made a list of twenty names in his journal: twenty men, not including Goffe himself, that the king had ordered imprisoned for their roles in the king's death.

Goffe wrote that all those men had been found and were locked in the tower—except one.

"Morgan," he reportedly wrote, "was not in the tower."[2]

* * *

Their baby was born in the summer of 1674. They named the boy Richard and moved to Billerica's northern border. How they got their house and land is a mystery—Martha's dowry, Thomas's savings, theft of a forgotten corner of the town. Thrushes in the oak trees, furrows in the stony earth. I imagined Thomas lending his strength and his name and Martha doing the bargaining, or, more accurately, the bickering, with buyers and neighbors. Within a few years, their farm appeared to be flourishing.

Where they did not do so well was in weaving themselves into the fabric of the town—to the point where Martha was described, two hundred years later, as "a woman of a disposition not unlikely to make enemies."[3] Things came to a head two years after their marriage, when the selectmen of Billerica ordered the town constable to give notice to "Thomas Carrier, alias Morgan, Welchman, that the town was not willing he should abide here ... and that he forthwith depart with his family, or give such security as shall be to the content of the Selectmen, on peril of 20 shillings per week while he abide without leave."[4]

Thomas and Martha and their toddler were being "warned out" of town, a common practice in which undesirables—mostly poor people and foreigners (like a "Welchman")—were told to leave or potentially pay a ruinous amount of money. At first, I actually thought whoever had written down twenty *shillings* in the Billerica warning-out notice had made a mistake. Twenty shillings is only the equivalent of about $230 today,[5] but it's more than twice the amount that Thomas would be paying in annual taxes a few years later.[6] To ask him to pay that every week would have been impossible.

But that was the point. Warning out usually involved asking for a sum that *couldn't* be paid, because the town didn't want the warned-out party to pay, they wanted them to leave. It was understood as a way of protecting New England's welfare system: local governments were required to offer some kind of poor relief to their citizens, and they didn't want to pay anyone they didn't have to, or let any one village become a magnet for the poor.

It appears, however, that Martha and Thomas did not leave Billerica. In 1679, three years after that warning-out notice, they were still in town—and what was more, Thomas Carrier had somehow become the third-highest taxpayer in Billerica.

Which hardly made sense. If his family was warned out for poverty in 1676, how did a formerly landless Welsh laborer end up paying that much in taxes in 1679?

Two options, and both may be true. The first: Thomas was taxed at a high rate to punish him for not leaving when he'd been warned out. The second: the Carriers weren't warned out for poverty (a theory supported by the fact that by 1677, they had hired a man to help on their farm[7]). People were warned out for other reasons, sometimes. Even those who could financially support themselves could be warned out for having what others judged as "bad character," which could mean anything from keeping a messy house to being lewd to—if you were a woman—having an "unruly tongue."[8]

It's possible that Martha annoyed the Billerica town council to the point that they sent a warning-out notice. She might have had such an unruly tongue that the town sent an official notice to tell her, *Just so you know, if you're ever on fire? We won't even spit.*

The logic was that sin, for the Puritans, was a communal concern. Part of what determined whether a person would go to Heaven was the godliness of their community. If your neighbor was sinning, your own chances of roasting after death increased. Someone like Cotton Mather would see this as a good thing, fostering a kind of interpersonal and civic responsibility—a way to understand the other as a part of the self—but what it did in practice was make everyone watch each other all the time to make sure no one was sinning. People spied on their neighbors and reported them to the church as a matter of course. Perhaps the best example comes from Salem Town, which established a formal town watch in 1644, men who walked the streets on Sundays to make sure nobody was breaking sabbath commandments.[9] A few years later, the town became worried the watchmen might be shirking their duties. They hired more people—to watch the town watch.

It was, in effect, America's first surveillance age. Martha, of course, had sinned publicly, exposing herself as someone willing to put her own personal desires above the godliness of the community. In another place or time she might have tried to hide how quickly her son was born, but there was no chance of deception in the small towns of Massachusetts. The same week they married, Martha was examined by a midwife, and both she and Thomas had to go to court and confess to "fornication" before marriage, a criminal act.[10] What sentence they received is unknown, but fornication was commonly punished with whipping or a fine, plus copious public shaming.[11]

Still, they stayed in Billerica. They lived in their house on the outskirts of town, and just a year after the business with the warning-out notice, the Billerica selectmen let Thomas Carrier take the oath of fidelity, allowing him to become a citizen of the town. Then they made him spend several days cutting a lot of brush along the roads, but it would have been worth it. They were townspeople.

Around the time Thomas became a citizen of Billerica, Martha gave birth to another boy, Andrew, and then to a daughter who died in infancy. A few years later they had another son, Thomas Jr., and another daughter, Sarah.

After fourteen years of marriage, Martha became pregnant for the sixth time. It was the autumn of 1688; she was around thirty-six years old. Martha and Thomas left Billerica for good and went home to Andover, where Martha gave birth to her last child, a girl they named Hannah, the following summer.

It's not clear why they left Billerica. Maybe Martha's parents were ailing; maybe she just wanted to go back to the place where she'd grown up. It hadn't been her family's land for very long—the English settlement of Andover had only been established in 1646, when a local Massachusett chief, Cutshamache, sold the land to a group of settlers for the price of "six pounds of currency and a coat."[12] But a child feels some attachment to the place where they grew up, regardless of whether their claim to the land is legitimate. In the years that followed, Martha took particular offense to anything she perceived as a challenge to her right to be there.

Those challenges began almost immediately. The selectmen of Andover apparently learned from their brethren in Billerica: nearly as soon as the Carriers arrived, the selectmen sent a warning-out notice to let the family know that if something should happen, the town would not be held responsible for their well-being.[13] Why they did this is unknown, but what seems obvious is that Martha would have turned up her nose at the notice. A town had tried and failed to warn her out before. What could Andover do to her that Billerica hadn't?

For the next year, the answer was nothing. The Carriers lived in as much peace as could be had.

And then came the plague.

6
The Plague

The notice sent by the Andover selectmen to Martha's relatives is reprinted here from Sarah Loring Bailey's Historical Sketches of Andover, Massachusetts *(1880). All deaths from smallpox are attributed according to the historical record.*

Billerica to Andover
September 1690

One morning in late September, the leaves beginning to crunch underfoot, Richard Carrier—sixteen now and not as tall as his father but taller than most—was splitting logs for the woodpile. His back was paining him, had been for days, but he gritted his teeth against it and kept chopping.

The world began to turn blurry, like a pane of expensive glass in rain. Richard swayed, the ax raised above the stump—and lost his grip, hands too slick with sweat. The ax buried itself in the earth at his feet.

His younger brothers helped him inside, one under each arm, while Martha gave orders and heated water over the fire. Richard's skin burned to the touch. She heated stones and wrapped them in rags, then packed them around his body, intending to sweat the fever out.

When the rash appeared on his tongue and inside his cheeks, Thomas rode hard for Billerica and Martha's brother-in-law, Roger Toothaker, the folk healer. He was back that same night, Roger in tow, but by then Martha hardly needed Roger's knowledge to confirm the worst. Red flecks had appeared on Richard's face and hands.

When the spots appeared, Martha's mother, Faith, sank down on creaky knees and began to pray. Martha joined her and then returned to work. Prayer had, on its own, proven inadequate against the smallpox: God needed proof, through hard work, that someone was worthy of being saved.

Roger bled Richard from the arms and tongue and ordered his windows be left open to let out the dark humors. He ground a paste from herbs and applied it to the spots, which Richard endured with bad grace. When Roger returned to Billerica, leaving instructions on how to proceed with treatment, Martha sent infant Hannah, five-year-old Sarah, and eight-year-old Thomas Jr.

with him to stay at her sister Mary's. Young children stood no chance in a sick house.

But neither did the old. Soon, Martha's father, dozing by the fire, realized he was too dizzy to rise. After helping his grandfather to bed, her son Andrew became shaky and feverish. Martha and Thomas boiled water, wiped sweat from foreheads, chopped firewood. When the red spots became blisters and the blisters leaked pus, Martha sponged it away and bound the sores.

In the first days of October, Andrew Sr. signed his will with arms shriveled with fever. He named his wife, his two sons, his four daughters. The day he did it, the spots appeared on Martha's hands.

In the end, Thomas went to the selectmen. The nights were lengthening, winter well on its way, and the harvest was in shambles. If they weren't to starve, they needed aid.

He was not fool enough to enter the meeting house. Sickness does not come alone on its dark horse. Behind it tramps famine and ahead, paving the road, slinks fear, the deadliest visitor by far. Instead, Thomas made it clear to the Andover selectmen that he was no danger to them—he'd survived the smallpox years ago in England—and implored them to listen to him through the open door.

From the point of view of the selectmen, whether to help was not a simple choice. The Carriers had chosen to stay despite being warned out; the town owed them nothing under the law. But Andrew and Faith Allen had been members of the community for many years. They were owed aid.

The selectmen made their decision. They had other constituents to protect. The Carriers—and, regrettably, the Allens, but what could be done?—would have to fend for themselves. The selectmen informed Thomas that he would be allowed to take a load of firewood home with him, but they would supply no aid.

Thomas stood in the doorway, clutching the frame with one hand. He wanted, in that moment, to kill them; hadn't wanted to kill anybody quite so much in a long time. The lintel creaked under his grip as he tried to master himself. Killing, against a plague, did as little as prayer.

"Then let others aid us," he begged them. "Enforce no quarantine. Let others bring aid."

They told him they'd consider it. A week later, they sent a notice to Martha's brothers that left no room for uncertainty:

> *Neighbors and friends—We the subscribers of Andover have been informed that your sister Carrier and some of her children are smitten with that contagious disease the small-pox and some have been soe inconsiderate as to think that the care of them belongs to the selectmen of Andover which [it] does not, for they took care when first they came to towne to warne them out again and have attended the law therein and shall only take care that they doe not spread the distemper with wicked carelessness which we are afraid they have already done: you had best take what care you can about them, nature and Religion requiring of it. We hope we have done faithfully in this information and are your friends and servants.*

Martha's brothers and brother-in-law came to help, bringing firewood and food. Thomas found himself pathetically grateful, right up until a frightened nephew shouted from the road that both Allen brothers and one of Martha's sisters, Hannah, were showing signs of the infection.

Then the selectmen did place the Allens under quarantine. The constable was not to allow any member of the family to go near any other house. If they truly needed something, like firewood donated from friends, they could tell the constable and he would drop it some distance away for them to retrieve. Thomas followed Roger's instructions, forcing beer down his family's throats and rubbing their blisters with ointment.

Martha's father died on October 24, his face a leaking mass of red. Two days later, he was followed out of the world by one of Martha's brothers. Her other brother died a month after that. The first brother to die lost a three-year-old boy. Martha's sister Hannah lost her husband and her infant and her husband's sister. Martha's cousin died, and her brother's widow, and her uncle's brother-in-law.

Faith, Martha's mother, who had collapsed when she heard of her oldest son's death, did not rise again from her bed. Her skin feathered and flaked, and she died at the end of December.

The earth was frozen solid. Thomas put his mother-in-law's body in the woodshed.

The plague killed thirteen people in Andover that winter, nearly all of them Martha's relatives. Eventually, word came from Boston—also suffering a wave of the pox—that the outbreak had begun by the docks. A slave ship, recently arrived from Barbados, had carried the infection. The ship had been quarantined as soon as the infection was discovered, but not nearly soon enough.

As winter thawed, Martha's sons recovered. By the time crocuses began poking their bright heads through the snow, she herself was well enough to work, and one morning she stood alone in the kitchen, listening to the sounds of her family waking. The quarantine had finally been lifted. She'd gotten word from her sister Mary in Billerica that both her girls and Thomas Jr. were in good health and would soon be sent home. All of Martha's children had survived the plague, as had her husband, and she herself.

Light-headed, slow-moving, she built a fire in the hearth that had been her mother's. It wasn't her mother's anymore. It had happened quite by accident, the plague's terrible gift. With her mother and father and brothers dead, with her sisters in their own houses with their husbands (those still living), and with Martha already installed in the farmhouse, she had made off with her father's farm.

7

The Murder Wall

If I had to choose a single factor that made Martha vulnerable to accusations of witchcraft, it would be the plague, both for whom it killed and whom it left alive. In a society that gave cosmic significance to the smallest of actions, a plague was unavoidably the work of the devil. Approved by God, perhaps, as the Puritans had been measured and found wanting, but the devil carried out the sentence.

If someone seemed immune to that plague, or worse, seemed to *benefit* from it, received an *inheritance* from it, it would not be difficult to arrive at the conclusion that such a person was associated with the devil.

In a time of peace this may not occur to anyone, but in a time of invasion, in fear—in a time of witch trials—a plague is the sort of thing that people remember. The Carriers came, and then the plague. When the devil appeared on your doorstep to make it his own, he could easily come disguised as a wayward daughter.

The morning I began to understand the full weight of the plague's repercussions I was sitting at a long table in the library's main reading room, buried deep in the work of historian Carol Karlsen. I was investigating where Martha fit into patterns of witchcraft accusation, and the first and most obvious pattern is gender. When Karlsen analyzed all the witch trials in colonial New England, she found that nearly four-fifths of the more than three hundred people accused of witchcraft from the middle of the seventeenth century to the beginning of the eighteenth were women.[1]

This didn't take me by surprise. I was so used to thinking of *witch* as a feminine-coded word that I'd taken it for granted that most of the Salem accused were women, the same way I took it for granted that most people killed in the witch hunts of Europe had been women. The European witch hunts, known as the Great Witch Hunts, lasted from the late 1400s to the late 1700s, and they killed as many as fifty thousand people.[2] Four-fifths of the victims were women, a stat that most people take in without blinking. Who else would witch hunts target? Men?

The historian Elspeth Whitney writes that the cultural expectation that witch hunts target women is so ingrained that we don't stop to think about what role gender actually plays and why. "Explicitly or implicitly it is assumed that a sort of timeless, 'natural' misogyny present in Western culture can adequately explain why the collective image of the witch was that of an ill-tempered, older woman," Whitney notes, writing on the Great Witch Hunts of Europe.[3] "Conversely, it is argued that misogyny has been so permanent a characteristic of Western culture that it cannot be considered the cause of so specific an event as the witch-hunts." But misogyny is no more natural, as in *not created by humankind*, than Puritanism was. What was it about the ways the Puritans were thinking—about women and the world, and at that particular moment—that caused women to be so overrepresented in Salem's victims?

For starters, the Puritans had inherited centuries of Christian theology blaming Eve for humanity's problems. Women were understood to be weaker of spirit, more likely to be drawn in by Satan's offers, more likely to be tempted by pleasures of the flesh and prone to lie and you get the point. Women were more likely to turn evil.[4]

They inherited this theology from Europe. The attitude can perhaps be seen most blatantly in a book called the *Malleus Maleficarum* (the *Hammer of Witches*). *Malleus* was written by the German Catholic inquisitor Heinrich Kramer and first published in 1486, right around the time the Great Witch Hunts began. It's a metaphysical treatise on witches—it purports to explain what a witch does, and why—and it is a witch-hunting manual. It instructs the reader how to identify a witch and what punishment she deserves. And for nearly three hundred pages it makes clear that witches are women and women are witches, expounding on female moral, physical, and spiritual depravity.

> *What else is woman but a foe to friendship, an unescapable punishment, a necessary evil, a natural temptation, a desirable calamity, a domestic danger, a delectable detriment, an evil of nature painted with fair colors. ... When a woman thinks alone, she thinks evil. ... When a woman weeps she weaves snares. ... If we inquire, we find that nearly all the kingdoms of the world have been overthrown by women. ... She is a liar by nature. ... Woman is a wheedling and secret enemy. ... All witchcraft comes from carnal lust, which is in women insatiable. ... The crimes of witches,*

then, exceed the sins of all others; and we now declare what punishment they deserve … [heretics] are punished in various ways, as by excommunication, deposition, confiscation of their goods, and death … but to punish witches in these ways does not seem sufficient.[5]

Kramer should have been a poet. I think he would have been happier. Instead he wrote a witch-hunting manual that was a bestseller in Europe for nearly two hundred years and was used by inquisitors and secular courts alike. I don't mean to give Kramer credit for the Great Witch Hunts; as much as he'd love that, he doesn't deserve it. He described the era's religious attitude toward women, but he didn't create it.

In the years leading up to and during the Great Witch Hunts of Europe, women were increasingly excluded from economic and social power in Europe as male control over the family expanded in the wake of the Protestant Reformation and the budding system of capitalism took hold. Activities that had been relatively accepted, such as premarital sex and early abortion, were condemned. Women were pushed out of a number of trade occupations, and female independence—sexually, economically, and socially—became understood as more deviant and more potentially threatening. Together, the changing attitudes toward women comprised what some historians have called the "new misogyny."[6] (Elspeth Whitney rather elegantly defines misogyny as "the cultural expression of patriarchy's distrust of women."[7] In other words, misogyny is fueled by the fear and disdain that those who benefit from patriarchy feel toward those who do not.)

The Puritans of Massachusetts were inheritors of the new misogyny. They believed that women were more likely to be susceptible to the devil's wiles, and so while men *were* accused and executed in Salem, the Puritans told all kinds of stories to justify killing them. They posited that the accused men weren't just witches but wizards, partners with the devil rather than in thrall to him. (Contrary to the modern witch as a strong, independent woman archetype, female witches were understood in Salem and in Europe to be subservient to the male devil. Only male sorcerers were thought to have true autonomy over their power.[8]) But the expectation that witches would be women remained strong—so strong, in fact, that the accusations of men in

Salem actually helped, in the end, to throw doubt upon the legitimacy of the trials.

The Puritans were especially obsessed with male control of family: a man's rule in the home was understood to mirror the rule of God over the cosmic sphere.[9] To obey one's husband and one's father was to obey God. To *disobey* was to defy God, as the devil had. The disobedient, ill-behaved woman was coded as devilish—and was more vulnerable to being accused as a witch.

Martha checked all these boxes. She had become pregnant out of wedlock, a classic way to disobey one's father. It was also Martha, rather than Thomas, who appears in the historical record as having clashed with their neighbors, signaling an inversion of who the Puritans would expect to hold power in the household.

I'd suspected from the beginning that Salem was a story about women and power, heard it now like a mosquito's whine in the back of my skull. Martha *had* gotten some power, not political or cultural power but the real, tangible, dirty stuff, the oldest power of all. Land. She had gotten the farm.

It is this convergence of womanhood and property, delivered by the small-pox outbreak, that made Martha exquisitely vulnerable to accusation. Carol Karlsen's analysis found that the majority of convicted and executed witches in New England were women who came from families that did not have a male heir to inherit the family's property—women who either stood to or did inherit property that would typically go to a man.[10] This made them, in Karlsen's words, "aberrations in a society with an inheritance system designed to keep property in the hands of men."[11] Women like Martha were an implicit challenge to the expectation of male inheritance. They were a snag in the system.

Anxieties over land ownership were already spiking in Massachusetts in the years leading up to the trials. New towns were declaring themselves left and right,[12] their populations swelling, and good farmland was getting sucked up like water through a reed. Billerica's tax-paying base had nearly doubled while Martha and Thomas lived there, and Andover was no different. The run on land likely exacerbated any existing discomfort that the Puritans felt about women owning property, meaning that female property owners would be seen not only as inappropriate but destabilizing to society's natural order.

Inheriting the farm also meant inheriting its enemies, and to say a land dispute does an accused witch no favors is to say that the Biblical Flood made the place a little wet. If you belong to a culture that believes all misfortune is the result of witchcraft, when your cattle die or your child gets sick, you'll look most suspiciously at someone you already consider your enemy. A neighbor with whom you've had a protracted land dispute is a prime suspect. You know they're angry with you. You know they'd like to see you suffer if they could.

Martha had a lot of land disputes, and she liked the shape of a good insult on her tongue. Once, she warned a new neighbor that if he farmed on her land, he'd repent before seven years had passed; she said she'd hold his nose to the grindstone and stick to him as close as bark stuck to a tree. Not long after, that neighbor grew a painful boil that discharged "several gallons of corruption."[13] When the trials came, he remembered it.

I no longer felt like I had any problem getting to know Martha. She was shaking off the cobwebs, putting herself back together—testy, cool-eyed, straight and sturdy as a telephone pole. What I didn't understand yet was how it had begun, how Massachusetts had gotten to a place where witch trials *could* begin. It wasn't enough to say that the Puritans believed in witches. The Puritans had believed in witches the whole time they were in the Massachusetts Bay Colony, and they only attempted to *hunt* witches for a small percentage of that time.

For a witch trial to occur, beliefs must be transformed first into fear and then into action. For a court to be called, and witnesses believed, people have to be convinced that witches are a real and present danger. The witchcraft court is primed by the court of public opinion, and that doesn't happen on its own. Someone sets the stage. Someone hoists the curtain.

Which meant that someone was responsible for Martha's death.

Like any government-sanctioned execution, a witch hunt is an impersonal way to kill. Martha, living through it, would have had no way to trace the origins of Salem's court. She would have had no way to know *who*, at the heart of it, had set the wheels of accusation turning.

But I could find out. I had the vantage point, the means, the motive. That feeling, again, of a quest leading out into dark streets. Whoever had killed Martha Carrier had gotten away with it, but they wouldn't get away unnamed.

* * *

I pulled together my notes on Salem—the place, not the trials. The Salem witch trials began in Salem Village, a small parish of the port of Salem Town. Salem Village paid taxes to Salem Town, but it was allowed its own village council for internal matters. It had its own church. It was home to farmers and was big enough for a couple of ordinaries, taverns where you could purchase a meal.

Two Salem Village residents emerged as candidates for the role of villain. Neither played any official legal role in the courtroom beyond, occasionally, court scribe. They weren't magistrates or judges. They didn't serve as jurors on the witchcraft court. But each, in his own way, shoved at the wheel of the trials until it started to turn.

The first was Samuel Parris, minister of Salem Village. His surviving portrait shows a man with large dark eyes over a blade of a nose, a face framed with soft brown hair. Parris was not an experienced minister; he came to preaching as a second career, after first trying and failing to distinguish himself as a merchant. He was not particularly well-liked in the village. He seems to have been about as charming as Martha, which is to say not very, and he was attempting to enforce an unpopular church policy that restricted eligibility for baptism to "full church members" only.[14]

All Puritans had to attend church services, but usually only a modest percentage were "full members" of the church. To become a full member, you had to make a spiritual accounting of your entire life before the whole community. It was a serious undertaking, something you weren't supposed to do if you *didn't* feel confident in God's historical and continuing presence in your life, but the rewards of full membership were tremendous. In many churches, only full members could take part in certain rites—including the rite of baptism, which was understood as a prerequisite for resurrection and salvation.

To address declining church attendance at the end of the 1600s, some Puritan ministers had adopted a popular policy known as the "halfway covenant." This policy allowed churchgoers who were not full members of their current church—but had themselves been baptized, for example as children in their parents' church—to baptize their children.

Samuel Parris rejected this newfangled radicalism when he became minister of the Salem Village church in 1689. He believed in full membership or nothing. For the next three years—the three years leading up to the trials—Parris urged his parishioners to become full members of the church. He did this largely through public shaming: in his weekly sermons, he derided resistant parishioners as unclean wretches, impugning their honor, their Christianity, and their intelligence.

It may be unsurprising that he failed. When the trials began, only 30 percent of the adult population of Salem Village had joined the church as full members.[15] But Parris wasn't backing down. The more unpopular his position became, the more he insisted it was the right one.

The other man who stands out in historical record as a prospective villain was named Thomas Putnam Jr. He was a farmer, and a leader in village politics and in the fraught effort to gain Salem Village's independence from Salem Town. The town, loathe to give up its claims to the village's taxes, had long denied them the right to full autonomy.

Putnam resented this. He resented a lot of things. He had been born into one of the wealthiest families in Salem Village but as an adult found his fortunes on a consistent downward slide. He was literate, intelligent, and belligerent, which we know because he had a penchant for filing lawsuits against his neighbors, and anyone else who caught his eye. The Putnam family had boundary disputes, inheritance disputes, moneylending disputes—you name a kind of dispute, they had it.

We don't know what Thomas Putnam looked like. No portraits survive, if any were made. We only know that he was a man who veritably buzzed with discontent, so in my mind's eye he has a swarm of bees for a face.

Once I had Putnam and Parris in my sights, I printed out charts on Salem Village church membership and maps of land ownership. I tore off pages from a legal pad and scrawled down notes: *"the surveillance age"* (Puritan fear-culture and the obsession with watching one's neighbors); *"original sin = self-interest"* (the concept of communal sin); *"outside threats"* (the war against the Wabanaki Confederacy in Maine, natural disasters, the French). Another said simply, *"VILLAIN?"*

Then I got out the tape and the red embroidery thread. My roommate indulged my dramatics and let me tack it all up on the kitchen wall: notes first, then string. When it was done, a jagged web of notes and red thread stretched from the staircase to the window. It was the first thing visible when anybody came in the front door. I don't remember who officially dubbed it the Murder Wall, but the name stuck.

"Does this, um, help?" a friend asked when she came over for dinner. As I sliced onions, she traced the string from a note that read *"Why has the story endured?"* (why do we keep telling it?) to *"loud women"* (Martha, and others) to *"apocalypse then"* (the long-awaited Puritan resurrection). "Does it actually make it...make more sense?"

"It helps," I told her. "To have everything up there, you know? Just to visualize it."

It wasn't fully a lie. Stretching the string from one disparate note to the next to make new connections—that *had* helped, a little. And it had felt good to have the pieces of the trials in my hands, to be able to move and arrange and manipulate them. To have Salem, for one brief shining moment, under control.

Also, let's be honest: I thought it was hilarious. Who hasn't wanted to tape a bunch of maps and notes up on the wall and connect it with a web of string?

So it wasn't a lie, but it was hardly the whole truth. The real reason I liked the Murder Wall was that I'd taped up notes on Samuel Parris and Thomas Putnam—three hundred years dead, sure, but there was no statute of limitations for pissing me off. I liked the Murder Wall because it pinned Martha's villains to the wall, giving her something like justice and me something like purpose. The red thread was a bowstring, drawn tight, and they were my bullseye, my quarry, the men I was going to hunt.

The Murder Wall

8
Putnam and Parris

For more information on how Salem Village's efforts to attain independence from Salem Town affected the trials, as well as the inheritance dispute between Thomas Putnam Jr. and his brother Joseph, see Paul Boyer and Stephen Nissenbaum's comprehensive Salem Possessed *(1974). The importance of the dispute over "full membership" in the Salem Village church is argued compellingly by Benjamin Ray in* Satan & Salem *(2015). Anything noted as material that Samuel Parris preached is based upon* The Sermon Notebook of Samuel Parris, *1689–1694, published by the Colonial Society of Massachusetts.*

Salem Village
Early January 1691,
two months before the first accusation of witchcraft

All night the trees had cracked like muskets as their branches froze. Thomas Putnam Jr. heard them as he lay in his bed, not sleeping, while his wife snored softly beside him.

At dawn, he layered three shirts before going downstairs. Their maid, Mercy, had lit the fire in the hearth, and he could hear her talking with his daughter in the kitchen. It promised to be warmer in that room than anywhere else, but he didn't want warmth this morning, or at least, didn't want company. Putnam pulled on his coat, scarf, and a woolen hat and let himself out the back door instead.

All was hush in the lanes, the trees black under a hard white sky. The winter air pierced his lungs as he set off, stepping carefully over patches of ice and deeper drifts.

There were, he thought, looking about him as he walked, too many houses. Or, more precisely, there were too many houses for the village to be a simple parish.

When Putnam was young, Salem Village had been a collection of rural homesteads clustered to the west of Salem Town, known only as the Farms. It wasn't that he wanted to return to that time, when becoming a town of their own had been a distant dream, but back then it also hadn't mattered if some of the land a man claimed turned out to be no good for farming. Whenever a family had need, they could simply move farther west. They'd have to contend with Indians, to be sure, but not with British law.

No longer. New towns were cropping up all around the village like weeds in midsummer. Putnam did not begrudge them this, in theory; he appreciated and understood the desire for township. But his village had been petitioning for their own independence for years, and had been denied. Salem Town, reliant upon the village's taxes, refused to grant them their rights.

Money, Putnam thought with a vicious twist of his cold mouth, was all that the Salem Town council desired. The town had become a breeding ground for merchants and foreigners, men who lived to fatten their purses rather than worship God. They held Salem Village in their vise, and even the village was increasingly filled with the town's sort. The lanes felt crowded with new houses, new families, with whom Putnam found himself having less and less in common.

He turned the corner at the frozen hawthorn tree and realized that his feet had taken him to the Salem Village meeting house. He stopped outside the gate, gazing up. Peaked roof, strong door, delicate diamond windows of expensive glass to let in God's light. They were fairly small, though, the windows. The meeting house was the home of the church, the heart of the village, but on the inside it was rather dim.

Putnam supported the Salem Village church—he was one of the founding full members, numbered among the select few entitled to baptism and the sacrament of the Lord's Supper—because having a church was a crucial part of Salem Village's fight for independence. A town needed a church. But Thomas Putnam would not say, if asked, that he was particularly *satisfied* with the state of the church in Salem Village.

"Mister Putnam? Is that Mister Putnam?"

It was a woman's voice, harsh in the icy air. Putnam winced and turned, steeling himself.

Sarah Good had rounded the corner. She came toward him, prodding at the road's icy patches with a stick. "Well met, sir, well met!" she called.

The cheerful words were at odds with the hard eyes that tracked him from under her wimple. Her dress was good, heavy wool, gone threadbare, and she wore a gray shawl about her shoulders. The effect, combined with her stick, made her seem like an old woman, though she wasn't more than thirty. She came to a halt a respectful distance away. "Your family is healthy, I trust?"

"They are," he answered politely. "And yours?"

"Well enough, sir. But my husband has no work and we are reduced to relying upon the charity of our neighbors." She cast her eyes down. "Mister Putnam, you know it pains me to abase myself in this way, but could you spare a coin for a neighbor?"

He felt a twinge of satisfaction at how quickly she revealed her true designs. Out loud, Putnam said, "I have nothing for you. Beg elsewhere."

Good's pretended humbleness evaporated, as it always did. She straightened, fingers tightening on her stick, and he wondered if she intended to strike him. It would go badly for her if she tried. But Sarah Good only muttered something that sounded like *parsimonious snudge* and turned away to stump around the corner.

Putnam waited until the sound of her stick had faded before he rubbed a hand through his hair and turned back to the meeting house, trying to recapture some of the peace of the wintry morning. He almost had it when he heard running feet, half-muffled in crunching snow.

He turned on his heel, ready to tell Sarah Good that she had been making a nuisance of herself for years and he had yet to see why it became his responsibility as soon as the weather turned, when he realized the footsteps were coming from the other direction.

John Indian rounded the meeting house and skidded to a halt in the snow, staring at Putnam with clear surprise. He recovered and closed the distance between them quickly, blowing on his dark hands. The minister's slave wore a cheap, undyed coat that was even shorter than Sarah Good's, but you didn't see *him* complaining, Putnam thought.

"Sir," John Indian said, nodding respectfully. "The minister sent me for you."

"What's wrong?"

"No wood," he said succinctly.

"I see." Putnam's mind began to flick through possibilities for redress. "How is the minister taking it?"

"Will you come back to the parsonage with me, sir?"

Which was answer enough. Putnam followed him.

They weren't even halfway down the quiet lane that led to the parsonage when he heard the shouting. The minister had a strong, clear voice, right now gone rather shrill, and it cut right through the parsonage door.

"Three months, Elizabeth! I thought it was a—a token protest, not something they would stand by in *winter*. It's not lawful, not Christian, I *dare* say—"

John Indian opened the door. The parsonage had been built by the village, not its current minister, with two rooms on the ground floor divided by a massive chimney and the bedrooms upstairs. Mistress Parris had decorated her home with the furnishings and draperies she'd brought from Boston, but even without adornment it was a fine example of what Salem Village might produce, if it was allowed to do as it saw fit with its wealth. The parsonage was also—Putnam felt immediately—only marginally warmer than the icy road outside.

He knocked the snow from his boots and followed the voices to the kitchen, where he stopped just outside the doorway to observe. The minister's daughter and niece were behind the oak table. The older girl had a knife and a loaf of bread, but she'd stopped sawing slices from it to watch her aunt and uncle with unblinking eyes. The younger girl was barely visible, peeking out from behind her cousin's elbow. The minister's other slave, John Indian's wife Tituba, stood behind them, by a hearth that was nearly all ash.

Tituba was the only one to see him in the doorway. Her eyes slid to Putnam immediately, but the others didn't notice him for a long moment, absorbed in the spectacle of the Salem Village minister stalking furiously back and forth across his kitchen like a cock skittering across the ring before a fight.

"They are trying," the minister was shouting, "to kill us!"

"Samuel, please." His wife was trying to reason with him, but she kept having to sway out of the way as he strode by. "We can purchase—"

Parris rounded on her. "We should not have to purchase it! My contract is clear. The village *must* supply this parsonage with firewood, and the villagers—" He spat the word. Putnam could relate, though he disliked hysterics. "This *place*, which I have attempted to save from itself for *three years*, is in violation of the *law*. And why? Those vile wretches resent that I am committed to making them *godly*?"

"Minister," Putnam said.

Parris nearly tripped. He swung around, relief clear on his thin face. "Mister Putnam. Oh, thank the Lord Christ in Heaven. How on earth did you get here so quickly?"

"I was out for a walk. Your man found me." He came into the kitchen. "I hear there's trouble with the wood."

"Yes," Parris said grimly, "that is certainly a way of saying it. Here—Tituba, take his coat. Some tea, I think, and corn cakes. Yes, Elizabeth, *I know* the wood is low, but we must have tea. The cake can be cold. Let's sit in the parlor, shall we?" He flitted through the kitchen door. Sometimes the minister reminded Putnam of nothing so much as one of the fancy dogs that Englishwomen took for walks in Boston, prancing things that threatened to blow away in a strong wind, but he knew the impression was deceiving. The Salem Village minister was a bulldog.

Putnam's family had led those who hired Parris, three years before. They had advocated for him, aided in his salary negotiations with the town elders. They continued to support him now; the extended Putnam family made up a quarter of all the full members of Parris's church.

It was those parishioners who were *not* full members of the church who were the matter. There were some who disliked how much Parris was paid, some who disliked his personality, and many who disagreed on theological matters. And hardly anyone enjoyed the minister's habit of preaching that those who were not church members showed the resistance that Judas had shown to Jesus.

The previous October, those Salem villagers who did not want to become members of Samuel Parris's church had finally rebelled. They took over the village council—which was rather a nasty surprise for Putnam himself, as the council had previously been controlled by his family. But it had been far worse for Parris. The village council could not revoke Samuel Parris's appointment as minister, but they could, and did, immediately vote to stop collecting taxes for his salary.

Parris had been astounded. He'd raged for days at the disgrace of parishioners wielding civil institutions against a servant of God. Putnam was accustomed to people twisting civil infrastructure for their own gain, but even he would admit the move was ruthless. Part of the minister's salary was the delivery of firewood, collected from his parishioners. It was January now, and Parris hadn't been paid in three months.

Putnam followed Parris to the sitting room. Once they were ensconced in the cushioned chairs with steaming tea and cold corn cake, Putnam said, "Well, minister. This is a right insult and no mistake."

"Oh, I think that we have moved far *past* insults, my friend," Parris said. He set his teacup down on the fine saucer with a click. "We have moved directly to an attempt on my life. On my *family's* lives." He shook his head. "They're saying it's the coldest winter anyone can remember. It was never this cold in London, and don't even ask me to think on Barbados. What I wouldn't give to be back there, Putnam. Do you know, when I tried to write my sermon yesterday, I broke the nib of my pen in the inkwell? Clean off. The ink had frozen solid."

"It is," Putnam said, "very cold."

"Quite." Something glinted deep in Parris's gaze, something that Putnam had no doubt he was not intended to see. He knew that Parris considered him an ally in his fight to build the pure Salem Village church, but he also knew that the minister occasionally enjoyed looking down on him—on all the Salem villagers—as rough, simple, country folk. Parris liked to flourish his hands when they sat together, hands as slender as his wife's, the hands of a man who (he never let anyone forget) had been born in London and had gone to the university of Harvard, while Thomas Putnam had weathered farmer's hands and had been nowhere at all.

To say that Putnam didn't mind Parris's disdain would have been a lie, but his own rage was a carefully banked thing, and reserved for others.

"Have you heard nothing of our suit?" Parris asked.

They'd submitted a complaint to the General Court back in November in a vain attempt to force the village council to pay the minister's salary. "Useless. Courts in this whole colony are useless. I've sued with them enough to know."

"Of course—when you attempted to reclaim your inheritance?"

Putnam deliberately lifted his teacup and took a sip. It was cooling fast, but he made himself swallow it. The man *wasn't* an ignoramus, he reminded himself. Parris was simply so preoccupied by his own failings that he was incapable of resisting the urge to bring up everyone else's.

When he had himself under control, Putnam said, "Aye. Useless, as I said."

"Then we must find another method of recourse," Parris decided. His wife came in with the teapot to refresh their cups. "We should call an emergency vote, on the grounds that the council is shirking their obligation."

"We can try."

"Perhaps," the minister's wife broke in, holding the teapot over her husband's cup, "you might consider adopting the halfway covenant, extending baptism to those who are not full members? Or at least to their children? The council might—" She stopped and flushed.

Parris had turned to stare at her. "And succumb to the *devil*?" he snapped. "I am attempting the Lord's work in this world. You would have me capitulate to *Satan*?"

Her head was bowed. "Forgive me. I spoke without thinking."

"I should say so," he muttered, turning back in his seat. "Get a hold of yourself. I know that you are frightened, Elizabeth, but the devil will always try to tear down God's works in the world." He looked over at Putnam. "We must stand firm, mustn't we?"

"We must."

The minister's wife left them. Parris sipped his newly steaming tea. "This village is afflicted by a great darkness," he mused. "Refusing to pay their own minister. A curse there is on those who shirk their vows before God."

"Aye," Putnam said again, and this time when he didn't say anything more, Parris shifted in his seat. His reticence was beginning to fray the minister's nerves, was it? Good. His own modest revenge.

Putnam supported the minister's efforts to create a pure church, but it went deeper than that for him. It went back to the day he'd knelt at his father's bedside, listening to the old man die.

The horribly clever thing was that what they'd done to his father's will had been legal. Thomas Putnam had received a hundred and fifty acres of land, more than his stepmother, Mary, and her child, his half brother Joseph. But acreage was a fool's measure: Putnam had received the *western* side, useless, soggy, barren ground, and his foul sixteen-year-old half brother had been given the good growing land, the heart of the farm, along with all his father's tools and cider mill and plow gear and even the house and grounds in town.

Which Thomas Putnam hadn't particularly wanted, to be clear. He hated Salem Town, disliked the crowds and the noise and the smells—give him clean cow shit over the sourness of human waste any day—but it was the principle of the thing. He was the eldest son and had been bilked out of his inheritance.

He had contested the will in court and lost, and tried again, and lost, and his young bespoiled half brother had gone and married the daughter of one of the wealthiest men in Salem Town. Sometimes Putnam was sure he could hear the devil laughing.

He had borne it—no one could say he had not borne it. He had supplied for his wife and their children, but what he couldn't understand was *why*. He had worked hard all his life, had spent half a decade trying to gain the village's independence, had supported Parris's attempt to establish a pure church. Had his efforts not pleased the Lord? Was he not worthy?

Putnam was a devout man, and he knew that God had already decided whether he was bound for Heaven or Hell. In mortal ignorance, a man could never know the truth until he stood before the Redeemer—but God, in his infinite wisdom, might occasionally give a man hints. If you prospered, that could mean something about your character and, perhaps, your immortal prospects. If you faltered, that could say just as much. Nights, turning in his cold bed as his wife snored quietly beside him, Putnam forced himself past rage into clear thought, to hold his grievance in his mind like a stone, examining its facets, looking for a fault line into which he could drive a spike and crack it.

"Putnam," the minister said. "Are you quite well?"

"No," Putnam said quietly. "I am angry. We—you—have done so much for your parishioners, and they are ungrateful."

"They certainly are. But—"

"But," Putnam continued. "Indeed. *But*. In any decent world we would not have been forced to share a meeting house with most of them. More than half the village refuses to join your church, minister. They refuse to confess their spiritual lives before the congregation. Why? What are they hiding? What lurks in their hearts that they cannot open them to God?" The minister was watching with his teacup lifted halfway to his lips, eyes sharp. "If you ask me," Thomas Putnam continued in the same quiet voice, "if they find our church so foul they should leave. They should leave Salem Village to those who truly care for it."

Putnam's young half brother Joseph, he of such good fortune, was one of those who had refused to become a church member.

"I don't disagree," Parris said finally. "But what do you propose we do about the wood?"

Putnam drank the rest of his tea in gulp. "For now we wait. I will get you what you need. Those sworn to the church will contribute it."

"That is not enough!" Parris snapped. "What the council—"

The minister broke off, and he didn't flinch but the movement was close enough to it that Putnam wondered what his face was doing to elicit that kind of response. "No," Putnam said. "It is not enough. I did not tell you to abandon hope, minister. I said only to wait. Our enemies, cursed as they surely must be, will sooner or later suffer God's justice. We need only to wait for the day when justice comes, gleaming sword alight as it was when sin was first driven out of Eden."

Samuel Parris was staring at him. He reached out and took his own cup of tea, lifted it, didn't sip.

"Well," Parris said, "Certainly. I couldn't have put it better myself."

9
Follow the Money

It wasn't long before I started to wonder if I'd made a mistake. Putting Putnam and Parris on the Murder Wall marked them as my enemies, but it also put them in my kitchen. I saw their names every morning when I woke up and every night before I went to sleep, and the exposure wore me down. I'd been trying to understand them, and I made the mistake of succeeding.

Understanding a villain doesn't disqualify them from the role, but it makes it a little more unsatisfying to blame *only* them. I couldn't ignore that by the time the trials began, Salem Village was less a place to live than a well-built trap. And the conditions that built that trap—the fear of God and going broke, the desire for political autonomy, the inferiority complexes—they were bigger than the men who lived under them.

I was sitting in a café a few days later, contemplating my suspect-houseguests, when someone called my name. If I really had been a detective, this would have been the moment to get a crucial tip from a skittish informant. As it was, I got beckoned up to the counter by the barista.

"Hey," she said, "I heard you're working on something about witch hunts."

The gossip mill at my university rivaled any in seventeenth-century Massachusetts. "Yep," I said.

"That's so fun. Have you read *Caliban and the Witch?*"

"Caliban like from *The Tempest?*"

"Yeah, but it's not—it's a book by a woman named Silvia Federici. If you haven't read it, you should really look into her. It's about the witch hunts in Europe, and capitalism, and how they, like, fed into each other, and it's just really good."

I added the book to my Sisyphean to-read list. "Thanks for the rec."

"No, really," the barista said, "I'm *serious.*"

Something about her tone and the way she was gripping the portafilter made me pause and reconsider, sending the book a few notches up in the list. I got it from the library that night and read the first three chapters sitting at my kitchen table.

When I finally put it down, the threads of the Murder Wall were shivering in the breeze from the open window, bits of paper flapping against the wall.

"Okay," I said out loud, "holy shit," and I started tearing new pages from the legal pad as fast as I could.

* * *

Silvia Federici is a feminist historian and an organizer, co-founder of the Wages for Housework campaign in the 1970s and the *Campaña por la memoria de las mujeres perseguidas por brujería* (Campaign for the Memory of Women Persecuted for Witchcraft) today. Her book *Caliban and the Witch* tracks how the Great Witch Hunts of Europe were spurred by and contributed to the new world order of capitalism and colonialism. It is too dense to sum up here, but a few things need treatment.

The first thing is timing. The witch hunts of Europe were not a medieval problem. They began in the late 1400s, and it wasn't until the following century that England, France, Spain, and Switzerland made witchcraft a capital crime.[1] Salem, at the end of the 1600s, comes closer to the end of the Great Witch Hunts than the beginning, but it should rightfully be understood as part of that wave of European witch hunting—with its own colonial flair.

Federici attributes the rise in witch hunts to the transition from feudalism, with its lords and peasants, to capitalism, with its bosses and workers. As the subsistence economies that defined life in feudal Europe were replaced by market-based economies, the upheaval—and the concentration of power in the hands of the upper classes—created intense conflicts between different strata of society. One form the conflict took was the witch hunt.

Since around the thirteenth century, landlords in Europe had been doing something called "enclosing" land: claiming fields and forests that had been communal, turning them into private property.[2] Forests that peasants had been able to hunt in and fields that were open to communities for grazing were enclosed within fences or borders. Enclosure was immensely profitable for the ruling class, as it concentrated wealth in their hands and those of their allies, but it was a harsh dispossession for those who relied upon those same lands for their livelihood.

The rate of enclosure ratcheted up sharply in the early 1400s, in the years before the Great Witch Hunts really took off. Over the next two centuries, enclosure destroyed thousands of rural communities as people who had relied on common lands were forced either to migrate or turn to waged work.[3]

But wages were going to hell, too.[4] In the 1500s, the colonial mines of South and Central America overloaded the European economy with silver, spurring serious inflation. Wages collapsed—especially for women, who, contrary to popular imagination, had worked as waged laborers throughout the Middle Ages, as everything from weavers to ironsmiths to brewers to doctors.[5] The wage collapse helped kick them out of the market and simultaneously made the most basic foodstuffs impossibly expensive.

In response to these increasingly untenable living conditions, the next two centuries saw a number of attempted peasant rebellions across Europe. But the aristocracy was too powerful and too well-armed. The rebellions were put down, most of them bloodily, and fledgling European states tightened their grip on the labor force and on land. Censuses emerged, as the new economic system needed to keep track of births and deaths. Such knowledge was necessary; you can't regulate labor if you don't regulate the workforce. And you can't regulate the workforce if you don't monitor and control the reproduction of laborers.

What is the reproduction of laborers? Not only pushing children into the world but raising them, feeding them, tending to and teaching them until they are old enough to use their hands. The reproduction of laborers is also understood as the everyday work—cooking dinner, washing clothes—that goes into making sure that an adult worker can return to work the next day. To make women the primary instrument of the reproduction of labor, Federici argues, the new capitalist system of workers and owners incentivized the state to crack down on their reproductive and social freedoms.

Abortion, which was often legal until "quickening" (when the fetus can be felt moving, usually in the second trimester), was outlawed in some places; midwives who refused to cooperate with the state were punished.[6] Nonprocreative sexuality was increasingly condemned. A more restrictive sexual division of labor emerged. Women were pushed out of guild membership by craftsmen in Germany. They lost the right to make contracts and to represent themselves in court in France.[7] The work they were allowed to do, largely domestic labor as maids, was coded as women's natural work and therefore undeserving of any significant compensation.

A primary method of enforcing this transformation of women, as a class, into "an instrument for the reproduction of labor" was the witch hunts.[8]

Accusations of witchcraft were certainly used to punish deviant sexuality—
Kramer's *Malleus Maleficarum* repeatedly associates witches with miscarriages,
abortions, impotence, and non-procreative sex—but the hunts had a broader
reach than that. Witchcraft was an accusation so broad, so frightening, and
so effective that it could be leveled against any lower-class woman to punish
deviant behavior and enforce compliance. For more than two centuries, witch
hunts effectively held the peasants of Europe hostage, subjugating women
and their male family members alike with the threat of the witch's pyre. The
Great Witch Hunts are best understood less as a terrified craze than an active
reign of terror.

That this terror campaign took the form of a witch hunt is understandable.
The idea that anyone could be a witch—that any woman could access magical power—was dangerous in the eyes of both the church and the ruling class.
"This anarchic, molecular conception of [witchcraft's] diffusion of power in
the world was anathema," Federici writes. "Magic seemed a form of refusal
of work, of insubordination, and an instrument of grassroots resistance to
power. The world had to be 'disenchanted' in order to be dominated."[9]

As magic became seen as a refusal of work, those coded as existing outside
the workforce became prime targets of witch hunts. One kind of woman was
particularly vulnerable to witchcraft accusation in Europe and Salem alike:
those who had been forced into vagrancy by the combination of the wage
collapse and the loss of the commons. Hunts targeting such women often
followed a simple pattern: a vagrant or impoverished woman would ask for
charity, be refused by the householder, and if some misfortune then befell
the household, the woman would be accused of witchcraft and, sometimes,
executed.[10]

After all, it's easier to fear a witch than to feel the guilt of withholding charity from a needy old woman. It's easier to ascribe misfortune onto witches
than to go up against an economic system creating haves and have-nots. And
by diverting class conflict into misogyny and religious dogma, it could even
be said that killing women as witches actually served as a kind of protection
for the very system that was helping to spur the accusations in the first place.

This same cycle migrated to Salem. In the late 1600s, New England's economy was transforming from a survival-based frontier economy to a more regulated, standardized, and male-dominated market economy. Women were increasingly pushed out and became more socially and economically marginalized.[11] As new towns declared themselves, land that had only recently seemed to be there for the taking disappeared in a growing system of fully privatized land ownership.

The person who is likely to have been the first accused witch in Salem was the village's local beggar, a woman named Sarah Good. Good had been born into a wealthy family, but lost that wealth when one parent died and the other remarried. By the early 1690s, Good was in her late thirties, married but impoverished. She spent her days living in a rented room, begging at wealthier houses. On one instance, she begged at Samuel Parris's parsonage and went away mumbling when she was refused—mumbling that was later understood by the witchcraft court to have been a spell of revenge,[12] a pattern that had played out in Europe for two hundred years.

But the Puritan discomfort with Sarah Good would have gone deeper even than the fear of a witch's revenge. Good—born wealthy, now destitute—was a walking reminder to the village's wealthy of how swiftly a life could come apart at the seams, and this was not a reminder anyone particularly wanted. The Puritans might have believed in predestination, but they were no less susceptible to the growing influence of capitalism than anyone else, and they were also starting to believe in money.

* * *

At the end of the seventeenth century, Puritan ministers were hotly debating the rightful place of prosperity in the lives of the devout. Was it something to pursue? To avoid? The Puritans had long believed that money actually belonged to God and was only stewarded by men. Ministers like Cotton Mather argued that pursuing wealth for oneself was morally hazardous, making men more prone to sin—though Mather did not object to people *having* wealth and spending it judiciously.[13]

This outlook betrays a discomfort not only with the new economic system but with the idea of poor people seeking to change their station. Some of this uncertainty likely stemmed from the belief that sudden wealth could be a sign of hard work or skill—or it could be a sign that someone had made a deal with the devil. Satan, after all, was regarded as a kind of merchant, offering a witch material wealth and luxury in exchange for a signature in his book. If a poor woman suddenly became wealthy, that might mean she had stewarded her wealth judiciously—or it might mean she'd dealt with the devil.

Puritans also wondered whether financial success might be a sign of God's love. Worldly success could, potentially, be a sign that one was heading to Heaven—which of course meant that you were a good person. The idea that wealth reflected moral righteousness was a handy framework to explain why some people's livelihoods flourished and others' did not. In the last few hundred years this idea has endured, losing only its religious trappings. Eventually it stood up on its own two legs and went to Washington. Greed was good, financial success probably revealed something fundamental about your character, and poverty was something you deserved.

This paradigm, filtering into the Puritan consciousness, was a blade with no handle. If you slipped, at any moment, it could cut you, for if financial success meant a man was a good person, then a man who found himself impoverished might have caused it with his own sinful nature. In 1695, exhorting those who lost money to consider if they'd brought it on themselves, Cotton Mather wrote, "Loosers [sic], consider your wayes."[14]

To be such a "loser" would have been intolerable for someone like Thomas Putnam. Like Sarah Good, Putnam had fallen financially: he had been born the son of a powerful, wealthy man and was himself neither wealthy nor powerful. Putnam knew he was the weak link in his family's legacy. He must have suspected that he had been judged and found wanting.

Samuel Parris was in a similar boat. His father had been a successful merchant with a plantation in Barbados, but economic pressures forced the son to sell. Parris had only come to preaching after failing to establish himself as a merchant. He was fond of denouncing those who worked for their own enrichment rather than for the glory of God—but the reverend doth protest too much, because his sermons were stuffed chock-full of trade metaphors. He spoke of his church as a ship laden with jewels, bound for the port of Heaven where,[15] presumably, the pickings would be fat and eternal life easy to purchase, and he wouldn't have to be afraid that economic failure was his own fault.

God had a plan, after all. Putnam and Parris both knew it. They were both just hoping this wasn't it.

Lucky for them, there was another way to think about it. There was the possibility that they *were* worthy, *were* owed more, and that their birthrights had been stripped away by an evil force, working through someone (a brother or a stepmother, or troublemaking parishioners) to steal their future and their children's future. Why blame God when you could blame the devil? Why blame yourself when you could blame a witch?

I don't mean to say that either Putnam or Parris had a unified theory of witchcraft—who witches were likely to be and why they were in Salem—before the accusations began flying. But they had enemies in abundance, and they subscribed to a religious framework that allowed them to understand their own blessings as a gift from God and their misfortunes as the work of the devil, while simultaneously seeing *other* people's misfortunes as ordained by God and other people's *good* fortune as the work of the devil. For a rigid religion, Puritanism was exceedingly flexible when it came to placing blame.

* * *

The night I finished reading *Caliban* found me gazing at the Murder Wall with a skein of red thread clenched in one hand. The lamp dripped a pool of yellow light over the wall, casting a second shadow-web behind the strings. "Thomas Putnam," I said softly. "Samuel Parris. Oh. You played yourselves, didn't you?"

Their names glared back at me from a wall that was getting pretty crowded. I'd taped up new slips of paper that read *"demolition of the commons"* (the loss of colonizable land in Salem) and *"dispossession of the oppressors"* (Putnam losing his spot on top of the pile) and *"follow the $$$"* (self-explanatory). At the center of the web was the source point of the thread, the core from which the rest spun. The note there read *"MARTHA."*

I'd been so wrapped up in finding a villain to pin her death on that I hadn't focused on her in days, and I missed her. *Sorry for ignoring you,* I thought to that tacked-up paper with her name on it. *I had to look at Salem Village. They're wack over there. But I'm getting closer. I'm getting closer to what happened to you. I just need a little longer.*

By the winter of 1692, Salem Village was slavering for some kind of blow up. The transition to a mercantile economy had them disorganized and discontented. Some villagers wanted independence from Salem Town and to be the richest fish in a small pond; some were angry at the growing merchant class; some were tormented about what the tangled Puritan wealth dogma meant for their own souls. The village was losing resources as the towns around them achieved independence, and inheritances within the village were being split up between multiple sons. As a parish of Salem Town, the village was limited in its ability to enact legislation aimed at solving public problems. In the village church, some wanted baptism for all and some wanted it only for a select few. And everywhere, all through Salem, people were so afraid of the devil that they saw him everywhere.

And then, at the end of January, two young girls—Parris's eight-year-old daughter and his eleven-year-old niece—began to show signs of what would soon be identified as demonic possession. They had strange fits, twisting their bodies and refusing to pray and saying things no one could understand. Parris was frantic. He was already hated by his neighbors, and now, it seemed, he was being targeted by Hell itself. I could almost see him, sniffing the cold air in the parsonage for a sign that the devil was near.

As for Thomas Putnam, his moment came. He knew his enemies, knew what they were capable of, and his rage, primed and ready, mixed with Samuel Parris's paranoia like glycerol with nitric acid. All it had ever needed to explode was a good hard shake, and something that smelled like sulfur.

10
Winter

The account in this chapter of the "witch" hanged in Boston refers to Ann Glover, who was executed for witchcraft in an unrelated episode in 1688, four years before the Salem witch trials. Glover, an elderly Catholic woman from Ireland, was accused of bewitching the children of the Goodwin family, for whom she worked as a housekeeper. The Goodwin children convulsed, spoke in strange tongues, and exhibited other symptoms of bewitchment that were understood as usual for the time. Minister Cotton Mather took in one of the Goodwin girls in an attempt to cure her and wrote a popular book about his experience that described the girl's afflictions (Memorable Providences, published in 1689). Samuel Parris's family was living in Boston when the Glover-Goodwin episode took place, and it's extremely likely that Parris would have read Mather's book. The comings and goings at the Parris household, including the fact that visitors came to see the girls' afflictions and that Doctor Griggs visited (and eventually made his diagnosis), are drawn from Marilynne K. Roach's The Salem Witch Trials (Taylor Trade Publishing, 2002).

The parsonage, Salem Village
January 2, 1692

Abigail Williams took another cautious step onto the ice. It held. She smiled.

"See, Betty?" she said, and swiped a booted foot through the snow-scatter. The ice underneath was opaque, but through it she could make out the flashing shadows of the trout. Her aunt Elizabeth, the minister's wife, had taught them all about how fish slept under the ice. She called the way they could survive in such an inhospitable environment proof of the majesty of God's creations.

Abigail Williams called it dinner. She was tired of the winter diet of milk and beans and corn cake and dried meat boiled with vegetables day after day. She wanted a new taste on her tongue; she wanted *variety*. Abigail took the awl from her apron pocket and knelt on the iced-over stream, the cold sinking in through the knees of her petticoats, and began to carve a rough circle into the ice.

She could hear her cousin shifting nervously on the bank. "Are you sure that it will not break, Abby?"

Abigail grunted, digging the awl into the ice. "It had better break."

"But if you fall—"

"I will fall in the stream. It doesn't reach my waist." Abigail blew a hank of pale hair that had escaped her bonnet out of her face. "We swim in the stream."

"In summer."

"So go home."

Betty stayed, as Abigail knew she would. She focused on her work. An awl wasn't the tool she'd have preferred—her father had used the combination of an awl, chisel, and hammer to knock holes through ice—but she was short enough for her eleven years that the awl had been the only thing within reach in the carpenter's shed. With some more time, she would have climbed up for the other tools, but she'd heard someone coming and fled.

Her father would have scolded her for thievery, but he was long gone, his tools lost with him, and the dead had no say in what a girl did, or what happened to her. It was the living you had to watch out for.

It took longer than she remembered to scrape the circle deep enough. Betty was shivering all the while and started whining that she wanted to go back to the parsonage, but Abigail commanded her to stay, and Betty did. She kept complaining, though, in a grating little voice, and finally Abigail turned around and chucked a bit of broken ice right at her face.

Betty squealed and ran. To tell Tituba, probably; it was her whom Betty tattled to, rather than her mother, who was mostly concerned with Betty's younger brother. Tituba could be counted on for a soft hug and a prayer, if you were young enough to need that sort of thing. She'd opened her arms to Abigail, too, at first, but Abigail didn't trust adults easily—she'd trusted her parents, and they'd gone and died—much less Indians. And she didn't tattle to anyone.

By the time the circle was deep enough, her fingers were stiff with cold, her nose dripping snot that froze on her upper lip, but the coiled fishing line was heavy as a promise in her pocket. Maybe Tituba would make fish pie. Abigail wiggled the awl into the crack, trying to pop the circle into the water.

The ice wouldn't budge. She strained until her hands slipped on the awl's wooden handle and slammed into the ice. She stuck her stinging fingers in her mouth, a thick knot of frustration swelling in her throat, and sat back on her heels. She was—there was no way around it—too small.

In a sudden burst of fury, Abigail stood up and slammed her boot heel down on the circle she'd made.

The ice creaked. Nothing more than that, but it was enough. She brought her heel down again, and then she started stomping.

A crack spread, then two, branching out from her foot. The circle had shifted, she'd swear it. She heard the slap of water against the ice's belly.

Abigail brought her foot down one more time.

When she walked back into the parsonage it was with one boot full of ice water and an enormous trout flapping weakly in her blue-knuckled hands. Her aunt gasped. The minister scolded her and gave the trout to Tituba to prepare. They had fish pie with their dinner that night and thanked God for the bounty, but Abigail, scraping up the last crumbs from her plate, wasn't sure what he had to do with it.

By the time the girls readied themselves for bed, Betty was shivering, and Abigail found that the urge to sink her teeth into flesh had barely waned. She went over to the window, unlatched the white shutters to peer out, and said, "Yes, I thought so."

"What?" Betty followed her to the window.

"It's the kind of night demons like," Abigail told her, matter-of-factly. "When it's this dark and cold, that's when they come out, the devils and the witches."

Betty looked doubtful. "You're telling stories, Abby."

"Haven't you been listening in church? Your father says it, not me." This was Abigail's winning hand: There were evil things in the world. Minister Parris said so, every single week. Abigail clasped her hands in front of her and imitated the minister's officious preaching voice. "The devil is watching, the devil is waiting, the church has got *enemies*, and if you aren't careful, God'll let the devil loose!" She snapped back to herself, leaning toward Betty over the bed. "And when the devil's servants do come out, you know they'll come here."

"No they won't!"

"They hate God's best children the most, don't they? Of course they'll come to the parsonage. They'll come right up to the window and pull the shutters open, so they make a sound, like *creeeeeaak*. And they'll look inside and see who might be sleeping—who they can take. Little girls are best. They'll slither over the sill and tiptoe across the floor, silent as anything, so the only warning you get is that *creeeeak*."

Betty didn't look so doubtful now. She was trying to be grown-up and knowledgeable, but her gaze dragged back to the shutters. Pleasure curled up like a cat in Abigail's stomach.

"Listen careful tonight," she said softly. "If you see the shutters move, don't go back to sleep. Or the witches will get you faster than you can say *our father who art in Heaven*."

"Child, that is the smelliest load of dung I ever heard come out a girl's mouth," an unimpressed voice snapped from the doorway. "What does a child your age know of witches?"

Tituba stood there, holding a folded blanket. Abigail bristled. She hadn't planned on having any audience but Betty, because Betty was easy. "Plenty," she told Tituba defiantly. "I saw that witch killed in Boston."

"Sure, and I told them not to take you when they killed Goody Glover. You were too young to see a thing like that."

"I was not. *Betty* was too young."

"Betty *was* too young," Tituba said. She heaped the blanket onto the bed and smoothed a hand over Betty's mousy brown head. "But Betty doesn't remember it, does she?"

"I remember," Betty protested, but Abigail knew she was lying and pinched her. Betty yelped.

"None of that," Tituba warned. "You stop telling tales and get yourself to bed, or I will give you something to be frightened of."

Mutinous, Abigail wanted to tell Tituba she wasn't scared of any Indian, but that lie was a little heavy, even for her. Tituba latched the shutters, blew out the candle, and pulled the door shut behind her. But before she closed her eyes, Abigail saw Betty eyeing the window, and the satisfaction kept her warm enough to fall asleep between the cold sheets.

* * *

A foot was kicking her, jamming into her thigh. "Betty," she groaned, half asleep, but Betty didn't answer. The kick came again.

Abigail opened her eyes, meaning to show her cousin that if she couldn't lie properly in bed, she'd be shoved out of it, and jerked back. Betty was thrashing, her head thrown back and her eyes bulging, limbs flailing uncontrollably.

"Betty?" Abigail asked, voice thin with horror. At the sound Betty went taut as a strung bow, and Abigail shoved herself further back, nearly falling off the bed. She was, in that moment, entirely certain that the story she'd told Betty had come true. Witches had come for them.

Betty collapsed back into bed. Abigail screamed.

Betty's mother dashed into the girls' room and gathered her child into her arms, checking for wounds, for an explanation she could touch and soothe. She called Betty's name, shaking her.

After what felt like a year, Betty opened her eyes, dark pupils taking up half of her wan face. Then she burst into tears and burrowed into her mother's neck.

Abigail opened one eye and then squeezed them both shut, and kept screaming.

By the time dawn had fully broken over the snowbound town, Abigail's head was aching. The adults had written off Betty's fit as a nightmare, but it wasn't like any nightmare she'd ever seen. Abigail was shaky with leftover fear, alchemizing into something bitter. And now Betty was being coaxed and coddled to her breakfast, while Abigail was scolded for her tardiness.

She glared at Tituba when she instructed Abigail to clean the ash from the fireplace, then kicked at her ankles.

"Stop it, you little beast," Tituba said.

The fear in Abigail's stomach bubbled and burst, searing like lye. She hated them, all of them, the adults who preached constant vigilance against the devil and the dark only to dismiss her when she saw something moving in the shadows. They didn't want to listen? Fine. Neither would she.

Abigail thought, *You want a beast?*

She growled, snapping at Tituba's hand.

The rest of the day went like this: Tired of talking, Abigail chittered. Tired of chairs, she crouched on the floor beneath them. The adults smacked her—of course they did—and she went to a place far inside her own mind and waited until it stopped. And then she kept on.

Betty was taken aback at first, but she caught on soon enough and joined Abigail under a stool. "What are we doing?" she whispered.

"We're playing Goodwin," Abigail whispered back, and Betty went wide-eyed with delight.

"In the *sitting room?*"

"Anywhere," Abigail told her. "Anywhere we want."

Three years back, when Abigail was only eight and Betty practically a baby, the Parrises had lived in Boston. They hadn't known the Goodwin family personally, but everyone knew about them: they'd been afflicted by the witch who'd been caught and put to death. Abigail remembered it clear as anything: the old woman's gray hair tumbling over her face, the strange language she shouted in. ("The devil's tongue," Minister Parris had informed them, though she'd heard someone else in the crowd call it Irish.) A minister in Boston had written a book all about the evil witch and what she'd done and described how horribly she'd tormented the Goodwin children. Minister Parris had read that book to Abigail and Betty as a lesson, to teach them what happened to children who had the bad luck to consort with witches.

It had made an impression, though not the one the minister had intended. It was the description of what had happened to the Goodwin children that had stuck. They'd convulsed, twisting their bodies all the way round, or had lain comatose for long periods, unable to be roused. They had refused to pray or listen to their elders.

Abigail and Betty had played at it a few times, mostly in the privacy of their bedroom, once in the meadow. They called it *playing Goodwin*. The game was to pretend that the witches had them and all they could do was thrash, tumbling about. Sometimes they would pretend to be beasts, or one of them would lie silently and do her best not to move as the other tried to wake her.

It was fun but rather boring; usually Abigail's patience for speaking in Biblical rhyme or inhuman screeches ran out rather quickly. She liked to be able to talk.

But it didn't bore her, she found, when she played Goodwin in front of the adults. She liked speaking gibberish to them, liked giving her tongue such loudness and her body such leeway, knowing they couldn't understand her no matter how hard they tried. She liked frightening them when she thrashed.

It was better yet with a partner. Abigail and Betty chattered and crouched and hopped across the floor. Betty spoke to her parents in her own voice from under the chair, but when they asked her to come out she chirped at them like a bird. When the girls were told to join the family for prayers, Abigail seized up, thrashing the way Betty had in the night.

Tituba ended up doing their chores, and Betty's mother sat with them by evening, worried, stroking their hair and praying that they might recover from whatever strange illness had gripped them.

Her aunt's hand moved softly over her hair and forehead. Abigail thought, *I'm never going back.*

January passed. The girls lived inside the game. They jabbered or went silent. They refused to sit still for lectures or punishments or sermons. And the more they acted like the Goodwin children, the more they felt like them. Sometimes Betty's body took over, arms and legs flailing without help or intention, bending so far backward that the girls weren't quite sure how she'd done it. Some nights Abigail felt twinges of pain up her back like someone was pinching her, and throbbing headaches kept her on the floor long after she wanted to stand up—but that was how it worked when you were bewitched, wasn't it? That's what the Goodwin children had felt.

A host of sightseers paraded through the parsonage all February to pray for the girls and, mostly, gawk at them. It rained for weeks, the creeks eating their banks and turning the village into a well of mud, and no one had anything better to do than go see the afflicted girls at the parsonage. Thomas Putnam brought his daughter, Ann, who was a year older than Abigail, and Abigail catapulted about the house and screamed extra loud for Ann's benefit. William Griggs, a doctor whom Minister Parris knew from Boston and hoped to set up his practice in the village, came to take a look at the girls. He brought his great-niece with him. Seventeen-year-old Elizabeth Hubbard, a maid in her uncle's household, observed the younger girls with interest.

Griggs wasn't the only physician to examine Abigail and Betty. Each one pronounced himself uncertain, but reiterated that prayer never hurt. The minister and his wife prayed over the girls and read the Bible to them, hoping to restore their health, until Abigail grew tired of that, too. Finally, she leapt up, snatched the Bible from her uncle, and tried to throw it into the fire. Parris wrestled it away from her, panting, his face twisted with fear.

On Sundays, Abigail sat in church and listened to her uncle preach that Satan was, without a doubt, at work in Salem Village. God was allowing the devil to afflict them. Why? It was the villagers' own fault, of course: they were sinful, unclean. Sinners had to be punished.

These sermons terrified Betty, who took them to mean that she herself was a sinner. Abigail only listened, and twitched.

Parris called again for Doctor Griggs at the end of February. Abigail and Betty had been having fits for nearly six weeks, and it was becoming more and more difficult for Abigail to remember that she hadn't always lived this way.

This time, after examining the girls, Griggs drew the minister into another room. Abigail, crouching on the floor, somersaulted over and over until she hit the door with a thump. She wriggled, bringing her ear close to the jamb.

The doctor was telling the minister that he was confident it was not epilepsy. In fact, the girls' symptoms did not resemble those of any natural illness. The only diagnosis he could give was that Abigail and Betty were under an evil hand.

The skin all down Abigail's back prickled, sharp and tingling as a mouthful of crushed-up pine needles. She lay perfectly still, listening, as the doctor and her uncle discussed the possibility that her fits were not just a punishment from God, suffered on behalf of the whole village, but that they'd been sent by someone *in* the village. That she was afflicted by a servant of the devil. By a witch.

Lying on the floor, Abigail's stomach swooped in a hot surge of discomfort. It almost felt like guilt. *Wait*, she thought. *It was a game.*

She imagined herself getting up and walking into the room and telling her uncle that they had been playing Goodwin, and she could stop if she wanted. She thought she could probably stop if she wanted.

She didn't move. She took a deep breath and felt a shudder start working its slow way through her body: it started in her hands, making them flex, moved up to her shoulders, and lodged itself in the crook of her neck.

And as it went, it burned away the guilt as easily as a feather in a candle flame. She wasn't *trying* to move her body, after all. Maybe it had started as a game, or she'd thought it had, but for a long time it hadn't felt like she'd been playing at all.

She'd *wondered* about that, as February's snow melted into slush and her body twitched and flailed. She'd wondered, listening to her uncle preach that the church's enemies would strike against them. The world was full of frightening things. People told those stories for a reason.

Maybe, Abigail thought, her cheek pressed to the polished wood grain of the parsonage floor, it *was* witchcraft. Maybe she was bewitched. She could have been bewitched all along. Maybe they were all bewitched, all of them, everyone in this cold, wet, stinking village, down to the last infant, and only Abigail had been brave enough to see it, and to act it out.

11
Under an Evil Hand

Abigail Williams and Betty Parris were the first of Salem's afflicted girls. Eventually, the cohort of girls who would have fits and claim to be afflicted by witches would grow to include a number of older teenagers, and even a few grown women and men, but the fits started with Abigail and Betty. An eleven-year-old and an eight-year-old, close as sisters. The questions start with them.

That fall I audited a seminar called "Witchcraft in the Early Modern World." It was mostly freshmen and sophomores, and the professor invited me to lead a conversation the week the syllabus landed on Salem. The class started by discussing Betty and Abigail's mysterious fits, and pretty soon a freshman boy raised his hand.

"I heard that the screaming and stuff started because the girls were tripping," he said. "Like, on acid?"

An excited murmur rippled through the class. In the warm months on campus, there was always someone tripping—so I'd prepared for the question. "You're talking about the rye theory," I told him. "It was suggested by a psychologist in 1976. She based it on the fact that rye plants, which were a staple crop in Salem, are susceptible to a fungus called ergot. Ergot fungus creates grains that contain trace amounts of lysergic acid. LSD."

The kid's face lit up.

"Eating ergot-contaminated food *can* cause convulsions and hallucinations," I continued. "And it's true that the conditions for ergot to thrive—rainy spring, wet, hot summer—were present the year before the trials."

"So they were tripping, holy shit!" He caught himself and glanced at the professor, who was leaning against the wall, amused.

I held up both hands. "Sorry. You take a closer look at the ergot theory and it doesn't really hold up."

First, convulsions and hallucinations are the exciting symptoms, but ergotism also causes vomiting, diarrhea, crawling skin, severe itching and tingling, and a ravenous appetite. There's no record of the girls experiencing any of those symptoms. Second, in outbreaks of convulsive ergotism, all members of a household are expected to show symptoms, especially all the young children.[1] If, somehow, tainted rye made its way into the parsonage, there is no plausible explanation for why only Betty and Abigail had fits for over a month when Betty had a younger brother. If it was ergot poisoning, there should have been an afflicted *boy*.

Finally, convulsive ergotism epidemics appear to occur only in places where people have severe vitamin A deficiencies.[2] Salem Village was a farming community with plenty of dairy, which means plenty of vitamin A. There would be no reason for girls like Abigail and Betty to be suffering from the deficiency that would make ergotism possible. Samuel Parris was running out of firewood, not food.

Here's where it gets interesting. The ergot theory was proposed in 1976 and was countered with the points I make above by two other academics, Nicolas P. Spanos and Jack Gottlieb, *later that same year*. But though the ergot theory has been dubious for nearly half a century, it remains exceedingly popular on the internet and in the popular imagination. It's on the wall of at least one museum in Salem—not presented as settled history, but held up as a possible explanation.

I get the enduring appeal. It's hard science, stripping history down to biology, wringing out all the sopping contradictions and complications and unknowables of the trials like a wet towel. It turns Salem's players into people who were forced into a terrible situation by bad bread and brain chemistry, rather than a series of very human choices.

The truth is that there were a thousand possible reasons for a Puritan girl to start screaming that someone was hurting her. I spoke with a child psychologist who suggested that the fits of the first accusers could have been the result of sexual abuse, acted out in the only way available to them. Another psychologist told me she thought the symptoms could indicate a psychotic break. There are accounts of Puritan children having something like mental breakdowns when they came to terms with the fact that, according to Puritan dogma, they were probably damned to Hell. It's a heavy burden for an eight-year-old to bear.

It's also entirely possible that the burden wasn't mental or theological but social. Abigail and Betty's fits included a refusal to say prayers, an inability to perform chores, and irreverence toward authority figures. They behaved in all the ways that little girls were not allowed to act. Maybe they were just tired of cleaning the ashes from the hearth and praying on cold flagstones and obeying their elders. Maybe they gambled that if they became uncontrollable enough the adults would stop trying to control them, the way that as preteens my friends and I kicked around the idea of screaming or hissing to get men to stop catcalling us in the street. When your humanity is under examination, there can be power in acting the beast; not much, and it's short-lived, but some.

It's also true that Abigail Williams spoke of headaches throughout her early afflictions. She could have had some underlying medical condition that spurred her behavior. There's no way to know.

The crux of it is this. There was one villain in the story the girls had been taught all their lives, the story that Samuel Parris had been repeating relentlessly from his pulpit for the last four months, ever since the village council canceled his firewood delivery: the devil and the devil's servants. The likeliest reason for the girls' fits is the simplest one. Abigail and Betty knew how bewitched children were supposed to act, and that was the way they acted.

I could see Abigail so clearly: orphaned, older and smarter and angrier than Betty, taking advantage of the adults' fear to show them what she really thought of them. Seizing some power, however and wherever she could.

The truth is that it was my choice to write her this way, and I did it because Abigail Williams is easy prey. Abigail has been a favorite scapegoat of Salem since Arthur Miller made her his villain in *The Crucible*. He aged her up to sixteen and invented a new plot point, making her drive the trials forward in order to continue an affair with local farmer John Procter.

I was waiting for one of the students in "Witchcraft in the Early Modern World" to bring that up, too. Shortly after we finished the ergot discussion—the class still clearly disappointed that there had been no acid trips—a sophomore girl obliged.

"Um, I have a question about *The Crucible*," she said. "How did Arthur Miller find out that Abigail Williams and John Procter were having an affair?"

"Great question," I said. "He didn't."

She blinked. "Wait. You mean—"

"Abigail Williams was eleven. John Procter was in his sixties." There were exclamations of disgust. "But more to the point, she was never a maid in his house. They didn't even live near each other."

They stared at me.

"So…" The sophomore looked genuinely perturbed. "He…made it all up?"

They all made it all up, I wanted to say, standing in the classroom while yellow leaves blew past the windows in long, silent streams. *Do you understand? The girls made it up, even if they believed, and the grown-ups made up what the girls didn't, and they believed it, too. They all made it up, and they all believed.*

"Miller never claimed his play was a true story of Salem," I said instead. "It was an allegory for McCarthyism."

"What about Tituba?" someone asked plaintively.

Yeah, what *about* Tituba? *The Crucible*'s other explanation for how the trials began is that Abigail, Betty, and some of their friends were learning magical practices from Tituba and had to come up with a story when they were found out. Miller came by this idea honestly: it was suggested by the nineteenth-century historian Charles W. Upham in his book *Salem Witchcraft*. Upham claimed that "during the winter of 1691 and 1692, a circle of young girls had been formed, who were in the habit of meeting at Mr. Parris's house for the purpose of practicing palmistry, and other arts of fortune-telling, and of becoming experts in the wonders of necromancy, magic, and spiritualism,"[3] and that they were being taught by Tituba. (Upham and his contemporaries also made the choice to reimagine Tituba as part African, though the trial records invariably refer to her as an Indian. Her history is somewhat shrouded, but she came with the Parris family to Massachusetts from Barbados, meaning that she likely belonged to Barbados's Indigenous Arawak or Carib populations.[4])

Nothing in the trial documents suggest that Tituba led any circle of the sort that Upham describes. In fact, there is no evidence that Tituba or John Indian, who may have been her husband, ever shared non-Christian practices or beliefs that they may or may not have held. Yet the idea that Tituba taught the girls of Salem magic remains lodged in the popular imagination, partly due to *The Crucible* and partly because it reinforces the stereotype of the straightlaced Puritan who would only attempt magic if taught or tricked by an outsider.

The Puritans tried to do magic all on their own. People in and around Salem Village read palms, tried out astrology, and created rudimentary Ouija boards.[5] They took part in myriad folk magic traditions that they'd carried with them from England, like using blessings based on Bible verses to find lost items or to heal small hurts.[6] Martha's brother-in-law, Roger Toothaker, was a folk healer of exactly this kind; he attempted small magics as part of his trade.

The girls in Salem may have done some folk magic on their own—things like cracking an egg into a glass to see if it would tell them the trade of the man they'd marry, the Puritan equivalent of twisting an apple stem off to the letter of your true love's name. But these weren't Barbadian practices, and there's no evidence that Tituba was ever involved.

As for *The Crucible*'s famous love affair, the relationship between Abigail Williams and John Procter, that was the prerogative of the writer. Every story needs a villain and if we cannot find them we will create them. I had Thomas Putnam and Samuel Parris; Miller had Abigail. It made an undeniably good story, the beautiful young girl carried away by her passion and leaving absolute ruin in her wake.

I expect Miller had his own reasons to feel compelled by that narrative. I don't know if he realized that the story he ended up telling was not unlike the one Salem's witch hunters told: that inside the women of Salem there was something dangerous, something related to female sexuality, that would bring catastrophe to the lives of innocent men if it ever got out of control. Sometimes the stories we end up with aren't the ones we set out to tell.

It makes sense that Miller chose Abigail, out of all of Salem's girls, to be his villainess. By the year 1700, only eight years after the trials, Abigail Williams doesn't exist. She disappears from the historical record, giving Miller the freedom to write the end of his story, and the end of hers, however he wanted.

At the end of *The Crucible*, Abigail escapes. She boards a ship in the dead of night, and before she goes, she asks John Procter, the man whom she has accused and condemned for something they both know is a lie, to come with her.

Procter refuses. Abigail disappears. I don't know if Miller meant it as a condemnation of her character or if he was trying to make it up to her, but he gets her out of there. He lets her escape, far from Salem.

In the story.

* * *

In 1671, twenty years before Abigail and Betty started screaming, a sixteen-year-old girl named Elizabeth Knapp started having similar fits in the town of Groton, Massachusetts. She yelled during prayer, barked like a dog, spoke with a deep voice that wasn't her own, and tried to throw herself into the well. She took to crying "money, sin, misery" and said she'd seen a man floating by her bed. She said the devil had given her a book in which other witches had signed their names. She even accused a neighbor of witchcraft.[7] Like Betty and Abigail, she lived in the house of the minister, a man named Samuel Willard. She was his servant.

But no one's ever heard of the Groton witch trials because there weren't any. Samuel Willard didn't believe Elizabeth Knapp. Oh, he believed she was possessed, that the deep voice that spoke through her was the devil's, but he didn't believe she'd become a witch. Her accounts of meeting with the devil were *inconsistent*, Willard wrote: she changed her story too often. It sounded more like she was possessed *by* the devil, perhaps through some indiscretion of her own.[8] But that didn't mean the people she spoke against were witches; it meant that the devil wanted Willard to *think* they were.

Samuel Willard took no action to find any other witches, and, after a couple of months, Elizabeth Knapp's fits stopped. Had certain people in Salem reacted like Willard, Abigail and Betty's fits might have gone the same way. But instead of Samuel Willard, Salem had Samuel Parris. Even before Doctor Griggs's diagnosis that the girls were *under an evil hand*, Parris was considering the possibility that they had been spiritually attacked.

And he knew whom to blame. The failure belonged to the Salem Village church, to those parishioners who shirked their spiritual duties. "For our slighting of Christ Jesus, God is angry & sending forth destroyers," Parris preached a month into his daughter and niece's fits. His flock must "war a good warfare, to subdue all our Spiritual enemies, if we would reign with Christ."[9]

When someone wants a war that badly, they'll find an enemy to wage it on. Samuel Parris believed that hunting God's (his) enemies was a moral responsibility, and he had a chance, every Sunday in church, to convince his parish. "Cursed be he that keepeth his sword back from blood,"[10] he told the congregation soon after arriving in Salem Village. "A curse there is on such as shed not blood when they have a commission from God."

12
The First Confession

The descriptions of Mary Sibley's folk magic attempts, Parris's reaction, and the first accusations are drawn from Marilynne K. Roach's The Salem Witch Trials *(Taylor Trade Publishing, 2002) and Stacy Schiff's* The Witches *(Little, Brown, 2015). The descriptions of the ensuing examinations are drawn from the trial records, including the "Examination of Sarah Good, as Recorded by Ezekiell Chever" and "Examination of Sarah Good, Written by Jonathan Corwin" (SWP No. 63.2 and SWP No. 63.4); "Examinations of Sarah Osborne and Tituba, as Recorded by Ezekiel Cheevers" (SWP No. 95.2); "Examination of Tituba, as recorded by Ezekiell Chevers" (SWP No. 125.3); "Examination of Tituba, as recorded by magistrate Jonathan Corwin" (SWP No. 125.4); and "Second Examination of Tituba, as recorded by magistrate Jonathan Corwin" (SWP No. 125.5). All records can be found in the Salem Witch Trials Documentary Archive.*

Salem Village
February 25, 1692

When Mary Sibley came in, she took off her mud-spattered shoes, placed them neatly by the door, and smiled at Abigail and Betty, who were crouched under the table. "Any better today, girls?"

Abigail eyed her and hissed something to Betty, who twitched.

Mary knelt in front of them, one hand at her back and another on her swelling stomach. "Goody Sibley, you needn't go down there," Tituba protested from where she was tending the fire. "I can fetch them out if you like."

"I would rather speak to them directly," Mary Sibley said. She was on her knees now, peering under the table. "You recognize me, don't you, girls? I live down the road. Your parents asked me to look after you while they are out."

"Not my parents," Abigail said. Her voice was perfectly clear.

"That is true," Mary Sibley replied. "But I know they have been greatly troubled by your afflictions. Wouldn't you like to do something nice for them?"

Only Betty's shoulder was twitching now. Abigail watched the gleam in Mary Sibley's eye and said nothing.

Mary Sibley dropped her voice to a whisper. "I know that you may be under an evil hand. I'd like to catch the witches who have done this to you. But I will need your help. Will you help me?"

Abigail stared at her for a long moment. She said, narrowly, "How?"

"Tituba?" Mary Sibley called. "Bring yourself and your husband over."

Mary explained that she knew something of the cunning folk's ways. All she would need was a bit of the girls' urine and a bit of help, and they'd be able to lift whatever enchantment was afflicting the children, at least enough to allow Betty and Abigail to catch a glimpse of their tormentors.

Tituba and John Indian exchanged long looks but did not attempt to dissuade her. Betty seemed to like the experience of peeing right into a bowl and wouldn't stop giggling. Mary Sibley had John mix the sloshing urine with rye flour until it formed a paste. Tituba, more impassive than usual, followed Mary's instructions and baked the cake on the hearthstone.

When it was cooked through, they fed it to the dog. He scarfed it down, which sent Betty into another round of hysterics. Abigail felt rather queasy about the whole thing.

The door opened. Samuel and Elizabeth Parris were home.

Predictably, there was shrieking. Unpredictably, for the first time in weeks, it wasn't from Betty or Abigail but from the minister himself.

Parris shouted at Mary Sibley until his face was red and sweating. Magic in the minister's own house was *not* permitted, not even from a church member, which Sibley was. She was also related to the respected Putnam family, the backbone of his church—but it didn't matter!

"Witchcraft," Parris bellowed, "is witchcraft!"

"Yes, minister," Mary Sibley said, her eyes cast down. "Of course, minister. Forgive me."

Elizabeth Parris ushered her out of the house before giving Tituba and John Indian their own dressing down.

Mary Sibley baked her witch cake on a Thursday. Over the next few days, Abigail and Betty's symptoms only grew worse. They thrashed harder, screamed louder. There was no doubt now, in anyone's mind, that they were bewitched. Parris began to demand that the girls tell him who was responsible.

And then—to Mary Sibley's immense satisfaction, which she did not express to the minister, though she ran out to tell her nearest neighbors—they did. That weekend, Abigail and Betty named three women as witches. The witch cake had worked.

The same weekend, Thomas Putnam rode up to the parsonage, his horse lathered. His daughter, twelve-year-old Ann, had begun to show signs of being under an evil hand.

Putnam and Parris were joined by a frantic Doctor William Griggs. It was his maid, his wife's great-niece, seventeen-year-old Elizabeth Hubbard. She, too, had begun to shake.

What had begun in the parsonage was spreading fast. Parris and Putnam and Griggs formed a plan of action while Abigail shrieked in the next room.

Monday morning, Thomas Putnam rode through a storm into Salem Town to press formal witchcraft charges before two Salem justices on behalf of his daughter, Ann Putnam Jr. She had named three women as witches, the same three as Abigail and Betty:

Sarah Good, the local woman who begged at the parsonage;

Sarah Osborne, a woman who had borne a child out of wedlock, married her indentured servant, and had not been to church in years; and

Tituba.

* * *

On the streets of Andover, half a day's ride away, Martha heard it said that seventeen-year-old Elizabeth Hubbard had seen Sarah Osborne transform. Osborne was a woman in the village green one moment, sickly and snaggle-toothed, all stench, and the next moment she was a great black hairy beast that chased Elizabeth into the dusk, a dog or a boar.

Well, which was it? One listener demanded. *A dog or a boar?*

The point is, the gossips insisted, the girl *saw* her: she was a woman and then she was a beast. Dog or boar, if it's got thick shaggy black hair and long shining teeth and big gleaming eyes, it's evil, isn't it? How clear does the devil have to make his footprints?

The Andover villagers murmured to each other. They didn't know Sarah Osborne personally, but from what they'd heard, she acted more beast than woman sometimes. The Hubbard girl's story required no real stretch of the imagination.

Sarah Osborne wasn't the only witch Hubbard had named, the gossips were quick to point out. There were two others as well, that beggar woman Good and an Indian. And three *other* girls had named the same women as witches— the minister's daughter, his niece, and Thomas Putnam's little girl.

Martha wasn't overly given to flights of fancy or fear, and when the news had first filtered into Andover that the Salem minister's children were having fits with no discernible explanation—long before they accused anyone of bewitching them—she had curled her lip. "What those children need," she'd told Thomas, "is nothing but a good hiding."

"Like your mother gave you when you were young?" Thomas said mildly. "Aye, I remember you telling me how well that worked."

She scowled at him. "I had no fits."

"Your sister Mary tells it differently."

"Oh, hush," she muttered. "Don't the cows need milking?" And Thomas had laughed and sent one of the boys to do it.

But now, with two more girls afflicted and three women accused of witchcraft, Martha was frightened. She knew there were witches in the world, after all; it was in the scripture. And she was the mother of two girls herself, one the same age as Betty Parris. What if the witches turned their eyes to Andover and attempted to bewitch her children?

Martha held Hannah a little more closely that night, the child squirming in her arms and wailing when her mother wouldn't let her toddle on her own. Thomas didn't remark on it. He only sang to the younger children, as he did on rare occasions, his deep voice mellowed and scratchy with age. The older boys hovered in the doorway, pretending not to listen. Martha held her baby, thinking of the devil, and of doors slamming shut in his way.

The next morning she woke before dawn, as was her habit. The bed was already cold, for Thomas had risen earlier, and Martha padded downstairs to the empty kitchen, busying herself breaking the crust on the fire to let it breathe.

She woke the children, sent the boys out to tend to the cows, and was back in the kitchen mixing cornmeal by the time the door swung open to reveal her grim-faced husband. "I've been in town," he said. "They've held hearings for the three accused as witches."

"No time to waste, I suppose." She checked the milk, heating over the fire. "What happened?"

"They meant to hold the court in Ingersoll's, the ordinary there," Thomas said, which wasn't what she'd asked, but he always took his own sweet time to tell a story. "But enough came they had to move it to the meeting house. It was a sight, by all accounts. They rode magistrates Hathorne and Corwin from Salem Town into the village with the pennants flying. Someone brought a drum."

"You'd think they were sending them off to war."

"Perhaps they are," Thomas said softly. "The devil's come to Salem. The witches confessed."

Martha froze, holding the bowl of cornmeal. "They *confessed*?"

"Not all of them," he amended. "They heard Goody Good first. She was sullen and quiet and denied it all, excepting that mayhap Osborne could be the witch they desire. But Good had a hard time saying the name of God, and her husband—he said she's got something that could be a witch mark on her shoulder."

Martha pressed the back of her hand to her mouth. "Next was Goody Osborne," Thomas continued. "She denied it as well, but she said she herself could be bewitched by another. Said she's dreamt often of a man, a figure like an Indian, who pinches her in her sleep."

"Wait," Martha said. "That's all? My sister Mary has had nightmares like that since she was a child. Our mother would try to frighten us from going into the woods by telling us we'd be taken. Mary's rather hen-hearted, but all the same, it hardly means the woman's *bewitched*."

Thomas shook his head. "No," he said, "it hardly does. But Tituba—the Indian—she confessed."

Martha felt cold. "To what?"

"To all of it," Thomas said, "and more."

Tituba hadn't confessed to anything at first: when they hauled her up before the magistrate, she'd been much like Good and Osborne, denying all familiarity with evil spirits. But Magistrate Hathorne seemed to sense some lie in her, and he pressed hard, questioning her again and again and again, until finally Tituba broke.

Magistrate Hathorne asked, "Did you never see the devil?"

Tituba answered, "The devil came to me, and bid me serve him."

Yes, Tituba said, Sarah Osborne was a witch, and Sarah Good, too. *They* were the ones who hurt the children, she said, and they had wanted Tituba to do the same, but she had refused. She would never hurt Betty or Abigail, and though she had no responsibility to the other girls, Putnam's daughter and Griggs's niece, she would never harm them, no matter how the witches might afflict her, threatening to hurt her if she refused.

"But did you not hurt them?" Magistrate Hathorne demanded, and Tituba relented. Yes, she had sent her spirit to pinch and prick all four afflicted girls. But never again, she said, now that she had been unmasked. She would never do it again.

The confession went on. Tituba had let the devil's creatures, imps and a hairy bird, warm themselves by the parsonage's own fire. She had met the devil himself, a tall man with white hair, dressed in rich black serge. She had seen unknown women accompanying him, dressed richly in silk hoods. The devil bade her serve him and promised he would give her many pretty things.

Magistrate Hathorne had asked if the devil had made Tituba write her name in his book. To sign one's name in the devil's book was to covenant with him, to swear oneself to him. It was the cursed inverse of the holy covenant that a person swore when they joined a church. And this, Thomas said, was where the gossips who told him story in town had turned serious and frightened and grim—although the grimness was the kind that came laced with pleasure, for there was vindication in having one's worst fears come true.

Tituba had confessed to signing the devil's book, and Magistrate Hathorne had asked if she had seen any other marks in it. If there were, in other words, any more witches.

Tituba said, "Yes. A great many. Some marks red, some yellow."

She hadn't recognized all the names, only two—Sarah Good's and Sarah Osborne's—but she had counted. In total, Tituba said, she had seen nine names in the devil's book.

"Nine?" Martha breathed. The kitchen was terribly cold, and she moved automatically to throw another log on the fire before realizing that it was crackling merrily. "So many?"

"If she's telling the truth, of course."

"Do you think she is?" She hated how uncertain her voice sounded, but Martha was—it couldn't be denied—frightened of witches. She feared the devil, as any godly woman would. Thomas was less devout, and so less frightened of the devil, which Martha thought was backward, given that only those who were vigilant of the devil's tricks could hope to escape them. But Thomas was contrary like that.

"I don't know," Thomas said tiredly. "Mayhap it's all true. But if she's a witch, how can they trust her?"

Abruptly Martha shook her head. She drew a sharp breath in through her nose and spit it out, forced her heart to quiet and her head to clear. "Enough of this. We must think on what to say to the children."

Thomas rubbed a hand over his beard. "You want to tell them?"

"Yes," Martha said grimly. "I do. If there are witches about in the colony, I want our children on their guard."

13
Prophets and Puppeteers

Somebody once told me that the angriest demographic in the world is teenage girls, and I agreed without asking for their sourcing. Reading the witchcraft complaints filed on behalf of Abigail and Betty and Ann Putnam and Elizabeth Hubbard, reading Tituba's confession over and over, I thought of that factoid. I thought of a moment in high school when a friend had asked, If you were given the power to kill someone who had hurt you, with no repercussions, would you use it?

We went around the table and every girl said yes. One of the boys exclaimed, "You guys are crazy. That's so messed up."

Three years later, that boy assaulted one of the girls who had been at the table. She did not kill him. She was older by then.

The most obvious channel for young, female, incandescent rage in the trials is the afflicted girls, but there is another. Someone who is usually overlooked because of her race and because popular representations have reimagined her as old. But Tituba *wasn't* old. No one knows her precise age, but according to one record, she could have been as young as twenty-five.[1] It is likely that she wasn't all that much older than the oldest of the girls accusing her.

It is also likely that Tituba was beaten into her original confession. John Hale, the minister of the nearby town of Beverly, noted that a physical examination the same day as Tituba's confession showed "marks of the Devils wounding of her."[2] In other words, visible bruising.

A man named Robert Calef, writing in Boston eight years after the trials, reported that Tituba eventually named the person who beat her that day as Minister Parris.[3] Calef didn't say whether he'd spoken directly to Tituba for this information or if it was hearsay. But the idea that Tituba was beaten into her confession makes more sense than anything else. Hers was only the fourth confession to witchcraft in all of Massachusetts history, because confessing to witchcraft traditionally meant signing one's own death sentence. Tituba would have confessed that day in March of 1692 thinking she was digging her own grave.

Well, not just her own. Tituba didn't only confess. She also claimed that Sarah Good and Sarah Osborne were witches, and that she had seen seven unknown signatures in the devil's book. Seven signatures in the book, seven Satanic saboteurs in the Puritan camp.

Tituba had been sold to the Parris family in Barbados twelve years before. She'd had twelve years to learn how the Puritans worked, and she spoke their language—not English but fear—better than they did. If this was revenge for enslavement, for abuse, for yesterday's beating and tomorrow's threat, it was a masterful one. Tituba told the Salem villagers a story, and they believed her, when she was disbelieved or ignored or belittled in every other conceivable context. They believed her when she told them that what they feared above all else was already happening. And then she watched them eat each other alive.

Tituba accomplished this feat by including in her confession what's known as *spectral evidence* (i.e., any witchcraft that took place on the spectral or spiritual plane, rather than on the physical plane, which would include potion-making or the use of poppets). Most often in Salem, spectral evidence was the report of a witch's "specter" or "shape," a ghostlike figure that looked like the witch who had sent it and could be deployed to perform all manner of mischief. A witch's shape could spoil cider, kill livestock, or afflict a minister's daughter. It could cause pain but could not usually be harmed, in the classic *the ghost can hurt you, but you can't hurt them back* paradox.

Spectral evidence in Salem also included the girls seeing a figure who was supposed to represent the devil, and whom they called "the black man." This was not, shockingly, a racial epithet—if they'd meant to describe a person of African descent, the Puritans would have used the word "negro." Most scholars today think that "the black man" is instead meant to refer to someone dressed in black. Tituba described the devil as a tall man in rich black clothes, and "the man in black" was an established devilish figure in English folklore; "the black man" was most likely a kind of shorthand for him. Eventually, that specter came to be understood as a *specific* man who wore black: a minister.

But all that came later. At the beginning of the trials, the matter of whether to even allow spectral evidence into court was far from settled. Spectral evidence is invisible to everyone except its victim: only the person afflicted by the witch could see the witch's shape. This created obvious legal issues. If one person claimed to see a witch's specter but the rest of the room saw nothing, who should be believed? Some ministers cautioned that spectral testimony was far too unreliable—not only because a person who claimed to see a witch's specter might be lying, but because the devil might use the specter of an innocent person to frame someone.

But while the ministers were busy hashing that out in Boston, the magistrates in Salem, John Hathorne and Jonathan Corwin, accepted spectral evidence without a peep. They also broke precedent in another way: they decided to interrogate the suspected witches in the middle of the village meeting house, and they let the afflicted girls attend.

They might as well have loosed a pack of wolves. As the accused witches were interrogated, the girls acted out their afflictions for all to see. They wept, convulsed, cried out that they had been pinched or stabbed. They gasped that they could see the accused witch communing with the devil. It was hard to maintain one's innocence under Magistrate John Hathorne's relentless questioning, but even harder when a twelve-year-old was choking, screaming, and pointing her finger right at you.

The audience in the meeting house watched the girls' performance, riveted—for they were an audience. What should have been a private legal process was transformed into public spectacle. With a little collaboration and the highly attuned perception of a teenage girl raised near the bottom of a rigidly stratified society, the Salem Village meeting house became a stage, and its men and women merely players in the most dangerous improv troupe Massachusetts had ever seen.

The cohort of afflicted girls evolved from the original four. Betty, the youngest, dropped out, and three new girls joined the star trio of Abigail, Ann Putnam Jr., and Elizabeth Hubbard. The new girls were Mary Walcott (Thomas Putnam's cousin), Mercy Lewis (Thomas Putnam's maid), and Mary Warren (a maid in John Procter's house). Walcott and Lewis were both in their late teens, and Warren was twenty. They may have been friends before the trials began.[4]

These six girls became the core accusers of the Salem witch trials. They were eventually joined by a swath of other afflicted, including grown women, like Ann Putnam's mother, and even a few men, but the girls were the heart of it. They spent the next six months having fits, seeing ghosts, and naming witch after witch after witch. They accused people as close as their own households and as far away as Maine, from enslaved people to powerful merchants. Before long, the afflicted girls were marching off across Massachusetts to discover witches in other towns.

Some of what they did was intentional fraud. The girls bit their own wrists and showed the judges the marks as evidence against the accused. They tied each other's hands and pretended a witch had done it. They listened to what an accused witch said and reacted in real time: if she yelled that they were lying, they screamed bloody murder and fell to the floor, and if she confessed, they stood up, perfectly fine.

I don't mean to say it was only fakery. The girls embodied the stories of witchcraft and possession they'd been told all their lives, until their afflictions seemed real to those around them—and likely felt real to the girls themselves. They are hardly the only ones to have experienced this kind of mind-body connection. In a recent case, from 2020 to 2023, doctors treated thousands of young people around the world, mostly teenage girls, for "tics"—convulsing, shaking, whooping—that they'd never previously exhibited. The *New York Times* reported that many of the girls were frequent consumers of TikToks made by content creators who claimed to have Tourette syndrome. The teens who watched them came to believe that they, too, had Tourette syndrome, and their newfound tics felt both real and uncontrollable. A psychiatrist told the *Times*, "We all recognize that the mind can make the body do things."[5]

The fits of the girls in Salem may have felt just as real, but reality was hardly the point. In Salem, a witchcraft affliction opened doors that were otherwise bolted shut. Adult women in the Massachusetts Bay colony could not vote, serve on juries, or speak in meeting. A woman who interrupted a minister was placed on the block in the town square for public ridicule. Meanwhile, in the midst of her affliction, Abigail Williams interrupted a visiting minister, informed him his sermons were boring, and walked out of the meeting house unscathed. Women who were sexual outside of the marriage bed were sinful and shamed accordingly, but one could not control one's witchcraft fits.

Some of the older girls clenched their legs together and threw their heads back when ministers prayed over them, crying out that they had been pricked. Was it still a sin to moan under the hands of a minister if a witch was making you do it? The answer, apparently, was no.

Three of the four older afflicted girls were maidservants, ranked among the lowest sectors of free society. Some of the girls were orphans, without support or a clear future. When their fits began, they received care and concern from the whole village. Girls with no prospects were suddenly the talk of the town, appearing in court over and over as the prosecution's star witnesses. Perhaps infamy didn't feel so different from purpose. Perhaps sympathy didn't feel so different from love.

Their afflictions gave them a voice. Name a woman as a witch and your opinion was sought after, respected, feared. For the first time in their lives, the afflicted girls could say something that contradicted a man's word and *they* would be believed. They spoke. Of course they spoke. A world that had told them to be seen and not heard was offering to treat them as prophets.

It wasn't as easy as I'm making it sound. The girls had to walk a thin line not only to be taken seriously but to avoid being accused of witchcraft themselves. They were regularly accessing visions and magical knowledge, which was historically the purview of Satan. They had to find a way to maintain their credibility as agents of God, not the devil.

They did this primarily by telling the court authorities and their parents exactly what they wanted to hear. The moment the girls failed to perform the cultural expectation of who and what a witch was and did, they would be disregarded. So they behaved as the court, the clergy, and their parents expected bewitched girls to behave. Prophets operate on sufferance of a higher power, after all. Others speak through them.

The Salem witch trials can be seen as a moment when people who were historically excluded from power caught and rode its wave, but they should not be understood as an attempt to overturn the colony's hierarchies. The afflicted girls arrayed themselves, always, on the side of power. They got their first leg up by accusing lower-ranked women: an enslaved woman, poor women, women who didn't go to church, women who had borne children out of wedlock or had mixed-race children. They moved on to women with whom their parents had property or inheritance disputes. Even the wealthy, high-status men that the girls eventually accused tended to have some other mark against them, such as being foreign-born, newly wealthy, or friendly with Indigenous communities.

Like so many white American women in the centuries to come, Salem's girls had discovered that the authorities, who so often disregarded them, would respond to their complaints with swift and brutal force if those they accused fit a certain mold. What power the girls were allowed to exert lay not only in their afflictions but in being afflicted by the right people. So they stuck to the formula. They didn't try to break the social ladder, only climb a few rungs themselves.

* * *

They couldn't make that climb alone. They needed backup.

On March 27, Parris gave a sermon to his congregation called "Christ Knows How Many Devils There Are." It continued in the same vein in which he'd been preaching since Abigail and Betty began having fits: Satan was targeting his church because the Salem Village parishioners weren't holy enough. But this time, Parris made clear that there could be agents of Satan among the parishioners. Among the church members, even. "There are such Devils in the Church," Parris told his congregation. "Not only sinners but notorious sinners."[6]

It was a declaration that anyone in Salem Village could potentially be a witch, anyone at all. One reason Parris might have made such a declaration is that a week before he gave this sermon, the afflicted girls accused their first church member, a woman named Martha Corey. Charges against a church member would need considerable backing to stick. (Corey showed total disdain for the accusation against her, calling the girls "distracted," i.e., mentally unstable, during her preliminary hearing.[7])

Parris supplied the necessary backing. In that same sermon, he said that while Satan would certainly *like* to send out specters of innocent church members to frame them, "it is not easy to imagine that his power is of such extent."[8] In other words, the devil could *not* take on the shape of an innocent person, as long as that person was sufficiently holy. So it was likely that every specter the girls saw belonged to a practicing witch—or at least someone sinful enough to be witch-like.

It's unclear why Parris thought he had the dogmatic authority to make such a claim, when ministers far more respected than he were still debating the matter and coming to conclusions that were far less confident. But make the claim he did, and then he went on to write ten separate depositions on Abigail Williams's behalf, many of which accused his own parishioners of witchcraft.

Which was nothing compared to how many depositions Thomas Putnam submitted. Over the course of the trials, Putnam penned more than *120* accusatory depositions and complaints, a full third of the total depositions and complaints submitted.[9] He filed both the first and the last official complaint of the trials. He personally testified against seventeen witches. He even sent the magistrates encouraging letters at crucial junctures, thanking them for their perseverance in seeking out the witches and returning Salem to its former glory.

His daughter, Ann, was the most prolific of all the afflicted girls, naming a staggering sixty-nine people as witches. Thirteen of those people were killed, meaning that Ann—and her father, who wrote down and filed each of her accusations with the court—had a hand in two-thirds of Salem's deaths. And Ann's weren't the only accusations that Putnam helped file. In total, his household accused more than 160 people of witchcraft, and given that the testimonies of his daughter, his maid Mercy Lewis, and his relative Mary Walcott were all submitted in his handwriting,[10] it is only a small exaggeration to say that Thomas Putnam literally wrote the Salem witch trials into existence.

He may have been as afraid as any of them, at the beginning. His home was the devil's punching bag. His daughter appeared terribly afflicted, and his wife, Ann Sr., soon became the trials' first afflicted adult. But even if Thomas Putnam was afraid, he was motivated. Plenty of those accused of witchcraft by members of Putnam's household were people he'd clashed with in the past—over land, money, village leadership. It doesn't strain credulity to consider that the adults closest to the afflicted girls might have realized what they could do with a prophet in their pocket, and from the beginning, Putnam seemed to understand the potential of the trials in a way few others did. As soon as the first accusations were in the air he snapped into action, writing indictments and depositions, wringing detailed accusations from the girls in his household. He kept track of the court's schedule, supplying the prosecution with evidence precisely when it was needed, like a general moving troops across a map. He was *good* at it. If the enemy had been real, Thomas Putnam would have been a war hero.

* * *

Samuel Parris, not to be forgotten, did one more thing. He sent his daughter Betty away. He did this around the end of March, the same time he gave the sermon, "Christ Knows How Many Devils There Are," and declared open season on his own parishioners.

Betty Parris spent the rest of the trials at the house of a relative in Salem Town, isolated from the other afflicted girls in a calm environment—which was, as it happened, the minister-recommended treatment for such afflictions at the time. And it appears to have worked: Betty didn't immediately stop having symptoms, but she did stop accusing people. Her name doesn't appear on any more warrants. Betty Parris's tenure as an accuser was over.

If Parris and Putnam were interested in helping the other girls recover— if their priority was to see Abigail and Ann and Mercy released from their fits too—one would think they'd have considered a similar course of treatment. Instead, the day after Parris's March 27 sermon, two young men were at the Putnam house, doting on Mercy Lewis. Later, the young men said that they had heard Thomas Putnam and his wife, Ann, putting words in Mercy's mouth that day, nudging her toward an accusation.[11]

Also on March 28, a group of villagers were at Ingersoll's ordinary, gossiping about the allegations over cider and ale. Some afflicted girls—the record doesn't name who—were there, too. One of the girls leapt up to say that she saw the specter of Elizabeth Procter in the tavern, which was the same as naming Procter as a witch.

But instead of taking the accusation seriously, the innkeeper's wife and the local villagers scolded the girl—and she immediately recanted. "The girl said that she did it for sport," one of the villagers who had been in the tavern that day later testified on Elizabeth Procter's behalf. As soon as the accusation was met with resistance, the girl recanted. She apologized. It had only been a game. Girls must, after all, "have some sport."[12]

14

The Witches' Sabbath

The description of the "witches' sabbath" was first reported by Abigail Williams in mid-April, later supplemented by sundry confessors. For detail on George Burroughs—the former Salem Village minister, who left after a monetary conflict with the Putnam family to become the minister of Casco Bay (present-day Portland, Maine)—see Boyer and Nissenbaum's Salem Possessed *(1976). Martha's interactions with Phoebe Chandler are drawn from the "Deposition of Phoebe Chandler and Testimony of [Bridget] Chandler v. Martha Carrier" (SWP No. 24.10) in the Salem Witch Trials Documentary Archive. Roger and Mary Toothaker's marital troubles are recounted in* Ancestry of Charles Stinson Pillsbury and John Sargent Pillsbury *by Mary Lovering Holman (1938).*

Andover to Salem Town
April and May 1692

Wind hisses through the empty streets of Salem Village. Shutters creak as clouds knit over the sun. There's rain coming, the smell of it sharp and cool in heart of the village, stronger on the outskirts of town.

The villagers are gathered in the meeting house for a day of fasting and prayer. All day they have prayed on the hard floor, entreating God to care for their holy outpost in the wilderness, asking the Lord to recognize the covenant they have made with him.

But unbeknownst to the good people of Salem, others, too, are gathering. In a dark mirror of the day of prayer, the witches are holding a sabbath.

They come one by one and two by two, by foot and by broom, riding the storm wind, some from Salem Village and others from as far away as Maine. They come to the pasture behind Minister Parris's own parsonage, and there they gather round a long table. The crowd swells until there are forty of them, witches all, sworn to the enemy of God. Newly budded branches click over their heads as the witches break bread, red as flesh, and dunk it in goblets of bloody wine in a dark sacrament. Dark beasts prowl the woods. A dark minister leads the mass.

"At least, that's what the child said," Goody Foster announced, perched on the seat of her cart. She was parked in the corner of the road that cut through the heart of Andover, a small crowd gathered around her. "Heard it myself in Salem Village. Whilst the minister held a day of prayer a fortnight ago, the witches made evil in the woods."

At the edge of the crowd, Martha adjusted the sack of ground rye onto one hip and took her daughter's hand more firmly. Martha disliked old Goody Foster—a neighbor who had long coveted Martha's father's land—but she'd stopped to listen regardless. It was a rare person who would turn away from a meal of news from Salem Village. Gossip was the new meat.

Even if it came from Goody Foster.

"Which child saw the sabbath?" someone asked.

"Abigail Williams, the minister's niece," Goody Foster informed the crowd. She was tall for an old woman and sat straight-backed, proud to be the one bringing the news. "She saw the witches in the minister's own pasture."

"It's true, then," another woman said. Martha craned her neck to see Goodwife Deliverance Dane, the wife of one of Martha's cousins, pale with worry. "The witches mean to tear down the Salem Village church."

Martha felt her daughter's hand twist in her own. "Hush," she murmured, though Sarah had said nothing.

"They've had a fair few years of strife there," Goody Foster said. "Their minister says it's made them weak. There's talk that witches have been recruiting for a long time, pulling folk from the church."

"Praise God that we've none of that sort here." Goody Dane pressed a hand to her breast. A few other women gave her skeptical looks, brows twitching, but no one said anything.

The idea that disagreements in a church could destroy it so easily was discomfiting. As if a parish were nothing but a raw egg, pinpricked on both ends, the yolk blown out, leaving behind a brittle shell to be crushed in the devil's hand. Martha didn't like that thought at all. She looked for a stick to spike Goody Foster's wheel.

And found one easily enough. "Goody Foster," Martha called. "If the witches had their sabbath back when Salem Village held its fast day, that's a fortnight gone. Why did the girl wait so long to tell anyone?"

Goody Foster stiffened. She didn't care for Martha any more than Martha cared for her; the thing about old neighbors was that they still remembered you as the Allen girl who'd gone and gotten yourself with child before marriage. "She didn't see it at the *time*. She saw it after, had a vision of what they'd done. But—" Quick flick of her head back to the waiting women, a clear dismissal; Goody Foster wasn't going to waste time arguing when she had a better story to tell. "There's more. The Williams girl saw two of the witches serving as *deacons* at the sabbath."

"Horrid," Martha said loudly, reinserting herself. Sarah shifted at her side, but Martha was enjoying the way Goody Foster's lips pinched. If she wanted a dismissal to take, she'd have to work harder for it. "Who were they?"

Goody Foster hesitated, but the urge to share what she knew won out. "One was Sarah Good."

There was a flurry of satisfaction in the crowd. "I shan't say I'm surprised," someone muttered. "I've met the woman, and she seemed beastly—"

"—she was on hard times, is all—"

"And the other," Goody Foster said, raising her thin voice, "Sarah Cloyce."

"Cloyce? Her sister's already been accused, hasn't she?"

"Aye, Rebecca Nurse. It runs in families, they say."

"I heard the Nurse family has bad blood with the Putnams."

"Where'd you hear a thing like that?"

"From Goody Bishop. Don't fix me that look, Goody Dane, I don't frequent her establishment. I was at Ingersoll's to visit my sister and Goody Bishop happened in."

"What did she say, then?"

"She said Goody Putnam bears a grudge against Mister Nurse. Something to do with her sister. I didn't catch it all, so if anyone else knows aught—"

Sarah was tugging at Martha's sleeve, a curious glint in her eye. Martha bent down, listening to the women with half an ear. "What is it?"

"What's Bridget Bishop's establishment?"

Martha clicked her tongue. "All this talk, and you managed to pick that right out, didn't you? It's a tavern, child." It wasn't even a particularly bawdy tavern, but there were games there some nights—so Martha had heard, anyway—and Goody Bishop was known to prance about in a coat of red, which was a disreputable color. "Don't trouble yourself about it."

She straightened. The others were still bandying about what they could remember of Goody Putnam's sister, who'd gone to her reward ten years back, and Goody Foster looked rather forlorn at having lost the crowd. It was time to go, Martha decided. She was interested in the witches, not in years-old gossip from a town she didn't even live in.

She gathered Sarah and started off down the road. As the women's voices faded, Sarah said, "Mother."

A different voice than when she'd asked about Goody Bishop. "Yes?"

"There aren't witches *here*, are there?"

Martha stopped. She put her sack down in the road, where wagons had whipped the mud into stiff peaks, and took Sarah by the shoulders. "Listen to me," Martha said. "We've no reason to think there are any witches here, and praise God for that. But if you see anything, *feel* anything, I want you to tell me first thing. Do you understand?" She waited until Sarah nodded. Martha remembered being that age only faintly, but she'd never forget lying awake at night, believing she could hear the devil whispering on the other side of the wall. *You can't get in unless I open the door.* "And I want you to pray, whenever you've a spare moment. Keep the Lord foremost in your thoughts. Stay true to him, and he will have charity for you. The devil will have no advantage."

"All right," Sarah whispered.

"Stronger than that. You must believe it. The Lord rewards our faith in him."

"*All right,*" Sarah said, raising her chin, and her voice came out like a clear little bell, made in a good strong cast. It would do. Martha squeezed her shoulders and let go. She picked up the sack and set them briskly for home.

* * *

In the weeks that followed, Martha repeated those words to herself and her family, used them like a walking stick, both to lean upon and to beat back snakes. *The Lord rewards our faith in him. The devil will have no advantage.* But still the fear crept closer, for as spring sped toward summer, the number of witchcraft accusations only grew.

Either Martha or Thomas made a point of going into town each day to get the news from Salem Village. Thomas would stop by the ordinary and Martha would chat with the women in the lanes, and so they heard when a woman named Elizabeth Procter was accused, and then accused again. Her husband, John, said that all the afflicted girls needed was a good hiding; soon the girls reported that his specter, too, was tormenting them. Both Procters were arrested and placed in jail. Bridget Bishop, who ran her tavern near the edge of Salem Town, followed them. And no one would stop talking about the witches' sabbath, the gathering behind the Salem minister's own parsonage. The sabbath meant (it was said) that Satan intended to destroy the village church, to sicken the village until it withered and died. The godly people of Massachusetts had seized the devil's land and made it holy. Starting with Salem, the devil was taking it back.

The gossip reached a fever pitch in April, when a fourteen-year-old girl from the nearby town of Topsfield named Abigail Hobbs followed in Tituba's footsteps and confessed to witchcraft. The Hobbs girl was said to be a disobedient child, one who'd tried to run away from home and made her stepmother's life a living hell. She admitted to witchcraft and to tormenting the afflicted girls in Salem with hardly any prompting.

The Hobbs girl's confession raced through Andover faster than wildfire at the end of a drought. She claimed to have seen the devil twice: first, four years ago while living on the frontier in Maine, just before Indians attacked, and again not long ago, in the woods outside Falmouth.

These two references were understood by all to mean that the witches afflicting Salem Village and the Indians afflicting all of Massachusetts might be connected. Indians were already making war on the northern frontier. If they were working with the witches, as Abigail Hobbs implied, then the afflictions in Salem were not the work of a few isolated agents but might be— it was possible—part of a full-scale devilish invasion.

Two weeks later, Martha brought home the most important revelation yet. It must have shown on her face as soon she came down the darkening lane, for Thomas, who had been repairing the wheel of their cart, stopped and motioned toward the barn. But Martha shook her head. Her children needed to hear this.

When they were gathered in the kitchen front of her, Richard and Andrew and Tom sweaty from the day's planting, Sarah grasping Hannah by the wrist so she wouldn't toddle away, Martha said, "They think they've identified the leader of the witches. He is a man named George Burroughs and he used to be the minister of Salem Village."

The children stared at her. Thomas, leaning against the latched door, said nothing.

"A minister?" Andrew said. He was usually the first to speak up. He had his father's curly hair and easy smile, and Martha's knife of a tongue. "I don't believe it."

"Fortunately, what you believe has absolutely no bearing," Martha said, which quieted him, briefly. "Two confessing witches, that girl from Topsfield and her stepmother, have said it. Burroughs is the one who led the witches' sabbath in Salem Village."

"Why would a minister do something like that?" Richard asked.

"I'm sure I don't know," Martha said. "Revenge, perhaps, against the man who took his place as minister."

Hannah wailed, and Martha realized that Sarah was gripping her baby sister's wrist too tightly. "Sarah," she reprimanded, and the girl realized and let go. Hannah plopped herself down on the floor and continued to cry.

Martha scooped the child up. "I do not say this to frighten you," she told the others, raising her voice to be heard over the noise. "It is good news. They've sent men to retrieve this minister. He will stand trial, and by the grace of God the witches will be stopped."

Thomas broke his silence. "Retrieve him from where?"

"Wells," she answered, bouncing Hannah. "Maine. He went north after leaving Salem. He was the minister in Casco Bay."

Thomas's brows lifted. The settlement at Casco Bay had been razed to the ground a few years before in a devastating Indian attack. It did not reflect well upon George Burroughs to have been the minister of a village that had been eradicated by the devil's servants.

Richard and Andrew were old enough to remember the Casco attack. Andrew, who loved stories of battles and raids, nudged his brother, then pretended he hadn't.

"My instruction for each of you," she said, fixing her children with a stern gaze and letting it rest on Andrew, "is to remain vigilant. If they are close to unmasking the witches, the devil may strike back harder."

There was a chorus of agreement, even from Andrew. She surveyed them a moment longer and then released them back to their chores.

"A witch minister," she heard Andrew whisper to Richard as they tumbled out into the yard. "His sermons must be *awful* to sit through."

It was not what she'd wanted him to take from her lecture. "Andrew," she snapped, and went after him.

* * *

Martha's fear that the witches might grow more active with their leader in custody proved all too true. Thomas brought home the unsettling news that allegations of witchcraft had been leveled against Philip English, one of the richest merchants in Salem Town, a foreigner from the Isle of Man. His wife had been accused a few weeks earlier. But when the constable had come to arrest them, the Englishes were gone.

"Did the witches get them?" Sarah piped up. She was weeding the vegetable garden. Martha hadn't realized she could hear what was said at the garden gate quite so clearly.

"No, child," Thomas said. He began unsaddling his horse. "They've gone into hiding."

"Hiding from the law," Martha said grimly, taking the horse's reins. "They certainly won't be able to clear their names that way. Nothing good on God's earth ever came of hiding from the law."

Her husband paused, then hoisted the saddle onto his shoulder. "We both know," Thomas said, "that is not true."

A few days later, word came that Sarah Osborne, one of the first three women to be accused, had died of illness in Boston prison.

It seemed impossible that life should go on while witches lurked in the colony, but it did: the harvest grew on work, not gossip. The first few weeks of May flew by, a blooming stretch of days that had Martha sweating in her apron. She deployed her children and her husband in the fields; Thomas took her orders with amiable grace. At meeting at week's end, Martha scolded eleven-year-old Phoebe Chandler for fidgeting during the singing of a hymn, demanding to know where the girl lived. She knew full well that the Chandlers ran a tavern just down the road, but Martha figured it was worth reminding anyone within earshot where, precisely, the parents of this misbehaving child could be found.

Then Thomas came home with news that made any sense of normality evaporate. He pulled her to the woodpile, out of earshot of the children. "A warrant's gone out for Roger."

It took her a moment even to understand. "Roger," she repeated. Then: "My *sister's* Roger?"

Thomas only looked at her grimly, and Martha gaped. "Roger's no witch! He says blessings over toothaches and most of the time they don't even work. I don't believe it." Her own words to Andrew, blowing back at her. *What you believe has absolutely no bearing.* She rubbed a hand over her face. "The magistrates can't think—why on earth would the devil want to recruit *Roger*?"

"Truthfully," Thomas said, "looking at it now, I'm surprised it took the magistrates this long to consider him. He's been living in Salem for years, and I know you say his treatments don't work, but he claims they do."

"He always did think his reach was further than it was," Martha murmured, pressing her knuckles to her mouth. "But he's a buffle-head, Tom, you know he is."

"Oh, I know," Thomas said. "But I don't like to think what this'll mean for Mary."

"I won't believe she knows a thing about it! *If* he's a witch, he left her near eight years ago, and she was innocent of his schemes even when they lived in the same house."

"But the magistrates might think she knows aught. If they make her testify, against her own family—"

"He isn't her family," Martha said. "He's a good-for-nothing who went off and left her first chance."

"Even so," Thomas said, and Martha went into the circle of his arm and gave herself a moment there before pulling back to ask him to cut more firewood while he was out here by the woodpile; or, if he was tired, to give her the ax so she could do it herself.

* * *

Ten days later, late enough that the younger children had been sent to bed but the older boys were whittling by the hearth, throwing the wood shavings into the fire and poking each other with the sharper fragments. Martha and Thomas were at the dining table, going over the farm's books, when something hard slammed into the door.

Thomas was on his feet before Martha even understood that it had been a knock. A heavy knock, the kind someone made with a staff—or with a broomstick. "Richard, Andrew," she hissed, and they sensed her seriousness immediately, rising to stand behind their father before she had to say another word.

Thomas called out, "Who's there?"

"Constables Ballard and Bradstreet, and Sheriff Corwin of Salem."

Martha jerked a glance at Thomas. He was staring grimly at the door, big hands open at his sides. "What business have you here?"

"Open the door, Carrier, as is your duty to God and the king."

Thomas Carrier had not been raised as one of the godly, and at this point in his life had no particular allegiance to the man who was called king in England. He cast a wary eye at his wife.

She nodded. He unbolted the door and swung it open, and for a moment she saw them only as a mass in the darkness, too many limbs and the slice of a face gone yellow in the firelight. Then one stepped forward, detaching from the others, and they were men again, three men on her doorstep.

Thomas folded his massive arms over his chest and did not invite them in. "A warrant for what?"

"For your wife," Bradstreet said. He glanced grimly around Thomas to where Martha was standing in front of the fire. "For witchcraft."

There was a moment of silence.

Then Martha set her hands on her hips, pulsing with astonishment. "Witchcraft? I have never heard such an absurd accusation in all my life. Did I not see you at meeting, sir, not five days past? And you come here now and wake my children and accuse me of *witchcraft*?"

"Not I, Goody Carrier. The girls in Salem say you've sent your shape to afflict them."

"My *shape*? In *Salem*?" The snort was involuntary, derisive. "I've never seen those girls in my life. Set the saddle on the right horse, sir. Some devil must have planted my image in their minds."

"Goody Carrier—"

"I am not done. Constable Bradstreet, you knew my parents. You know that my family and I have never failed to attend meeting, and you come to my home at this time of night bearing slander? How dare you, sir?"

"Enough." It was the dark-bearded, sallow-faced man behind Bradstreet. Martha didn't know him, but he had to be Corwin, the Salem sheriff. He stepped around Bradstreet, ignoring Thomas, to look only at Martha. "You will accompany us."

"I'll do no such thing!"

Corwin took a single step forward, and Thomas shifted. It was just a shift of his weight, but there was no mistaking it for anything but a threat. Corwin stopped and looked up at him, consideringly, for a long moment.

Then Corwin seemed to make a decision. He turned back, as if to say something to his fellows, and then in one quick movement he was swinging the long musket off his shoulder and sweeping it up to point at Thomas's heart.

Martha saw the next few moments as if her sitting room had been plunged underwater. Thomas grabbed for the ax hanging from its hook over the door lintel, and a chair scraped across the floor as Richard bumped into it in his haste to seize hold of his brother, who was lunging forward. Bradstreet's free hand flew to the hilt of his saber, and through it all the musket was rising. "Stop!" she shrieked.

Their movements stuttered. Martha was already turning toward Bradstreet to pluck the warrant from his belt. He let her take it and read it, her fingers slipping on the curling paper.

She read it twice through. It proclaimed what he had said it did and was signed by two names that were familiar to anyone in gossiping range of Salem. Magistrates Corwin and Hathorne had been running the preliminary hearings for two months, and nearly everyone who appeared in front of their bench ended up in the Salem jail. Martha had taken this as proof that the witches were being rapidly unmasked—but *she* was no witch.

She could feel Thomas's eyes on her the same way she could feel heat from the hearth fire, could almost hear him thinking. He didn't have the ax in hand, but he was close enough to the lintel to take it in an instant, and if he was slower than he'd been twenty years ago he was still quick enough to bull inside the range of Corwin's long, unwieldy musket, now half-lowered. He could have Corwin's hands off before he made the shot.

Damning himself in the process. These were the appointed representatives of His Majesty the King. If he killed any of them, he would face the noose. And her sons were not out of musket range.

"I am no witch," Martha said. She folded the warrant crisply and flicked it to Bradstreet. "I have nothing to fear under God or the law. I shall accompany you to Salem Village and set this absurd accusation to rights."

Corwin's eyes raked over her, and then, finally, the musket drifted the rest of the way down.

Martha turned to her husband, calmly, so the boys would heed her composure. "I shall return as soon as I am able."

"You will," Thomas said.

He hardly ever looked at her that way, with black iron in his eyes. She nodded once and turned to her boys. Richard looked sick, freckles standing out and gaze darting between the constables. Andrew's mouth was half-open, as if he wanted to say something but wasn't sure, for once, what it should be. "Mind your father," Martha told them. "And the little ones. Don't plant the peppers without me."

She waited for them to nod. And then she let the constable take her arm and guide her through the door and into the waiting cart.

Only then did she look back. Thomas was still in the doorway, a tall silhouette in a weak bubble of light, the night around him turning unfamiliar by degrees. The trees seemed to loom closer than they had that morning, and small animals rustled in the undergrowth, hissing almost too quietly to hear. Even the sloping dark eaves looked strange, as if someone had taken apart the house she'd been born in and fitted it back together wrong.

Something reared up in her throat and she turned away, setting her jaw tightly. She would not be afraid. This accusation was a mistake; she would resolve the mistake and return home. Her hands were not trembling. She gripped them tightly to be sure.

"On with it, then," she said sharply to the constables, and one of them murmured to the horses. The cart jerked into motion, rocking her against the railing, and they rolled forward into the dark.

15
All Maps Useless

And so we come to it. The snare tripped, the rabbit quivering. Salem's gravity finally strong enough to pull her in.

And me right along with her. This was where I'd been heading since I found the red book in the library, since I started this quest to map the contours of her world—political economy, religious paranoia, gendered mutiny—to make sure I understood what I was seeing when I looked back. To clarify the landscape in which Martha stood, so that she would show clearly against it. I thought I'd managed well enough, even at such distance, even in such slanting light.

But the night she was taken, the night Martha's story and Salem's converged, I found there was no distance. Not between us; not between any of us. That night flooded me, tied me in the cart beside her. Fear transports us through time. So does lineage, and in that moment I felt all lines of analysis unraveling, all villains rendered untouchable, all maps useless. In that moment, truth wasn't enough. I wanted revenge. I didn't care, anymore, that Martha was already dead.

16

The Examination of Martha Carrier

The description of Martha's preliminary hearing comes directly from the trial records: "Examination of Martha Carrier," May 31, 1692, (SWP No. 24.3) in the Salem Witch Trials Documentary Archive. Nearly all dialogue in the hearing is direct quotation; modifiers of speech are inspired by the original transcript, including speaking verbs like "cried" or "complained." Physical movement and action have been inferred from the transcript. According to the historical record, the jail did indeed flood in certain conditions.

Salem Town
May 31, 1692

Martha ran her fingers over the shackle underwater. The Salem Town jail flooded when it rained at high tide, an unholy combination of moon movement and bad weather. When her shackled ankle bled, the seawater swirled pink.

The cell was large, in near darkness, and crowded, stinking of sweat and excrement and salt. Her dress had gone soggy, blackening at the edges with mud, and the skin of her ankles was raw, and she was hungry, but the physical discomfort was bearable.

What was harder to bear was the whispers of some of the other women in the jail cell. *Other women.* They weren't other women. They were witches. Confessed witches, who said that they had done exactly what the girls accused them of doing, who said they had trafficked with the devil. They were in the cell with her. She had never imagined they would all be penned in together, innocent and witch. She did not speak to them—did not look at them.

But she couldn't stop listening, because some of them said there might be a way that a person could be a witch and not know it.

Martha knew that she had never treated with the devil, but this was something else entirely. She found herself running over moments of strangeness and malice like probing at a rotten tooth with her tongue. Once she had hurled a curse at her nephew Allen Toothaker, Mary's boy, and afterward the wound in his leg from the Indian Wars festered with yellow pustules and refused to heal. And there was the day she had screamed at the Fosters for trying to move the boundary line between their properties, and a few days later their calf had sickened. Coincidence, she'd thought, if she'd given it half a thought. But what if it wasn't? If you could be a witch and not know it—and these women, these confessed witches, said that you *could*—

She'd thought she was clever, all these years, facing off with the devil through a locked door, but maybe the door was already open and the devil was leaning on the jamb.

Her head was swimming with hunger, with the sharp crawling eyes of the witches on the other side of the cell. She couldn't be sure, sure to the tips of her fingernails and the ends of her hair, that the girls in Salem were wrong.

But how could such a thing have *happened*? Who could have made her a witch? Witchcraft ran in families, but her mother—that, she could not believe. There wasn't a chance that Faith Allen had ever dealt with the devil. But who else?

Perhaps no one had made her a witch. Perhaps God was letting the devil use her specter to afflict the girls as punishment for her sins. She had sinned, certainly. She was overbearing and abrasive, indulged her children, had disobeyed her father and taken Thomas to her bed unmarried simply because she had wanted to direct her own life.

What a fool she'd been. No one was given leave to direct their own lives, not on God's earth. She stared at her feet, submerged to the ankle, watching her blood curl in the water. Even the smallest things, in that moment, felt like sins: red was one of the devil's colors, but she'd always liked it. Couldn't help herself. It was so bright and bold, the color of heart's blood, of a baby when it drew its first breath, the color of dawn when a storm was coming, and the beady-eyed interrupting rooster. In the right light, her own dark hair shone russet.

"*No.*" Martha found herself speaking aloud, digging her fingernails into the flesh of her legs. Another woman looked dully at her, then away, but the pain grounded her, brought her back to the surface.

No. That *was* prideful, to think herself important enough to bring ruin upon a town through her own small preferences and indiscretions. To think she was important enough for the devil to wear her shape. And—the thought slamming into her—why should she trust confessed witches, anyway? They could be lying; were liars by nature. Why should she listen to a thing they had to say?

She was as guilty of sin as any other, but if that made her a witch, then all her neighbors were witches, every one of them. She had never seen the devil, had certainly never sent her spirit to afflict the Salem Village minister's children. She was no witch. She would tell the magistrates as much.

If she stayed true to the Lord, Martha thought, clenching her eyes shut, the Lord would have charity for her, and the devil would have no advantage.

They came for her then, as if the Lord had been waiting for her to pull her wits about her, to rid herself of the confessors' hideous whispering. A constable she didn't know and the man who ran the jail unlocked her shackle, tossing it to the floor with a splash and a dull thunk, and took her out of the cell. She ignored the other women and marched forward fast enough that the constable was pressed to keep up. This was her chance to speak with the magistrates directly, to clear up this mess. This was the chance she'd been waiting for.

Only then, all at once, it wasn't.

* * *

"Abigail Williams," the magistrate called, perched at his table in the Salem Village meeting house like a black-robed bird of prey. "Who hurts you?"

"Goody Carrier," the girl answered promptly. Her voice went clean through the courtroom like a flute, a voice made for singing children's songs. "Of Andover."

Martha stood before the magistrates' table, bracketed by constables. She could feel the girl's gaze, but she kept her eyes on the man who'd introduced himself as Magistrate Hathorne. The other magistrate sat beside him, but Hathorne, with his papery skin and thin-lipped frown, was doing all the talking.

She hadn't understood the girls would be here to speak against her—or that there would be ranks of spectators gathered behind them—but it mattered little. The girls might be bewitched, but she had not done it. She'd been told this hearing was supposed to be her chance to address the magistrates directly, and that was how she planned to use it.

Also, it was difficult to turn and look at the girls when the constables were gripping her arms hard enough to bruise. If Martha strained, she could just barely see the children lined up on her right, a neatly buttoned troop.

"Elizabeth Hubbard," the magistrate said. "Who hurts you?"

"Goody Carrier." The voice of an older girl.

"Susannah Sheldon, who hurts you?"

"Goody Carrier. She bites me, pinches me, and tells me she would cut my throat, if I did not sign her book."

"And me!" a new voice cried. "She afflicted me. Goody Carrier brought the book to me."

The magistrate leaned forward. "What do you say to this you are charged with?"

His tone was strange. He sounded stern, Martha realized with a swell of disbelief, as if she was a disobedient child who required correction.

She raised her chin. "I have not done it."

"She lies!" a girl called. "She looks upon the black man even now!"

Martha wanted to demand exactly what that was supposed to mean, but the magistrates were already twisting around in their seats, toward the back corner. Martha followed their gazes, her stomach clenching, frightened to see—

The corner was empty.

A girl shrieked. It was a different voice, younger, and from the corner of her eye Martha saw a prim child in a starched white wimple stumble forward. She was clutching at her stomach. "I'm stuck!" she exclaimed. "She's stuck a pin in me!"

One of the constable's hands tightened convulsively on Martha's arm, making her suck in a breath. She tried to turn to better see the child, but they held her firmly. She could only listen to a run of footsteps, a man's concerned voice.

Magistrate Hathorne pounded his table for order. When the room had settled, he leaned forward, eyes on Martha, and motioned to the corner. "What black man is that?" he demanded.

Martha stared at him, and then at the corner, which was still empty. "I know none."

"Yes there is!" A little girl's whimper—the pin-stuck girl. "There is, I see him!"

Another girl made a pained noise behind Martha, low and hard, like someone had shoved her. "I'm stuck," she moaned. "She's pricked me."

"What black man did you see?" the magistrate repeated. He raised his voice to be heard over the girls. His brows were drawn tight, clearly angry at the state of his courtroom and Martha's lack of cooperation, but she couldn't cooperate when *there was no one in the corner*. There was wood, empty air, light sliding down the molding, nothing else. And she hadn't pricked anyone; she knew that for certain.

The girls had to be deceived by the devil or afflicted by someone else, some true witch who was fooling them all. It was the only explanation. Martha opened her mouth to tell the magistrate so.

A flash of white, in the corner of her eye. One of the girls had come forward, one of the young ones, and Martha couldn't see her face but there was something about the movement that distracted her. The girl was on her tiptoes, practically hovering.

When the thought clarified, it was so unexpected that it took a moment to sink in: it wasn't the way a child moved when she was frightened. It was the same way that Sarah leaned around the jamb when her brothers were telling a story she wasn't supposed to be listening to, and she was afraid her parents would tell them to hush.

It was curiosity. The girl wanted to know what was going to happen next.

Martha's mouth snapped shut. The room felt sharper, as if the windows had been flung open, and a kernel of outrage was swelling in her breast. That girl wasn't afflicted by *Martha's* specter, that was for certain—but she'd stake her farm on it that the girl wasn't afflicted by anyone at all.

Some of these girls, she thought suddenly, wildly, *are lying*.

And the magistrates were *letting* them. The kernel in her chest popped, billowing outrage. "I saw no black man but your own presence," she snapped at him.

Hathorne recoiled, then swept a hand toward the girls. "Can you look upon these and not knock them down?"

Was the man a fool? "They will dissemble if I look upon them."

A dull thud: the sound of a body hitting the floor. Martha twitched in the constables' grasp. In the corner of her eye she could see that one of the girls had fallen to her knees.

Then, like scythed wheat, the rest followed, a series of knees slamming into floorboards. Children cried out, gasping, and something scraped on wood. A girl's fingernails.

"You see?" Hathorne demanded. "You look upon them and they fall down."

"It is false," Martha snapped. "The devil is a liar. I looked upon none since I came into the room but *you!*"

A girl screamed. There was the sound of a scuffle, and then one of them was on her feet, limping forward. She stopped in the middle of the courtroom, in front of Martha, and stood there stock-still.

If Martha would not turn to look at them, it seemed, they would put themselves before her. The girl was about Richard's age, her wimple knocked askew. Her eyes were closed.

A woman's voice broke the silence, calling out frightened from the gallery. "Susannah?"

The girl's eyes snapped open. Her gaze was unfocused, glazed.

"I wonder," she murmured, as if answering a question no one had asked, and then sucked in a hiss through her teeth. "What?"

The woman in the gallery had gone silent. Something about Susannah's stillness was even more unsettling than the hysterics of the children. It was an animal stillness, foreign in a room of law, hardly human. Slowly, so slowly she hardly seemed to be moving, Susannah turned her head.

Her gaze came to rest on Martha—focused—sharpened. Against her will, Martha felt her skin prickling.

The blood drained from Susannah's cheeks, leaving her the color of curdled milk. In a high-pitched, ragged voice, she asked, "Could you *murder* thirteen persons?"

Before Martha could react, another girl stumbled forward. "There!" she gasped. "There they lie!" She pointed off to Martha's right, and the constable on that side flinched. "Thirteen ghosts!"

Martha didn't know which of the girls screamed first, but suddenly they were all shrieking, climbing to their feet and ripping at their arms and legs as if to tear away the skin. The little pin-pricked girl flinched back, throwing up her hands. "She killed them!" the child screeched. "She—!" She choked, grabbing at her own throat. "Thirteen!" she gargled. "In Andover!"

Understanding opened like a chasm at Martha's feet. The children meant to call upon the plague.

That she would not stand for, would not let the *magistrates* stand for. Martha ignored yet another girl who was raising a finger and pointing at nothing. She raised her voice to carry to the magistrates, to the watching crowd, to the whole damned village. "It is a *shameful thing* that you should mind these folks that are out of their wits!"

Hathorne slammed a hand down on his desk. "Do you not see the ghosts?"

"If I do speak you will not believe me!"

"You do see them!" one of the girls cried. "The thirteen. You *do* see them."

"You *lie*. I am wronged."

"The black man!" the girl shrieked. "He whispers in her ear!" She stumbled, and another girl grabbed her arm to support her—and cried out, letting go as if she been scalded. The first girl tumbled violently to the floor, and the others fell after her.

This time they didn't stay still: they writhed and twitched, moaning, crying out for the torment to stop. One girl bent backward, her body arching like a bow. There was clamor from the spectator's gallery, people rushing forward. The pile of contorting bodies only screamed louder.

The magistrate shouted something, pounding on his desk, and Martha could hardly hear it over the noise but the constables seemed to understand. They wrenched her wrists behind her and bound them there. She spat a curse at them, and one flinched, but the other ignored her and knelt to hobble her feet.

As soon as the last knot was tied, the moaning stopped like a door had been slammed. The girls sat up, slowly, looking about them. Martha wanted to laugh, or possibly scream, but before she could speak the magistrate was ordering the constables to take her away.

Over her shoulder, Martha heard one of the girls, in a voice hoarse from screaming, say, "Forty years. This woman told me she has been a witch these forty years."

Forty years before, Martha had been inside her mother's stomach. They dragged her out of the meeting house.

17
Naming Names

At the turning of the year, as the world began to slingshot back toward warmth, I had a dream that my mouth was sewn shut. The dream was an unformed thing, only impulse and color, but I knew I had to say something—my mother was there, and I had to tell her something, urgently—but I couldn't speak. I struggled as hard as I could, wrenched my lips apart, and came awake panting. I'd been trying so hard to speak that I'd spoken out loud, in my bedroom in the world.

Salem's silences shout as loudly as its voices. There are the potentially deliberate blank spaces in the archive, the gaping holes where the missing Salem Village record books should be. There is the general Puritan silence on surrounding Indigenous communities, who remained a wraithlike "other" in the Puritan worldview. There are individuals, like Tituba, who disappear after 1692. Tituba survived the trials only for Samuel Parris to refuse to pay the jail fees that he, as her enslaver, owed the prison-keeper for her long imprisonment. Parris didn't want to pay, so instead he seems to have sold Tituba, out of Salem and out of the historical record. There's no more information to be found about her, after that. Tituba goes silent.

Martha was known for her voice, her unruly tongue. She was the last person I'd associate with silence, but there it was, in the transcript of her preliminary hearing. Martha had told the magistrates, *If I do speak you will not believe me.*

That was it, I realized, watching red light from the crosswalk outside blink against the ceiling. That sentence marked the moment in which Martha had realized she could say nothing to get through to the judges, that her words meant nothing. Which was, admittedly, a particular nightmare of mine. I put a lot of faith in the idea that there was such a thing as *the right words*, that you could find them and organize them, and that they could make a difference, or at the very least an impression.

There were no right words for Martha to find. Her voice had been useless. Her mouth might as well have been sewn shut.

The witchcraft court in Salem was officially called the Court of Oyer and Terminer, Latin for *To Hear and Determine*, but the judges there, like the magistrates who ran the preliminary hearings, seem to have been more interested in the determining part than the hearing part. They were only interested in *hearing* what an accused witch had to say if it was a confession. Words of confession had value. Words of innocence, of protest, were useless, currency for a lost time, as devalued and disbelieved as forgeries.

If your words are stripped of all value, if you can't convince the court that you're telling the truth about your innocence, then you're left with only one choice: whether to say what they *will* believe. Whether to confess. For if the judges on the court of *hearing and determining* did not hear, neither were they the ones who truly had to do the determining. In the Salem witch trials, it was the *accused* who had to determine what she believed. Whom she trusted.

Do you trust yourself? Your memory? Do you believe you know who you are, and no one else can tell you? Do you believe someone else might have made you a witch? Do you believe the accusers, those charlatan surgeons, who say that they have cut you open and laid bare your rotten soul? Or do you believe in the court? In due process? Do you believe the court will hear you? Do you believe it can distinguish the innocent from the guilty? Do you still believe some people are guilty?

Standing in the Salem Village meeting house that day, Martha would have had to make all those choices. Confession wasn't the obvious answer, not at the beginning, not to anyone. Here's the thing about confessing to witchcraft in Massachusetts before the Salem witch trials: it wasn't something a person could do and survive. The colony got its list of capital crimes directly from the Bible, and one of the earliest versions of the legal code, the "Body of Liberties," stated the punishment for witchcraft in no uncertain terms: "If any Man or Woman be a Witch they shall be put to Death."[1] Before Salem, only four people confessed to witchcraft in Massachusetts,[2] and all those who were found mentally competent were executed.

But somehow, in Salem, those clear instructions got muddled. In Salem, confessors were *not* killed. Instead, confession became a way to escape the noose, flying in the face of tradition and law alike, illuminating an entirely different paradigm of belief.

It started with Tituba, the first confessor. After her confession, Tituba should have had a trial and, assuming the jury took her confession as (uncoerced) proof, been executed. But none of this came to pass.

What saved Tituba's life, at least at first, was a combination of timing and politics. Authorizing a trial and execution was the purview of the governor's office, and in March of 1692, when Tituba became Salem's first confessor, the Puritans hadn't had a governor in three years.

It was their own doing. They'd overthrown their last governor, a man named Edmund Andros. Bear with me for a minute. It happened like this: In 1684, angry with the Puritans for a number of indiscretions (e.g., breaking trade laws, harassing Quakers) the king of England revoked the Puritan charter, the document that gave the Puritans sovereignty over Massachusetts. He appointed Edmund Andros to rule New England in 1686. Andros promptly got rid of the Massachusetts legislature, took away special privileges for Puritans, and appropriated a Puritan meeting house for an Anglican service. He levied heavy taxes and fees on the common people and redistributed the property of the wealthy among his own friends. At one point, he told a Puritan, "Either you are subjects or you are rebels."[3]

They were proto-Americans, and they decided to be rebels. In 1689, when William of Orange invaded England in what would eventually be called the Glorious Revolution, the Puritan clergy in Massachusetts seized the opportunity of a coup in the mother country to organize one in the colony. Aided by a citizen's militia, the clergy overthrew Governor Edmund Andros and put him in prison.

Then they asked William, the new king of England, for a replacement governor and the reinstatement of their beloved Puritan charter. But William, understandably busy, didn't get around to the issue of Massachusetts for a couple of years. Andros's replacement wouldn't arrive until two and a half months after the *first* accusations were made in Salem.

In the meantime, the interim governor, Simon Bradstreet, refused to authorize any trials for witchcraft. This may have been a reluctance to step on the incoming governor's toes—by the time Tituba confessed, everyone knew a new governor was on his way. Whatever the reason for Bradstreet's reticence, Salem's jail was stocked with accused witches and a few confessors when the new governor's ship finally sailed into Boston Harbor in May of 1692.

The governor, a New England man named William Phips, was not part of the Puritan elite. He was a wheelwright turned treasure-hunter, more of a soldier than a politician. When he found himself in the middle of a witchcraft outbreak, he knew he was out of his depth.

On the advice of his deputies, Phips created a special court to handle the accusations: the Court of Oyer and Terminer. He appointed his lieutenant governor, William Stoughton, to be chief justice. Stoughton had experience with witchcraft accusations—he'd served in the government that had hanged Goody Glover as a witch in Boston, four years prior—but not with an outbreak. To figure out how to try the cases (what methodology to use, what theology to rely on) the court accepted advice from the colony's preeminent ministers.

One minister who gave the court advice was Cotton Mather, whose grandfather John Cotton had been the one to write the Body of Liberties legal code in 1641—the text that promised death to all witches. On the same day as Martha's preliminary hearing for witchcraft, Cotton Mather wrote a letter to one of the judges on the newly formed Court of Oyer and Terminer that departed from his grandfather's instructions. The judge was a member of Mather's church, and Mather was advising him as to how he thought the court should proceed.

Mather believed that spectral evidence wasn't reliable enough to convict someone of witchcraft. At most, he thought, spectral evidence like the afflicted girls' visions could justify searching a suspected witch's home for material evidence, such as poppets or ritual objects. Instead, Mather said, the court should value a different kind of evidence. The most credible proof of guilt was confession.

He wrote that if the witches who were "lesser criminals"—those who had been pressured or tricked into doing witchcraft by more experienced witches or devils—confessed,[4] the court might consider granting them a reprieve. If a confessor showed "solemn, open, public, and explicit renunciation of the Devil,"[5] the court should go easy on them.

Mather was recommending the possibility of a plea deal for a witch. If a witch recanted, and if the specific crimes she admitted to were under a certain threshold (some light affliction was permissible), she could be forgiven. Confession was a well-established method of repenting and reconciliation in Puritan Massachusetts, after all. Puritans confessed to things all the time. When they joined churches, they told the stories of their spiritual lives; when they sinned, they recounted transgressions in front of the whole community in order to gain forgiveness. Confession was normally used to address smaller indiscretions, certainly, but perhaps it could even reconcile a witch.

It was a gamble, but the witch's plea deal, for Mather, seems to have slotted nicely into a much grander theological ambition: that of a religious revival.[6]

As the witchcraft accusations began in Salem Village, Mather had led a meeting of ministers in Boston to discuss the "most heavy and wasting judgments of heaven upon our distressed land."[7] They believed that the hardships facing Massachusetts had been brought upon the Puritans by their own moral failure. This generation of Puritans was less devout, less committed to the project of a new holy land. If Massachusetts was ever going to become a shining city on a hill, its settlers needed "the recovery of practical religion in our hearts and minds"—and they needed it now.[8]

What you have to understand is that Cotton Mather believed it was the end of the world. According to his calculations, the Day of Resurrection was only a few years away. In the first week of April, while the afflicted girls ramped up accusations in Salem, Mather preached a sermon in Boston's North Church about Armageddon.

"The Lord is at hand," he told his congregation. "We are doubtless very near the Last Hours of that Wicked One, whom our Lord Shall Destroy with the Brightness of his Coming. ... We should always be also Preparing for that Stupendious Revolution."[9]

Mather saw the witchcraft outbreak in Salem as a precursor to this "Stupendious Revolution," proof that the devil (angry with the Puritans for trying to create their shining city on the hill) was striking back. For as the trials went on, the story of what the witches wanted twisted and grew. The witches had not, it emerged, simply come to afflict Salem Village by pinching its children. They had not even come to tear down the Salem Village church.

The true aim of the witches—the true aim of the devil—was to destroy *all* the churches of New England. To destroy the colony and establish Satan's kingdom in place of God's.

The witches, then, were fundamental enemies of the Puritan project. Which does not seem to square with Mather's recommended plea deal. If the witches were trying to tear down the Puritan project, why would he recommend that any of them be allowed to live?

Perhaps they could help him reinforce the Puritan project in another way. The other thing the witchcraft outbreak proved to Mather was that God, angry with the Puritans' moral deterioration, was letting the devil afflict them.[10] To fight the witches, then, they needed to regain God's favor. To regain God's favor, they needed that national reformation.

They needed confession. It was an avenue through which a sinner could repent and be redeemed, a version in miniature of what Mather thought the whole colony needed. Confession was a theological weapon in the holy war. And there had never been an opportunity for widespread confession like the witch trials.

Where do you place your faith? I think Mather put his in God and the court, in the concept of the court as God, hearing and determining. In the idea that each confession returned a lost soul from the devil to God, and so proved that the Puritans were successful foot soldiers in the divine battle against evil. In the idea that the confessions of the accused would be true, and valuable, like coin that could be banked against divine displeasure.

It should be mentioned, at this juncture, that the Puritan project was in some real, non–witch-related danger. Along with their new governor, Massachusetts had indeed received a new charter from the king. But it was a shriveled husk of the document that had given them permission to colonize Massachusetts, and a heavy blow for the Puritan project in the New World.

The new charter ensured religious tolerance for all other Christians (except Catholics) in the colony. Once it went into effect, any non-Catholic Christian man with a substantial enough income would gain the right to vote, regardless of whether he was part of a Puritan church.[11] Puritans would be unable to bar people like Anglicans and Baptists, often their enemies, from serving on juries. Infidels were about to get political rights in the Puritan holy land.

It is hard to imagine that the threat posed by the new charter never became linked, in the minds of the political men running and advising the court, with the "witches' plot" to destroy New England. The threat was the same: the end of Puritan supremacy. It is easy to imagine that they saw similarities between the specter of a witch and the specter of religious tolerance, between the spiritual consequences for a village afflicted by witches and the very real political consequences for a village forced to share power with non-Puritans. For the Puritans, the spiritual was political.

And it is easy to imagine, too, that battling the witchcraft outbreak and resisting the diluted Puritan charter might have begun to bleed into each other. The trials could have become a kind of proxy war. What better way to assert Puritan power in Massachusetts than a religious revival, in the face of Anglicans and Baptists and even the devil himself? And what better way to prove to God that the Puritans were worth saving, that their holy project was *worth* protecting, than to coax witches away from the devil and bring them, through confession, into the light?

* * *

Mather's advice in that letter never became official court doctrine. The court never said outright that "lesser criminals" would be spared if they confessed. But as the trials progressed, it became understood by the accused that sparing confessors was, indeed, the court's modus operandi.[12] No one who confessed to witchcraft in Salem was hanged. Not a single person.

And so, over the course of the trials, an unprecedented fifty-four people confessed to witchcraft. This spread of confession is what transformed the Salem witch trials from an isolated tragedy to an unmitigated disaster, running wild across the colony, because to prove that your confession was valid, that you had really renounced witchcraft and repented, you had to give the names of other witches.

This was in part because everyone knew witches didn't work alone. The Court of Oyer and Terminer was charged with ferreting out all the satanic soldiers in the colony. It follows that they would demand confessing witches give the names of their compatriots. But the court's demand for names cannot be understood solely through the lens of identifying witches, because by midsummer, the court was accepting confessions even if all the witches a confessor named were already in custody.

In the 1970s, the journalist Victor Navasky developed what he called the Informer Principle to analyze the political endeavor that we now call

McCarthyism, when Congress held hearings to try to identify Communists. Beginning in the late 1940s, people were brought before the House Un-American Activities Committee and pressured to inform on anyone they might know who harbored Communist sympathies. Navasky wrote:

> *The Informer Principle held not merely that there was nothing wrong with naming names, but that it was the litmus test, the ultimate evidence, the guarantor of patriotism. If the witness was "cooperative" in the legislative hearings, he was generally (though not always) permitted to return to society. If not, he remained on the political index, which at a minimum meant career purgatory. It was a corollary of the Informer Principle that the act of informing was more important than the information imparted.*[13]

Navasky could have written it about Salem. By confessing before the Court of Oyer and Terminer and naming comrades in the devil's plot, a confessor proved that her break with Satan was genuine. She demonstrated that she no longer wanted to destroy the Puritan project. She proved she was worthy of being saved. Confession was, indeed, a litmus test, the guarantor of both patriotism and piety.

Which meant that the accused witch who did not confess and identify others was considered to be unrepentant, un-pious—in a word, an *unbeliever*, the worst thing a Puritan could be. The witch who refused to confess proved herself to be on the side of the devil. She was marked as unfit to be part of the community. She would not be allowed to return to it alive.

This is the witch the Court of Oyer and Terminer would hang by the neck until dead. What made someone worth killing in Salem in 1692 was not the practice of witchcraft. It was the refusal to believe that you were one.

Some confessors do seem to have decided to believe that they *were* witches. I don't just mean they lied; I mean they seem to have believed. Lying was a sin, after all, and to lie in a court of law was to perjure oneself in the eyes of God (sin). And to name others was to bear false witness (sin). If people believed themselves to be lying when they confessed, they faced not only ethical recrimination but damnation.

So they looked for loopholes. As the trials proceeded and more accused witches were coerced into confessing to save their lives, it became common for confessors to claim that someone else had made them a witch. A mother, or a grandmother, usually, since witchcraft ran in matrilineal lines. This allowed them to believe they were witches *and* that it wasn't their fault. Confessors told the court they had only just realized their true natures and were ready to repent. They assimilated to the court's belief system in a way that should have expunged their souls.

They had varying degrees of success. Cotton Mather noted that some confessors were terribly tormented after confessing. He wrote that they appeared to have "undergone the Pains of many Deaths for their Confessions."[14]

Mather interpreted these pains as the handiwork of demons, torturing confessed witches for breaking the covenant they'd made with the devil. I read it another way. To accuse someone of witchcraft in Salem was to place them in the role of the witch, the role of someone who has fundamentally violated the social contract and should therefore be excised from society. But to be an accuser was, in fact, to become the real violator of that contract, and this kind of violation corrodes. It poisons integrity, eats away at honor. And even if you manage to convince yourself that someone else made you a witch, that you're an innocent victim, on some level you know. Belief can only carry us so far. It was possible to survive the Salem witch trials if you were willing to confess, but it was impossible to do so with your soul intact.

Arthur Miller was right to call it *the crucible*. Salem's where you find out what you're made of. Will you be fooled, speak out, stand by? Refuse to sign a false confession, or become convinced it isn't false? Will you sacrifice your neighbors? Sacrifice yourself? Choose mortal or immortal life? When your words don't matter and you're under the knife, do you name someone else to take your place?

18
In the Jail

The quotations Thomas reads aloud from the ministers' letter are direct quotes from "The Return of Several Ministers," later published in A Further Account of the Tryals of the New-England Witches *by Increase Mather and Deodat Lawson (1693). The description of the search for a "witch teat" is drawn from the trial records ("Physical Examination of Bridget Bishop, Rebecca Nurse, Elizabeth Procter, Alice Parker, Susannah Martin, and Sarah Good, No. 1" June 2, 1692, SWP No. 13.20 in the Salem Witch Trials Documentary Archive). The description of Bridget Bishop's trial and the use of the touch test draws from Cotton Mather's account in* Wonders of the Invisible World *(1692). The rumor about Joseph and Thomas Putnam is reported by Charles W. Upham in* Salem Witchcraft *(1867). Other details, including the content of Roger Toothaker's examination and the resignation of the judge, draw from Marilynne K. Roach's* The Salem Witch Trials *(2004).*

Salem Town
May 31–June 15, 1692

When Martha was brought back to the Salem Town jail after her preliminary hearing, the cell seemed more crowded with frightened, bedraggled women than it had even a few hours before. The jailer towed her to an empty space on the bench, near a woman who sat with her left ankle manacled and her head bowed and a girl with her knees hiked up.

Martha was so distracted, the shrieks of the afflicted children ringing in her ears, that she didn't recognize them until the girl looked up and cried, "Aunt Martha!" and Martha stumbled before the jailer even pushed her down next to them.

"Mary," she whispered as he shackled her. It was her *sister* sitting on the bench, and the girl was Mary's ten-year-old daughter, Margaret. Martha reached out her hand and Margaret clung to it. "Ouch, child, I'm here. Mary, what's happened? Who's accused you? Those girls are liars, they are dissemblers, they are not—"

Mary was shaking her head. "None of them," she said. "Roger."

It kicked Martha in the face like a mule. "Your *husband*?"

"No, he did not accuse me, but he's—" Mary choked, closing her eyes. The words came out strangled. "He's confessed."

Martha leaned back against the cell wall. Her shackle clanked. "That . . . fool."

"Martha—"

"That good-for-nothing *dung heap of a man*. If he was in here, I would *skin* him—"

"Martha!" Mary snapped, and she drew herself out of righteous fury to realize that Margaret was crying.

"Oh, child, don't." Martha squeezed her niece's hand. "Your father is no witch. He's simply an addle-pated—" Mary's fingernails dug into her elbow. "He is simply wrong."

"He's no witch," Mary agreed. "But he told the magistrates—Martha, he told them that he had used magic to fight a witch, mayhap even kill one. I suppose he thought they wouldn't mind that he'd dabbled in the devil's arts if it was *against* the witches, but—"

"Roger Toothaker," Martha interrupted, "a *witch killer*?"

Mary's fingers dug in harder. "Stop *laughing*," she grated out, more savage than Martha had seen her in many years. "He claims he can—" She choked again, and grasped at her breast, struggling for air.

Martha had seen Mary's fear choke her like this when they were children, though not in many years. She placed her hand on her sister's breast, pressing gently. "Breathe, Mary. It's all right. There you are."

Mary dragged a breath in through her nose. "He claims he taught Margaret," she managed.

Any urge to laugh vanished. Margaret was sitting hunched over her knees, and at her mother's words her head sunk deeper into her shoulders as if in anticipation of a blow. Her eyes flicked to Martha and then away.

It dawned on Martha that Margaret was afraid that she might believe what Roger had said.

Martha had hardly ever believed *anything* Roger Toothaker said. "What a load of dung," she told her sister firmly.

Margaret sniffed and gripped her knees more tightly, but the lines at the edges of Mary's eyes smoothed out. Martha took her hand and said nothing, letting her sister hold on to her.

That night, as Mary snored, Martha thanked God for Roger Toothaker. She would never have wished this stinking place on her sister or her niece, but it was an unbelievable comfort to have them beside her. Forget their differences; forget that Mary had never truly forgiven Martha for getting herself with child while she'd been living in Mary's house. None of it mattered. A sister is a fact of life like the sun or the sky. Mary had been there when Martha was born, and to be with her now transformed the jail from a sucking hole of fear into something endurable.

The sisters fell into a routine. They would braid their hair back, eat the rations of bread and milk the jailer brought them, and then either Martha or Mary would recite a Bible story to Margaret. Afterward, the three of them would discuss it, and sometimes another woman would join in. Susannah Martin, the widow of the old Salem Town blacksmith, often had an opinion, and talking in the evenings Martha discovered that Susannah had an ear for the best gossip and a tongue as sharp as Martha's own. She, too, had scolded the judges for idiocy at her hearing, and shared Martha's opinion that at least some of the girls were not bewitched at all.

The cell was terribly loud. Women breathing, farting, weeping, snoring, drowning out the men down the hall, insisting to the jailer that they were innocent. Sarah Good's five-year-old daughter, Dorothy, was in the cell, and she didn't seem to understand what was happening. She sang children's songs and tried to jump rope with the chains and screamed when they fell on her feet. Her quiet, steadfast dismissal of the afflictions was deeply heartening.

The confessors and the unconfessed stayed on opposite sides of the cell. There were fewer confessors than Martha had originally thought—it was really only the Indian, the Hobbs girl, and the girl's stepmother—but they mostly went unchained and kept apart. Martha did not speak to them. She no longer trusted the authority of the court, nor of the afflicted girls, but there was always the chance that one of the *confessors* was telling the truth. There was always the chance that one of the women in the jail with her was, indeed, a witch—perhaps even the witch who had afflicted the judges, addling their brains, twisting them to her dark designs.

And if there was no witch, if the girls were entirely dissembling, then the confessors were either gullible or they were cowards. Martha had no time for either.

Word came that the witchcraft court had set its first session. The court would be made up of nine justices. Eighteen men had been summoned to serve as grand jurors and forty-eight to serve as regular jurors, if the case moved to full trial.

"And they all came?" Martha said derisively when she overheard the other prisoners discussing the appointments.

"So many?" Martha curled her lip. "And they all came?"

"Yes," Mary answered. "Of course they came."

Martha scoffed, partially because she knew that it would comfort Margaret. It was a bit of a performance, both of them acting as they were supposed to: Martha rash and dismissive, Mary cool and thoughtful, besides her moments of choking fear, which both sisters tried to hide from Margaret. It was easier to be here with a role to play, with someone else to look out for. "One of them must realize that they are being deceived."

"Be grateful there are so many," Mary said. She was looking past Martha, one hand on her daughter's hair. "Perhaps one of them will prove immune to Satan's charms."

The first person to be tried was Bridget Bishop, who ran the tavern on the outskirts of Salem Town. There had always been rumors about her, Martha learned. She'd been accused of witchcraft years ago, although she'd been found innocent at the time by the minister of the nearby town of Beverly.

The jailor came for Bridget Bishop on a sticky morning just a few days after Martha's hearing. He took five others along with her, including Susannah Martin.

The five other women were returned to the cell in the early afternoon in varying states of distress. Sarah Good was spitting with fury, old Rebecca Nurse nearly catatonic. It was Susannah Martin who spoke for all of them, when she turned and saw their cellmates' darting, ravenous looks.

"Searched us for a witch teat," Susannah said evenly.

Someone made a noise. A witch teat was the place where a witch was said to suckle her familiar, the devilish creature that came to her when she made a deal with the devil. It could resemble a natural blemish, but the familiar would latch on and draw succor.

Martha liked Susannah, warily. It prompted her to ask, "What did they find?"

Sarah Good and Elizabeth Procter glared at her. "Nothing," Susannah said, unfazed. "Bit of flesh, that's all."

"On all of you?"

"No," Elizabeth Procter said shortly. "They said they saw something on me, Goody Bishop, and Goody Nurse."

"Bit of flesh," Susannah Martin repeated.

"Where?" Martha asked, and Mary elbowed her sharply.

"By the anus, dear," Susannah Martin said. Martha couldn't quite keep her gaze from dropping to Elizabeth Procter's stained skirts, hiding whatever was behind them. "Why, afeared they'll find one on you?"

"Watch your mouth, Goody Martin," Martha said, loud enough for the whole cell to hear. She didn't have to speak loudly; everyone was listening. "I'm no witch."

"Nor am I," Elizabeth Procter said sharply. She jerked her chin sharply at Rebecca Nurse. "Nor is she."

"And Goody Bishop?"

"Goody Bishop is in for trial," the last of the women who'd been searched said. Alice Parker, the soft-spoken wife of a fisherman from Salem Town, had come through the search for a witch teat unscathed, though she still looked shaken. "They have been hearing the evidence against her all day."

Bridget Bishop was brought back a trembling mess a few hours later. Martha watched as Alice Parker and another woman crept forward to murmur to Bridget, laying tentative, soothing hands on her arm.

Bridget mumbled something, and her face fractured like a frozen stream in the first thaw, something caving in and floating away. Alice Parker turned to the cell and told them, speaking quietly to no one and to everyone, that the grand jury had indicted Goody Bishop on five formal counts of witchcraft.

The only sound was Sarah Good's child sucking on her fist. Bridget had, of course, pled not guilty, Alice Parker continued, but the court heard the accusations against her, and the report of the witch teat, and the Salem girls' spectral testimony. The girls had been there in the courtroom, their afflictions on full display. Martha could imagine it only too well.

Each time Bridget turned her eye upon them, the girls screamed and fell to the floor, limbs thrashing and contorting. The only thing that relieved them was the touch of Bridget's hand, pressed by the court officer against their skin. When the accused witch touched the girls, they relaxed, as if the afflicting spirit had been sucked back into the witch who sent it. This was the touch test, a well-known method of divining a witch.

In the face of such clear evidence of affliction, the court could do nothing but find Bridget Bishop guilty.

Almost before the damning words left Alice Parker's mouth, the cell exploded with noise. One of the confessors pointed a horrible finger at anyone who moved; Sarah Good was shouting; her child had started to wail. Martha heard her sister say, "Oh, Lord, have mercy," and Martha took her hand automatically, though it was unclear to her if Mary was praying for Bridget or for those now stuck in the cell with her.

"It's all right," Martha whispered back. "I don't believe they'll execute her."

Mary looked at her strangely. "Why not?"

She struggled to explain. It was faith, really, that was all. Faith that someone would recognize the accusers for the dissemblers they were, recognize the trick the devil was playing on them all. Faith that someone would realize they had been, all of them, deceived, and the true architect of their suffering was chuckling to himself somewhere close by, on the other side of a door.

"I just don't," Martha said. "You'll see. If Goody Bishop is innocent, the Lord will see her through."

A week later, on the tenth of June, the jailer and the constable took Bridget Bishop away. Her shrieks rattled in the empty space between Martha's ribs for hours, only growing stronger as the day lengthened and shuttered and Bridget did not return.

The women in the jail found out, later, that there hadn't been time to build a scaffold. Just a week after her conviction, on the tallest hill in Salem Town, Bridget Bishop had been hanged from the branch of a tree.

* * *

The next few days were awful. Martha was grim, Mary choked on her words, and Margaret flinched at anything that moved. Most of the women seemed to be in a kind of blurred, suspended state, one ear always cocked toward the cell door.

But then word came—through Susannah Martin, who seemed to have struck some kind of gossip deal with the jailer—that zinged through Martha, burning away the dull horror. "See?" she whispered to Mary. "They are beginning to realize."

Salem Village's accusers, it seemed, were going quiet. A few of the afflicted girls were still having fits, but no new witches were arrested in the days after Bridget Bishop died. No new women joined the crowded cell. No one left it, either, but that seemed less important. What mattered was that accusations were slowing down, arrests had stopped entirely, and—perhaps even better— one of the judges on the witchcraft court had resigned his post. There were doubts, it seemed, about how Bridget's case had been handled.

It made Martha hopeful enough that when Thomas finally paid the requisite visitation bribes to the jailer, later that same week, she greeted him in strong spirits.

The jailer let Thomas stand on one side of the bars and unchained Martha so she could stand on the other. There was no privacy, but Martha pressed herself close, sticking her hands through the gaps.

Thomas took them, gripping hard. His gaze traveled down her body and back up again. He looked stricken.

Before he could speak, Martha told him, "You look exhausted."

It startled something like a laugh from him. He opened his mouth, shut it, gripped her hands more tightly.

"How are the children?"

"Well enough," he said, which she took to mean, *no one is ill.* "They miss you."

"Don't bring them here." Bile hit the back of her throat at the thought of her children seeing her in her tacky dress, manacled to the wall. "Tom, don't bring them."

"I won't."

"I mean it."

"I won't, love." It was whispered. She shut her eyes and gripped him tighter. "Come home."

"Don't trouble yourself." Martha opened her eyes and fixed him with the calmest, coolest look she could manage, to show him she believed it. To show him there was no reason for anyone to disbelieve it. "I intend to."

"Anyone giving you trouble?"

"Aside from him?" She cast a glance in the direction the jailer had gone. "No."

"The witches who've confessed—"

"Fools," she said. It was what she'd decided on. "Cursed fools. Bewitched or lying." She raised her chin, drawing herself up to her full height. "Did you hear about the judge who left the court? I wouldn't be surprised if they let the rest of us out soon. No, listen to me. Don't fret. You'll tell the children that, won't you? That I'll be home soon?"

"I'll tell them," Thomas said. He was holding her hands so tightly it almost hurt. He hardly ever forgot his own strength, but she supposed she'd forgive him for it, this once. "I'll tell them," he said again, and then his gaze slid past her, into the cell. "Martha. Listen. I need to tell *you* something."

His voice was grim. Martha drew back. "What is it?"

"Roger," Thomas said. "He died last night, in the Boston jail."

Mary spent the night weeping on Martha's shoulder. Margaret did not. When Mary had finally cried herself into an exhausted, shaky sleep, Margaret looked up at her aunt and said, quietly, "I hate him."

Martha reached over her sister, trying not to disturb her, to pet Margaret's cheek. "No, child," she said gently. "You don't."

"I do," Margaret whispered. "He said he taught me witchcraft, but he didn't teach me anything. If he'd known something, I wish he might have told me."

"Margaret," Martha said softly, "your father was many things. But he wasn't a witch-killer."

Margaret looked as if she might say something else, but she'd inherited her mother's habit of biting down on words before they could escape. In the end she shut her eyes and rested her head against the stones, but Martha thought she pretended to sleep for a long time before she managed it.

* * *

Their routine changed. Nights, Mary wept—too much, Martha thought privately, for a man who'd left her years ago. Days, the sisters still taught Margaret scripture, but more and more often Mary would excuse herself midway through a conversation, pleading exhaustion, to burrow into the corner of the cell and gaze at nothing, and Martha would have to rope in Susannah Martin to help with Margaret's lessons.

By the middle of June, wet heat hung heavy over the jail's windless corridors. Salt grooved its way into Martha's forehead, her neck, her thighs. Her ankle was braceleted with raw flesh.

But on Thomas's next visit, he reported that a number of ministers had sent the Massachusetts council—which included several of the judges who sat on the witchcraft court—a promising letter. "They advised the court to take spectral testimony under careful advisement," he told her. "They think that the devil *can* plant the image of an innocent in the mind of an afflicted person, after all."

"I *knew* it." Martha clutched at Thomas's hand through the bars and turned to the cell, viciously triumphant. "Hear *that*?" she spat at the knot of confessors. "The shapes the girls see—the shapes *you* see—they could be sent by anyone."

Muttering rose, but Thomas had managed to get hold of a copy of the ministers' letter. He dug it out of his pocket and unfolded it carefully. "'There is a need of a very critical and exquisite caution,'" he read, "'lest by too much credulity for things received only upon the devil's authority, there be a door opened for a long train of miserable consequences.' And they urge"—he squinted. "'Exceeding tenderness,' toward those accused persons who are 'formerly of an unblemished reputation.'"

"That's all very well," Susannah Martin called out, "but what about the rest of us?"

Martha smiled. Thomas did not, but Martha soothed him, reminding him that if the court decided not to allow reports of spectral evidence, she was as good as out, for it was the only kind of evidence they had against her. She had made no confession. All she had to do was wait.

Late that night, when Thomas had gone and Mary and Margaret were dozing, Martha slumped on the bench. It was too hot to sleep. She shifted restlessly, mopping the sweat from her forehead and the back of her neck with a dirty sleeve, and caught Susannah Martin watching her. She could just make out the shine of Susannah's open eyes in the dark.

"What?" Martha whispered.

Susannah was quiet for a moment. Then she said, "'Persons formerly of an unblemished reputation.' I'd wager anything they mean Rebecca."

Martha's gaze slid to the lump of darkness that was Rebecca Nurse, slumbering on a bench with her head in her sister's lap. She had gleaned from jailhouse gossip that no one in Salem Village was more pious, devout, or respected than Rebecca Nurse, though it hadn't stopped the searchers from finding a witch teat on her body.

"Rebecca is unblemished," Susannah murmured, so quietly that they were only the suggestion of words, offered into the dark. But then she added, delicately, "Which isn't to say she hasn't any enemies."

"Who?" Martha asked, a matching breath, and Susannah explained that Rebecca's maiden family, the Townes, had been fighting with Salem's Putnam family over a certain plot of land for generations. It was Thomas Putnam who had filed the complaint against Rebecca, Susannah murmured; the accusation had come from his daughter and from his wife. If that wasn't enough, Rebecca's husband had been allied, in his tenure on the Salem Village council, with Thomas Putnam's half brother Joseph, who was Putnam's most bitter enemy.

Martha listened with increasing consternation, trying to keep the various Salem families straight. "I think," she said finally, "that Salem Village might be under a curse after all."

Susannah snorted. "No more than elsewhere."

Rats squeaked nearby. Martha leaned her head back against the stone, listening to her sister breathing beside her.

She was halfway to dozing when Susannah spoke again, so quietly that Martha nearly missed it. "The half brother. Joseph," Susannah murmured.

Martha rolled her head to the side, resting her cheek on the cool stone. "What about him?"

"I heard—this is only rumor, mind—but I heard that Joseph Putnam went to his brother Thomas, and told him that if he dared to touch anyone in Joseph's household with his foul lies, he would answer for it. And now Joseph keeps a horse saddled, and he won't go out without a gun."

The way she said it, whispered in the still night air, gave the words a sense of unreality, like a child's rhyme that became more senseless the more you thought about it. "What?" Martha said again. "Then he believes the accusations are lies?"

A slight shift in the dark. Susannah was inclining her head one way, then the other.

"Why has he not spoken publicly against his brother? If he believes they're lies—will he speak for us?"

"He might speak for Rebecca Nurse," Susannah said. "She is, after all, of unblemished reputation."

Martha absorbed this. She thought, without conscious direction, of her oldest son, Richard, who had avoided being a bastard by the thinnest margin. Of her sister, who had married a man who claimed to kill witches.

Before she could gather her thoughts, Susannah asked, "Will your husband speak for you, do you think?"

Martha straightened, jarring her manacle. It sent a little rip of pain through her, which she ignored. "Of course he will. What do you mean to imply?"

"It was only a question. Goody Corey's husband turned on her, said he thought she might well be a witch. Goody Good's, too."

"I fail to see how that bears on my own."

"Fair enough." Susannah bent her head. "I never thought I would miss mine so," she murmured.

Susannah's own husband was dead. With Mary on her other side, Martha was bracketed by widows. She groped for some condolence, but before she

could speak, Susannah cleared her throat and spat into the dark. It hit with a
dull slap. "You know what else I miss?" she said. "Butter."

It startled a laugh from Martha, choked off as Mary stirred beside her. Butter was an indulgence, not to be enjoyed indecently. Some would take Susannah's words as a sign of impiety.

"Cornbread," Martha said.

"Berries with cream."

"Carrots, cooked crisp."

Susannah groaned. Martha found herself smiling. "A goose," she continued. "Thomas brings one in each autumn, and I roast it on the fire until the
skin goes brown and crackling, and the meat falls from the *mmph*—"

Mary had jerked upright to throw a hand across her mouth. "*Stop,*" she
groaned sleepily. "Lord *God.*"

Martha laughed under her sister's hand. "Mary loves goose," she tried to
tell Susannah, but it came out garbled. Mary let go and clasped her hands over
her ears, and Martha felt a growing lightness despite their blemished reputa-
tions, despite the shadows pooling in the corners of the cell.

Joseph Putnam didn't believe the accusations. A judge had resigned from
the court. The ministers were advising caution. Bridget Bishop had been lost,
but Martha still had faith. It was only a matter of time.

19

No Return

The old year slithered into the new. Books piled up on my desk until they threatened to topple and snow followed in deep drifts outside. I thought of Martha in the jail at midsummer, in the heat, waiting for word that the charges had been dropped.

She did have reason to hope. As soon as the ministers' letter (a document called, unimaginatively, "The Return of Several Ministers"[1]) began to circulate, the afflictions stopped. For three days, not a single person reported that she'd been harmed by a witch's specter. Maybe after Bridget Bishop's death, some of the afflicted girls began to reconsider their chosen sport—or maybe, with the ministers advising exquisite caution, they didn't want to make any accusations that wouldn't be believed. The result was the same. There was a lull in the terror.

Then, on June 18, a young man named Jonathan Putnam—a cousin of Thomas Putnam Jr.'s—fell ill. The family called in Mercy Lewis to divine if the illness was magical in origin. Mercy confirmed that he was afflicted by witches and named two tormentors: Rebecca Nurse and Martha Carrier.

Between the plague and her personality, Martha was an easy target, someone people were willing to believe was a witch. Rebecca Nurse was not. Accusing them both at the same time should have discredited Mercy Lewis, even delegitimized her other accusations. It should have been a chance to stop and think, a chance for cooler heads to prevail.

But two days later, a joint force of Algonquin and French soldiers attacked the town of Wells, in modern-day Maine, then the northernmost reaches of the Massachusetts colony.[2] It should have meant little to the people of Salem, but Wells was the town where George Burroughs had recently served as minister. In April the afflicted girls had accused Burroughs of being a powerful wizard, the leader of the whole coven. The authorities had sent men to Maine to bring him down to stand trial. By the time Bridget Bishop was killed, Burroughs occupied a cell in Salem Town.

Cooler heads didn't stand a chance. An attack by Indigenous Americans (understood as the devil's servants) and the French (the hated, ungodly Catholics) on a town associated with Burroughs would have confirmed that the

"Indians" and the "witches" were allies. Satan was attacking on all fronts. The raid on Wells would have read, to the Salem villagers, like a flashing sign: *WE'RE COMING FOR YOU NEXT.*

* * *

A week later, five accused women—Susannah Martin, Sarah Good, Elizabeth Howe, Sarah Wildes, and Rebecca Nurse—were brought before the Court of Oyer and Terminer.

The first four women were quickly found guilty. Each maintained her innocence, but fear had brought spectral evidence back into play. The cautionary "Return of Several Ministers" was mostly ignored.

Mostly. The fifth woman's trial—Rebecca Nurse's—began like the others had. Twelve-year-old Ann Putnam Jr. and her mother, Ann Sr., described how Rebecca had set her specter upon them. Abigail Williams testified that Rebecca's specter had confessed to murder. Elizabeth Hubbard testified that Rebecca had tempted her to sign her name in the devil's book. Most damning, Goodwife Deliverance Hobbs and her stepdaughter, Abigail, both confessors from the nearby town of Topsfield, said that they had seen Rebecca at the storied witches' sabbath behind the parsonage in Salem Village.

Then a thirty-six-year-old woman named Sarah Bibber flung herself screaming from a pew. Bibber had recently joined the ranks of the afflicted, and she yanked up her skirts in front of the judges. There were pins stuck in her legs—placed there, she said, by the specter of Rebecca Nurse.

It took some time for Bibber to quiet, not to mention the rest of the courtroom. But once all the afflicted were done testifying, Rebecca Nurse's adult daughter, Sarah Nurse, took the floor.

Sarah Nurse said, "I saw Goodwife Bibber pull pins out of her clothes and held them between her fingers and clasped her hands round her knees and then she cried out and said Goody Nurse pinched her. This I can testify."[3]

It was the first time that a witness had claimed to see an afflicted person faking their affliction in the courtroom. Sarah Nurse was calling Sarah Bibber a liar—and, by extension, casting doubt upon all spectral evidence, and upon the court that had already executed one woman.

Sarah Nurse's revelation was astounding. And if that wasn't enough to make the jury pause, there was other support for Nurse's innocence: a group of nearly forty respected men and women from the area had signed their names to a petition attesting to her good character. Nurse was, truly, someone known for her godliness, exactly the kind of person the ministers had advised be treated with exceeding tenderness.

Taking all the evidence into account, the jury found Rebecca Nurse not guilty.

The courtroom exploded with noise. The records note the dissatisfied exclamations of at least two judges and piercing wails from the afflicted girls.[4] "Not guilty" meant spectral evidence hadn't been enough. It meant the ladder upon which the trials were built, upon which the afflicted girls and their parents had been climbing to new heights, was shaking. It meant—if you believed—that one of the witches was about to escape justice.

The court recessed. And when it reconvened, William Stoughton, the chief justice of the Court of Oyer and Terminer and lieutenant governor of Massachusetts, spoke up.

Stoughton, the records show—though they don't tell us his exact words—objected to the verdict. He told the jury that Rebecca Nurse had incriminated herself.

No, Nurse had never confessed, Stoughton admitted, but she had said something very curious when Goodwife Deliverance Hobbs and Abigail Hobbs of Topsfield were brought to the courtroom to testify against her. At the sight of those two confessors, Nurse exclaimed, "What! Do these persons give in Evidence against me now? They used to come among us."[5]

They used to come among us—did that mean she was confessing to being at the witches' sabbath, where the Hobbs women claimed to have seen her? Stoughton heard it that way, chose to hear it that way.

Some of the jurymen clamored to revise their verdict, taking this new evidence into account. The jury foreman stopped them, giving Rebecca a chance to clarify her statement.[6]

Half deaf and ill—before being arrested she'd been mostly bedbound—and confused about Stoughton's allegation, Rebecca Nurse didn't answer.

The jury had no choice but to go out and deliberate again.

Later, Rebecca Nurse wrote a statement for the court, attempting to explain what she had meant. "Being something hard of hearing, and full of grief," Rebecca wrote, she "had not the opportunity to declare what I intended, when I said they were of our company."[7] She had only intended to say that she and Deliverance and Abigail Hobbs had all been *prisoners* together.

That was all she'd meant. Deliverance and Abigail Hobbs, accused of witchcraft themselves, had been in the cell with her. Rebecca had recognized them, and had been foolish enough to imagine some kind of solidarity among the accused.

* * *

I pinned a picture of William Stoughton up on the Murder Wall. He had sunken eyes, a straight nose, a double chin, and shrouded motives.

As chief justice of the court—not to mention lieutenant governor of the colony—Stoughton holds the extremely dubious honor of being the court's highest authority *and* one of its foremost proponents of spectral evidence. It's William Stoughton who, as chief justice, allowed the court to take spectral accusations seriously, and ignored the moderating voices advising that spectral evidence was not enough. Stoughton even lowered the standard of conviction: the mere intent to harm others through witchcraft, whether or not it had been successful, would be enough to convict in his court.[8]

But why? Stoughton seems to have believed wholeheartedly in spectral evidence, but belief has never been enough for a witch hunt. And he didn't have any of the obvious baggage that plagued most of Salem's players: unlike Putnam and Parris, he had no obvious grudges against anyone in Salem Village. He had no personal paranoia that the witches were out to get him specifically. Unlike the girls, he neither feared for his life if the witches weren't caught and killed nor, as far as we know, was he doing it "for sport." The lieutenant governor of the colony, one imagines, could make some sport of his own.

But Stoughton actually *did* have something in common with the girls. He too had the chance to climb the trials like a ladder.

Stoughton had held high posts in the Massachusetts government before. He had, in fact, occupied almost *every* high office that the colony had to offer, save that of governor.[9] He'd made only one rather blatant political mistake:

he'd been deputy president under the deposed and despised former Anglican governor, Edmund Andros.

Stoughton took that post against the advice of prominent Puritan ministers, and when Andros was overthrown, Stoughton was seen as a collaborator. Increase Mather, Cotton's father, named Stoughton an enemy of the people.[10]

Now, restored to a high post, he had what may have seemed like an opportunity to redeem himself: the chance to stop another takeover of Massachusetts. As lieutenant governor, Stoughton was tasked with protecting the colony. As the chief justice of the Court of Oyer and Terminer, he had the chance to do so. And this time it wasn't an Anglican who threatened the Puritan way of life. This time, it was the devil himself.

Stoughton was manifestly ready to use any weapon within his grasp, spectral or not, whether the ministers advised it or not, to combat the witch invasion. The question of *why* he believed so staunchly that the witches were a danger has two answers. First, it's hard not to wonder if the new Puritan charter might have been particularly stressful for a man with Stoughton's history. Here was a document that threatened to reopen Massachusetts to non-Puritan influence, the very thing with which he'd been stained and reviled. As when he'd served under Andros, Stoughton could do little to fight the incursion directly—but indirectly was another matter. Stoughton may have seen in the trials a chance to shore up the failing Puritan wall and rewrite his legacy, to purge any lingering shame of having been Andros's collaborator.

If that wasn't enough, the English settlers' ongoing war with the Wabanaki Confederacy and the French would have increased Stoughton's sense of imminent peril and responsibility in particular. Four years before the trials, he had mismanaged a hostage exchange with the Wabanaki, spurring a series of raids that left more than a dozen English colonists dead.[11] Now, with the witches associated with Indigenous people, his past looked to be coming back to haunt him. With the Wabanaki attacking in the north, witches in the Puritan heartlands, a feeble charter, and an inexperienced governor, it's easy to see why Stoughton would have been susceptible to the idea that the Puritan project was under attack on all fronts.

And—I have to wonder—if, for the consummate politician within spitting distance of the governorship, the trials might have looked like an opportunity. Stoughton was in every way more qualified and connected for the governor's seat than Phips, who had royal favor but no political experience. If he managed to free the colony from Satan, William Stoughton might well become the man who saved New England.

If it was in a man's ambition to become such a savior, to purge New England of witches whatever the cost, it might well lead him to send a jury back out despite the evidence, or the lack thereof. Stoughton did. And when that jury came back in the second time, it found Rebecca Nurse guilty of witchcraft.

Not long after Nurse's trial, Governor William Phips decided he'd had enough of Salem witchcraft. He turned his full focus to organizing an expedition to Maine to fight the Wabanaki-French alliance and announced he would be leading the militia himself, leaving William Stoughton in charge of the witches.[12]

* * *

Two weeks after Rebecca Nurse's trial, in the second week of July, a woman in Andover came down with a fever and complained that she couldn't breathe through a pressure on her chest. Afflicted girls Ann Putnam and Mary Walcott were brought to town, a pair of traveling prophets, to see if it was witchcraft, which of course they said it was. (Their visit turned out to have unfortunate aftereffects for Andover: Their affliction was catching. Soon, the teenagers of Andover began to show symptoms of witchcraft affliction.)[13]

At some point during Ann Putnam and Mary Walcott's visit, they accused old Ann Foster, Martha's neighbor. Foster was questioned in Salem Village beginning on July 15.

At first, Foster maintained her innocence, but over the course of six days—and in the face of four afflicted girls (Ann Putnam, Mary Walcott, Elizabeth Hubbard, and Mary Warren, maidservant to John Procter) screaming and choking in front of her—her story changed.

The record of her confession, edited for modern spelling, reads as follows:

After a while Ann Foster confessed that the Devil appeared to her in the shape of a bird at several times, such a bird as she never saw the like before.

And that she had had this gift (of striking the afflicted down with her eye) ever since.

And being asked why she thought that bird was the Devil, she answered because he came white and vanished away black, and that the Devil told her that she should have this gift and that she must believe him, and told her she should have prosperity. ...

And that it was Carrier's wife about three weeks ago that came and persuaded her to hurt these people.

Ann Foster, examined, confessed that it was Goody Carrier that made her a witch ... that Goody Carrier came to her ... and would have her bewitch two children of Andrew Allen's, and that she had then two poppets made and stuck pins in them to bewitch the said children, by which one of them died, the other very sick.

She and Martha Carrier did both ride on a stick or pole when they went to the witch meeting at Salem Village and that the stick broke as they were carried in the air above the tops of the trees and they fell, but she did hang fast about the neck of Goody Carrier and were presently at the village. ...

She further saith that she heard some of the witches say that their [number] was three hundred and five in the whole country, and that they would ruin that place the Village.

And further confessed that the discourse amongst the witches at the meeting at Salem Village was that they would afflict there to set up the Devil's Kingdom.[14]

Ann Foster's confession set the wheel of the trials rolling again, heralding a new phase. It was Andover's moment to see an explosion of accusations, and it began with Martha. It began with the plague: the accusation that Goody Carrier had made Foster *bewitch two children of Andrew Allen's.* Andrew Allen was Martha's father's name; Foster was, it appeared, saying she had bewitched Martha's brothers, who died of the smallpox.

As for why Ann Foster confessed—it might not have been clear, quite yet, that confessors would receive mercy from the court, but it was clear that people who did *not* confess would be shown *no* mercy. For in the middle of

Ann Foster's multiday confession, five women who had refused to confess to witchcraft were taken to Gallows Hill. They were Susannah Martin, Sarah Good, Sarah Wildes, Elizabeth Howe, and Rebecca Nurse, and all five of them were hanged.

20
Neck and Heel

The accusations that Ann Foster, Goody Lacey, and Mary Lacey Jr. make in the prison cell are drawn from the trial records, reflecting what each woman said in her preliminary hearing or confession ("Examinations of Mary Lacey, Jr., Mary Lacey, Sr., Ann Foster, Richard Carrier, and Andrew Carrier, Copy" July 21, 1692, SWP No. 87.2 in the Salem Witch Trials Documentary Archive). Beginning with Hathorne's line "Did Richard not join with you in several things," much of the dialogue is direct quotation from the trial records ("Examinations of Richard Carrier, Mary Lacey Sr., Mary Lacey Jr., & Andrew Carrier, Copy," July 22, 1692, SWP No. 25.2). Before that line, the substance is accurate but there is no direct quotation, as the records only provide description of what was said, not a line-by-line transcript. John Procter's letter is an excerpt of the original letter he wrote while imprisoned, edited for modern capitalization and punctuation. ("Petition of John Proctor from Prison," July 23, 1692, SWP No. 107.19.) As a note, many contemporary writers spell Procter's name as "Proctor." The Puritans played fast and loose with spelling, recording the same name three or more ways, but as the signature on the letter reads "Procter," I have used John Procter's spelling of his name throughout.

Salem Town
July 21, 1692

The key scraped in the lock, scattering Martha's dreams. There had been a ship, sails billowing in a keen wind, a gray salt sea. She could nearly taste the spray.

"Move aside." The jailer's voice grated and something kicked her ankle. She opened her eyes and glared at him.

He shoved her ankle aside with his boot to make room for a limping old woman, gray hair falling loose about her face. She looked familiar. *Susannah*, Martha thought, half caught in sleep—but it couldn't be. Susannah was dead.

Already they were replacing her, refilling the empty manacles. Two younger women were pushed into the cell behind the older one, and with a jolt, Martha realized that she knew them all. "Goody Foster," she said, rubbing salt-grit from her eyes and pushing her hair away from her face, ignoring the way it crackled. "Goody Lacey? Mary? *All* of you?"

Three generations of Andover women stood before her. The oldest was Ann Foster, Martha's neighbor; she hadn't recognized her because Ann looked as though she had gained twenty years in two months. She was half bent over, her perfect posture wrecked. The matron with the watchful blue eyes was Ann's daughter, Goodwife Lacey, who had grown up on the farm beside Martha's. The youngest of the three, a pretty girl with her yellow hair falling loose from her wimple, was Goody Lacey's daughter, Mary Lacey Jr.

Ann Foster said nothing, her head hanging. Only young Mary Lacey Jr. spoke, cringing away from Martha to reach for the jailer. "Please, sir, do not leave me here—not with her—"

He shoved her back. "She's in chains."

"She'll send her specter! The birds, she has the birds, she'll send them—"

Mary was stirring beside Martha, roused by the voices. Others were waking to watch Ann Foster and her daughter and granddaughter with narrowed, frightened eyes.

The jailer's eyes flicked to Martha. "Don't go killing anyone in my jail."

She waggled her chain. The jailer was unconvinced. "It'll be worse for you if you kill her."

Martha closed her eyes for half a second. "And why, pray, would I want to kill her?"

"These three told the magistrates what you are." The jailer spat to the side, barely missing a dozing woman. "They testified what the devil promised you."

A spark raced down Martha's spine. They were confessors, then. She turned her head, slowly, and fixed her gaze on Ann Foster, then on the other two. Ann had her face turned into the stone wall. Goody Lacey looked ravaged with weariness, and young Mary seemed to be keeping some distance between her and her mother. There were tear tracks on the girl's face.

"The devil promised me nothing," Martha said. "These women are liars. Ann Foster, if you have said that I am a witch, you are nothing but a greedy, craven, leasing-monger of a woman. And look what you raised."

Ann Foster didn't answer. It was her daughter who spoke. "It's too late, Goody Carrier," Goody Lacey said tiredly. "They know. You made my mother a witch, and she made me one."

Martha snorted. "What does the devil offer you for your lies, I wonder?"

"The devil gives me nothing. God gives me grace."

"You wouldn't know an angel from the devil if they were standing afore you—"

"Martha," Mary said behind her, but Martha ignored her.

"You have been deceived," Martha told the three women. Her voice cracked a little. Goody Lacey thought *she* had the right to sound tired? Martha had been in the cell for a month and a half. She cleared her throat. "You are deceived and you shall be punished for it, if not in this life then the next."

"You are the one who shall be punished," young Mary Lacey snapped. Her voice was strange, too high. More hair was falling from her wimple. "You killed your own brothers."

She'd thought the pain of that accusation might lessen the more it was repeated, but it did not. "Don't be doltish."

"I saw you at the sabbath," Mary Lacey insisted. "I saw the red wine, served in earthen cups, and the reddish-brown bread, and there wasn't enough of it, some went hungry—"

"What on *God's good earth*?" Martha interrupted, but the girl went on in that high, tight voice. "And the devil called your name and the name of seventy-seven witches, and he promised that you would have a crown, and the pretty little man, the minister—"

Her mother murmured, "George Burroughs."

"Burroughs," Mary Lacey affirmed breathlessly, "the minister who's been locked up, I saw him and I saw you—"

"You did *not*—"

"Yes, I did, I saw you! You and Burroughs did it together, you said you would take down all the churches in this land and set up the devil's kingdom! You told me yourself the devil promised you would be queen in Hell!"

For a long moment no one moved. No one was sleeping now, and Martha could feel them, a mass of breathless women, their face blurring at the edges of her vision. She felt the urge, unbelievably, to laugh.

Susannah Martin would have laughed.

"There is no queen in Hell," Martha heard someone say behind her. Her sister. "Only in Heaven. Mary, who bore Christ."

"The devil turns over the natural order of things," Goody Lacey said.

"You're a witch," Mary Lacey continued, as if no one had spoken at all. "You're a witch and your son is a witch and I never saw so terrible a woman—"

Martha was on her feet. "Say that again."

"You—your son," Mary Lacey said. Her face was suffused with fear. "Your son Richard, he—he hurt Mary Warren, I saw her in the courtroom, he sent his specter to the magistrate's table. But it's your fault, *you* made him a witch, you gave him some writing that the devil gave to you and he hurt Mary Warren. I saw him. I saved her and I hope they arrest him and take him—"

Mary Lacey cringed back against the stone wall. Martha kept coming, the other women scrambling out of her way. She made it as far as her shackle would allow, the chain screeching against the floor as it stretched to its limit. Goody Lacey stepped between them, her face a mask, but Martha leaned around her until she could meet Mary Lacey's gaze.

"If I had the power you think I have," Martha told her, "I would use it upon you, right now. This breath would be your last."

No one moved.

"Martha," a voice said behind her, barely audible over the thud of blood in her ears and the noise that someone was making, a high keen like the scream of wind through driftwood, and then her sister Mary was there, a hand on her arm. Mary tried to tug her gently back across the cell to their corner, where Margaret sat. Mary's child—Martha couldn't look at her sister's child when *her son*—

"Martha," Mary said. "Hush."

She hadn't been aware she was the one making noise. She shook off Mary's hand. "Goody Foster," Martha called across the cell, to the grandmother who should have kept her child and grandchild in check. "If any harm comes to my children, I will see you die in this cell."

"Martha," Mary said, sharply.

The rage inside her crystallized into something terribly sharp, something that would kill her if she didn't wield it. She whirled on her sister. "You want me to *hush*? You will not spare a word of defense for your nephew? For me?"

She shoved at Mary and Mary went, moving away without protest. Martha fell past her, dizzy with rage, and she didn't go back to Margaret's corner. Instead, she dragged her chain as close as she could to the bars and sat there, her back to the others, so that she would be the first to see if they brought her child in.

* * *

"Have you been in the devil's snare?"

"No. Never."

"Is your brother Andrew ensnared by the devil?"

"No."

"How long have you been a witch?"

"I'm not a witch."

"How long has your brother been a witch?"

"Sir, please, we are not witches."

"Have you not joined in afflicting these persons?"

Richard Carrier, three days past his eighteenth birthday, swallowed hard. Magistrate Hathorne hadn't moved, gaze fixed and hunting. They were not in the Salem Village meeting house but in Beadle's ordinary, the judges squeezed too closely together at the low tables. The afflicted girls were lined up at the edge of the room like a row of trembling aspen trees. Each time Richard denied guilt, a shiver went through them, one passing it on to the next.

The magistrate rapped on the table. "Have you not joined in afflicting these persons," he barked.

Richard tried not to flinch. His brother Andrew stood beside him, and their father was watching from somewhere in the crowd that filled the ordinary. "No."

"Who was in your company when you covenanted with the devil?"

"I never covenanted with the devil."

"Who was at the village meeting when you were there?"

"I know nothing of any meeting."

"Mary Lacey," Hathorne said abruptly. The girl sat beside her mother on a bench close to the judges, hands clasped demurely in her lap. "Did not Richard join with you in several things?"

"Yes," Mary Lacey Jr. said, and Richard did flinch then. It felt impossible to him that this was the same laughing girl from whom he'd once stolen a kiss in Foster's meadow. She said in a clear voice, "He burned Timothy Swan with his tobacco pipe."

"Who else joined in it?"

"Goody Carrier," she said promptly, and added that her own grandmother and her mother had been there, too.

Hathorne repeated the question to Mary's mother, Goody Lacey, who affirmed that, yes, she had been there, and Richard, too. "Now, Richard Carrier," the magistrate said. "What say you to these two evidences, that saw you with Timothy Swan?"

"I did not do it!"

Hathorne pitched his voice to the confessors. "Mary Lacey, when you went to afflict Goody Ballard, was not this man with you?"

"Yes, it was about a fortnight since we went upon poles in the night. We got into the house and Richard afflicted her by pinching and choking her."

"Goody Lacey, do you remember anything of afflicting this Goody Ballard?"

"Yes. And this Richard was there, and he afflicted her by pinching, choking, and laying his hand on her stomach."

"Richard," Mary Lacey Jr. said, and he flinched again, fought it down, the sound of his name in her thin voice. "Richard, please. Tell them. We used to talk together, and you would tell me that you would afflict people." Tears were welling up in her eyes. Richard wanted to hit something. "Tell them. You cannot deny it. You have a heart as hard as a rock if you will deny it!"

Andrew shifted his weight beside him. Richard gripped his brother's arm to hold him still, and in a flash Mary Lacey Jr.'s eyes had shifted to the movement. Without knowing entirely why he did it, Richard let go.

It was too late.

"He told me," Mary Lacey Jr. was saying, "he used to tell me he would go and afflict people, he said he would kill Goody Ballard, and he told me he would make his *brother* a witch."

"As I thought." Hathorne turned his gaze to Andrew. "How long have you been in the devil's snare, Andrew Carrier?"

Andrew swallowed. But before he could open his mouth, one of the girls shrieked. Richard didn't recognize her—fair-haired, only a few years older than his sister Sarah. She was shrinking away from him, clawing at her arms as if she would rip the skin from the flesh.

Mary Lacey Jr. screamed, pointing at her. "Andrew!" she shrieked. "Andrew, let her go!"

Andrew jumped. "I didn't—" he began, but with the first word out of his mouth another of the girls let out a scream that pierced Richard's ears. He clapped his hands to his head.

One of the girls copied him, slapping her hands to her ears, and another followed, and then they were all slapping their own faces, falling to their knees. One of them let out a sound that he had only ever heard come from a hog's throat, not a girl's.

"Enough!" Hathorne bellowed. "Bailiff! Remove these boys."

Two constables took Richard's arms, yanking him forward. Another had Andrew in hand. As he was towed toward the door at the back of the ordinary, Richard twisted around—ignored the way the girls twisted and spun when he did—and found his father in the crowd. Richard didn't have time to do anything but look, but his father nodded at him, a strong, quick nod of recognition, urging courage, and Richard held it close as they pulled him away.

* * *

It was hours, once the boys were taken away from the ordinary. Thomas waited as long as he could, but in the end he was forced to turn for home. The oldest child left in the farmhouse now was ten, the youngest was three, and their neighbors had turned their backs: no one wanted to keep an eye on a witch's children. Thomas had to go home.

He should have stayed.

* * *

When the constable brought Richard Carrier back before the judges, it was dark. Richard was red-eyed, moving unsteadily, wincing with each step. When he wiped a hand across his nose, it came away wet and red.

"Though you have been very obstinate yet," Magistrate Hathorne said stern and magnanimous at once, "tell us how long ago it is since you were taken in this snare."

And Richard said, "A year. Last May, no more."

Yes, he told the magistrates, what Mary Lacey Jr. said was true. Yes, he had seen the shape of a man one night when he was walking home alone. The man had worn a high-crowned hat. The man had said that he was Christ Jesus and bade Richard serve. And Richard had set his hand to the devil's book. He'd signed it.

And yes, Richard said, finally. Yes. When he went to afflict people, when he was sent by the devil to afflict people, "My mother was with me. Sometimes but not often."

Richard Carrier confessed: "We met in a green, which was the minister's pasture. I heard Sarah Good talk of a minister or two. One of them was he that—" He hesitated, trying to remember what he'd heard. "He had been at the eastward? His name is Burroughs. I saw the devil open a great book and we all set our hands and seals to it."

"For what engagement?"

"The engagement was to afflict persons, and overcome the Kingdom of Christ. And set up the devil's kingdom. And we were to have—happy days—"

He broke off, unable to speak, and Mary Lacey Jr. filled the silence. She affirmed that at the sabbath she had heard the witches talk of throwing down the kingdom of Christ and lifting up the devil on his throne. She affirmed that Martha Carrier had been there, and Goody Toothaker and her daughter, too.

"And Roger Toothaker," Richard said, finding his voice. It had occurred to him, when blood began to slip from his nose, that his mother had been arrested in the first place because his uncle had claimed to know something of witches and their ways. "My uncle Roger was one."

Hathorne said, not ungently, "Richard, can you name any that were at the witches' meetings?"

He listed names with no regard for if they were living or dead. John Willard. John Procter and his wife. Goody Nurse. Goodman Corey and his wife. Goody Howe, Mrs. Bradbury, Goody Oliver.

"And what happened when they signed the book?"

"The devil told them they should overcome and prevail. The witches are all afeared they shall all come out. And the devil threatens that if I come not unto his quarrel, he will tear me in pieces—"

He was crying. He did not know when he had begun crying. He turned toward the line of girls, reached out a hand toward Mary Lacey and the girl next to her, the one who'd first claimed he'd afflicted her. She was a thin girl with a coarse dress and sharp cheekbones, like she hadn't been eating. "Please," Richard said. "Will you not forgive me?"

They watched him, wary as cats. The thin girl—he didn't even know her name—lifted her hand. Breath hissed through the room, but she reached out, slow as thick snow falling, to touch Richard's hand.

Fingertips brushed, knuckles, and then their palms were pressed together and she did not collapse, did not even cry out. She held on to him with a shockingly strong grip, and the room swayed with relief. If he could touch her without hurting her, that meant he had renounced the devil and his craft. It meant that Richard Carrier had proven himself to be on the side of God.

* * *

The next day, John Procter sat facing the wall in one of the men's cells in the Salem Town jail, trying to keep the sheet of paper steady on the stone.

The Carrier boys dozed beside him, curly heads bent toward each other. Carrier's sons were both big boys, and the older of the two had the beginnings of a beard, but the younger was still carbuncle-faced. They were hardly more than children. On Procter's other side, his own son William was curled close, his head at his father's hip. All three boys had identical red marks circling their wrists, ankles, and necks.

Procter dipped his pen in the inkwell and scratched out the names of the five most prominent ministers in the Boston clergy who he thought might be sympathetic to his plea.

Reverend Gentlemen,

The innocency of our case with the enmity of our accusers and our Judges, and Jury, whom nothing but our innocent blood will serve their turn,

*having condemned us already before our trials, being so much incensed
and engaged against us by the Devil, makes us bold to beg and implore
your favourable assistance of this our humble petition.*

*Here are five persons who have lately confessed themselves to be witches,
and do accuse some of us of being along with them at a sacrament, since we
were committed into close prison, which we know to be lies.*

*Two of the five are (Carrier's sons) young men, who would not confess
anything till they tied them neck and heels till the blood was ready to come
out of their noses, and 'tis credibly believed and reported this was the occa-
sion of making them confess. My son William Procter, when he was exam-
in'd, because he would not confess that he was guilty, when he was innocent,
they tied him neck and heels till the blood gushed out at his nose.*

*These actions are very like the Popish cruelties. They have already
undone us in our estates, and that will not serve their turns, without our
innocent bloods.*

*If it cannot be granted that we can have our trials at Boston, we hum-
bly beg that you would endeavour to have these Magistrates changed, and
others in their rooms, begging also and beseeching you would be pleased
to be here, if not all, some of you at our trials, hoping thereby you may
be the means of saving the shedding our innocent bloods, desiring your
prayers to the Lord in our behalf, we rest your poor afflicted servants.*

John Procter.

He put his quill aside and set a hand on his son's shoulder. The boy's chest
rose and fell, the raw red places on his neck beginning to crust.

The trials were a wheel that had been set into motion, Procter understood,
and the ministers to whom he appealed were bound to it, turning with it, as
much as anyone else. But they, perhaps, had the power to break it. He prayed
that they would. He prayed someone would, that there would be some movement, some answer, before they were all broken, as the bodies of witches had
been broken on wheels in the Old World for so many years.

21
The Grave

They tortured her children and the only thing I could think was that it didn't make sense.

Which is not, perhaps, the usual criteria for assessing torture—if it's sensible—but you have to understand that in Salem there was very little court-sponsored torture. In the European witch hunts, torture was so constant as to be almost unremarkable, but in Salem only Richard and Andrew Carrier and John Procter's teenage son are known to have been tortured during their preliminary hearings. Tituba was beaten into her confession by someone unaffiliated with the court. There is one person, a man named Giles Corey, who was tortured to death near the end of the trials when he refused to plead innocent or guilty to the charge of witchcraft. But counting all of them brings us to only five people who were physically tortured in Salem, and two of them were Martha's children.

That they were tortured at all was against legal protocol. Torture was legal in Massachusetts to extract the names of a person's co-conspirators in the case of a capital crime—*after* conviction. When Richard and Andrew Carrier were tied neck to heel, they hadn't even been formally indicted.[1]

Why would the magistrates break legal protocol on some teenage boys, and why so soon after their arrests? Why wouldn't the court wait, as they had waited in the case of nearly every other accused witch, for the terrible jail conditions and the promise of survival to induce a confession?

The answer that hovered in front of me, beating its wings, was that the magistrates needed Richard and Andrew to confess. A surge of confessions at the end of July—Ann Foster, Goody Lacey, and Mary Lacey Jr.'s among them—had helped to reveal the scope of Satan's plot, the conspiracy to destroy the Puritan project. Martha was thought to be a leader in this plot, a woman who had worked closely with the dark minister George Burroughs. A woman the devil himself had promised would be Queen of Hell. This was not one of Cotton Mather's "lesser criminals," one of those who might be allowed lenience. The Queen of Hell would have to hang.

Martha had refused to play the role the prosecutors wanted: she would not confess. But a confession from a witch's child went a long way toward securing a guilty verdict. Martha was an immovable object, the court an unstoppable force. They wanted her, so they went for her children.

One rainy February night I sat perched on top of my kitchen table, staring at the Murder Wall and thinking about Martha's children.

The end of thesis season was beginning to tick in my peripheral vision like one of those incense burners that dangle from chains in churches, pendulous swings wafting pungent smoke. Nearly every senior I knew was panicking, but the truth was that I was less worried about finishing my thesis in time than about what would happen *after* the deadline hit. It was starting to feel like no matter what I turned in, the work wouldn't be done. The story wouldn't be over. Salem had revealed itself to be a haunted house after all, spinning out new rooms and doors and staircases every time I blinked.

There had to be something I was missing, some magic word that would pick the last lock, make me feel that what I had learned about Martha was enough. But even her children oozed mystery. Richard and Andrew: What had happened to them after the trials? What would it do to you, if you confessed to witchcraft under torture as a teenager and named your mother as a witch? Where would you go? How—

I stopped. Rain hissed against the windows. *Where would you go?*

"You're an idiot," I said out loud, and dove for my computer.

I knew that after the trials, Thomas had moved the children to the Connecticut town of Colchester, but I'd never actually checked where Colchester was. And *I* lived in Connecticut. And it's not that big a state.

I mapped the route and sat back. Colchester was only twenty miles away, but that wasn't the worst of it. The town of Marlborough was even closer.

Marlborough was where Thomas had been buried.

My roommate, Brackets, who had long become resigned to the fact that living with me meant living with all my ghosts, drove me to the Old Marlborough Cemetery the next afternoon. It wasn't far off Route 66, a small square on the side of the road, and didn't have its own parking lot, so we left the car at an abandoned Bank of America and slipped in through a gap in the fence.

The grass wet and yellow, the air slick with mist. Cemeteries either welcome you or make you feel you're trespassing, and this one, empty of other visitors, fell firmly in the latter camp. I felt like we were going to get caught; by whom and for what didn't matter.

But then I saw Thomas's grave, and every other thought evaporated.

His headstone was eight inches thick and taller than me, a six foot behemoth of gray-brown sandstone. A hot pink elastic tie was knotted around the center, as if someone had wanted to mark out this grave in particular. The inscription read:

THOMAS CARRIER
DIED MAY 16, 1739
AE. 109 Yrs

ANDREW CARRIER
HIS SON DIED JULY 23, 1742
AE. 74 Yrs

At Thomas Carrier's Grave

I'd already read that Thomas lived to be over a hundred years old, but seeing it there, inscribed in rock, sent something zinging through me. There were six more names stacked beneath those—a son of Andrew's, and the son's son, and the women they'd married. The last death date was in the late 1880s.

This wasn't just Thomas's grave. This was a cache of ancestors. Andrew was my great-great-etc.-grandfather too, after all. I was descended from Martha and Thomas through him.

I traced the carvings while Brackets took photos of the grave. The stone was pleasantly rough, and I knocked my knuckles against it.

And froze.

"What is it?" Brackets asked.

"Listen." I rapped again on the stone just over Thomas's name. The sound was strange. Impossible. Unmistakable. "I think it's *hollow.*"

We jumped into action, tapping at different parts of the stone. At about eight inches thick, it was plenty big enough for an empty space inside. Brackets spotted a tiny crack on the side face, like a long thin seam, that started where the stone was sunk into the dirt. It reached all the way up to the stone's arched top and, as best as we could tell, curved over it to come back down the other side.

There was a similar crack an inch from the headstone's back face. It looked, in other words, as if two flat stone slabs had been stood upright and pressed against either side of a six-inch-wide stone arch.

After years of wet New England weather, the seams were beginning to split. At the base of the gravestone, one had started to crumble, leaving a half-inch gap of darkness. I knelt on the hem of my overcoat in the wet grass and angled my phone flashlight into the gap.

It was too small to make anything out. I sat back on my heels and looked up at Brackets. "This is weird, right?"

"Were hollow gravestones a thing for the Puritans?"

"Not that I know of. I mean, why would anyone build one? I can't imagine it would be cheaper or easier than a tablet." The most common kind of grave in Colonial America was a tablet stone, a single piece of cut rock, easy to carve and simple to sink into the earth.

"Bones," said Brackets.

"What?"

"I bet there's bones inside."

"Nah, for Puritans to stay unburied was, like, capital-*B* bad for getting into Heaven."

"What if it was someone who wasn't supposed to have a gravestone?"

"You mean like—someone else was buried here, but secretly? So they just put their bones in the stone?"

"Yeah."

I didn't say anything. Brackets examined the seam. "You know," they said neutrally, "we could split this pretty easily."

"We can't break the stone, dude."

"Sure we can."

"I'm not robbing my ancestor's grave."

"It's not grave robbing if it's your own ancestor."

"Pretty sure it doesn't work that way."

Brackets gave me a look. I held up a finger. "No."

"Okay, what do *you* think is inside?"

"Ideally?" I thought about it. "Thomas or Martha's perfectly preserved diary, with a firsthand account of the trials."

"Did either of them keep a diary?"

"I have no idea."

"But you think—"

"No, I don't. I don't actually think. But God, that would be amazing." Against my will I started to imagine it, each thought more fanciful than the last: a stack of letters, tied with a bow, in Martha's own hand, wrapped in oiled cloth to keep them safe from the weather. Or Thomas's diary. Or Samuel Parris's missing diary, the one where he recorded the progress of Abigail's and Betty's afflictions. He'd kept one and it had gone missing. Or better yet, the missing chapters of the Salem Village Book of Transaction, the ones that covered the months of the trials. The missing court records. The ax that Thomas had used to kill King Charles I—

I told my brain to cut it out.

"It would be wrong to go grave robbing," I said. "Also, illegal."

Brackets gave an eloquent shrug. I groaned and towed them toward the car.

When we got home, I scoured the internet for any mention of hollow gravestones. Nobody seemed to have heard of them, either on official sites or on New England ancestry message boards. I called up the Marlborough Historical Society and left a voicemail asking if they'd ever heard of people building hollow gravestones in Connecticut.

The idea of finding something inside the headstone was outrageous, but Thomas Carrier's story was *already* outrageous. Thomas Carrier, who might have killed the king of England. Thomas Carrier, who was nearly seven feet tall and known for fleetness of foot. Thomas Carrier, who lived to be 109 years old. In 1735, a newspaper reportedly noted:

> *His head, in his last years, was not bald nor his hair grey. Not many days before his death he traveled on foot six miles to see a sick friend, and the day before he died he was visiting his neighbors. His mind was alert until he died, when he fell asleep in his chair and never woke up.*[2]

Legends beget legends, and Thomas was already more mythos than man. I *wanted* it to be true, wanted him to have left something behind in a hollow headstone. If he had, and I got to be the one who found it—it was the kind of thought you can't look at straight on, fantastical and self-important and so, so sweet. Maybe *this* was what I'd been looking for. Maybe this was where the story had been leading me, all along: to find whatever Thomas had left behind in the damp, hollow dark.

People are always looking for magic in Salem, even me. That night I dreamed of crowbars.

The next morning, the logical and cowardly voice in my head coolly pointed out a variety of problems that might accompany hasty action. I was almost done with college, and getting arrested for grave robbing right before graduation was too absurd to contemplate. To break open the headstone would be deeply irresponsible, seeing as I was hardly the only descendant with a claim to the historical artifact. And, of course, the most likely outcome of breaking into Thomas's gravestone was that I'd find nothing but beetles and dust.

It was that last thought that stopped me, more than anything else. I didn't want to have to leave that graveyard with the legend dismantled, the myth fact-checked, the magic exposed as a lie.

So I stalled. It wasn't like the grave was going anywhere. That headstone had stood for hundreds of years; it would last a few more weeks. I buried my head in finishing the thesis and the frenetic buzz of senior parties.

February passed that way, and then March. By the time I got the phone call, the thesis deadline was only a few weeks away.

I woke to a voicemail from a lady at the Marlborough Historical Society. No, she said, she'd never heard of anybody building hollow gravestones in Connecticut. That seemed very strange to her. She wasn't sure why they would.

That afternoon I sat before the Murder Wall and went back to the beginning, looking for any clue that might point me to which of Thomas's sons had buried him and why they'd chosen Marlborough. Desperate, I ended up on WikiTree, "where genealogists collaborate"—I couldn't cite it in my thesis, but if they had any clues, I wanted them. Needed them. And it was there that a post informed me, matter-of-factly, that Thomas hadn't originally been buried in the Old Marlborough Cemetery at all.

When Thomas had died in 1735—the date on the headstone was *wrong*, I realized with a wrench of betrayal, off by four years, something I should have clocked immediately but hadn't, too swept up in the mystery of a hollow headstone—he had been buried on his homestead in Colchester. When Andrew died, he'd been buried there as well, as had his family members. Their bodies had remained there for nearly two centuries, until a road crew looking for gravel in the 1930s unearthed them near the intersection of South Main Street and Kellogg Road in present-day Marlborough. Only then were the remains apparently taken to the cemetery and reburied.[3]

The headstone wasn't original. It hadn't been built by Thomas or Andrew or any of the children—which meant that even if it *was* hollow, there wasn't anything of Thomas's or Martha's inside.

There was a mystery about the stone, just not the one I'd been imagining. According to a WikiTree post, quoting an article from the *Lowell Sun* newspaper that wasn't available online, the town of Marlborough apparently had no record of who had created the headstone. It had most likely been some historically minded citizens in the '30s, but there was no way to know. The only thing certain was that the headstone was far younger than the bones of the men buried under it.

I borrowed Brackets's car and drove back to the cemetery alone. It was early spring, new grass beginning to wriggle up at the base of Thomas's grave. I sat cross-legged in the dirt and ate an apple, staring up at the dappled stone.

The feeling that I should have realized something was off about the stone was chewy and bitter as the apple seeds. The names and death dates were far too clear to be nearly three hundred years old, and too evenly spaced to have been carved before all the family members were dead. Plus, Andrew's name was on there *twice*, which I had noticed but written off, assuming that Andrew had shared a name with a son.

The truth was easy to see, now that I was looking for it. The headstone had clearly been carved by someone who didn't know as much about the Carrier family as they thought they did.

All that time spent dissecting my villains, studying how easy it is to fall into stories that promise to give us what we want, and I'd fallen right for it. I should have known better. It's Salem's fundamental tenet: you see the omens you look for. If it fits together too neatly—witches' sabbath in the pasture, nine names in the book, a hollow headstone stocked with all the answers you've ever wanted—it's not real.

"Thomas, you ass," I said finally, throwing the apple core into the grass. "You had to have a hollow gravestone. You had to have a *traveling, hollow, unrecorded gravestone*. You couldn't just let things lie?"

The grave was silent, as graves tend to be, but it felt good to say it out loud. Obsession is like a sugar high: at first, in the wild throes, you're limitless—and then the slight shuddering decline—and before you know it you're left with a headache and exhaustion balled up at the back of your throat, and it makes you angry, a little, that your body has metabolized it so quickly, leaving you with the same nothing you had before.

And I was supposed to walk away. The thesis was nearly done, and I had what I came for. I'd found Martha, and her villains, and the stories that shaped them. By any measurement my quest was over. By some measurements it had been over 325 years before it began.

I didn't want it to be over. Didn't want to let the story go. Sat for a long time at the foot of Thomas's grave, wondering what you do with a mystery when solving it doesn't matter, and then I got in the car and drove away.

When I finally showed a geologist photographs of the stone, he told me that the seam didn't look man-made. There were too many protuberances and embankments, whatever that meant, that indicated natural joints inside the rock. The seam had most likely formed naturally, he said, and as the stone froze and thawed and froze over a hundred winters, the passage of water through the rock had worn away at it, creating space inside. Creating echoes. The headstone hadn't been built hollow. It had become hollow. I'd been asking the wrong question all along.

It's only sand. Headstones hollow out, and history follows, the books get rewritten or go missing and the archive caves in on itself until there's nothing but bones, thrown in the ravine. Magic is a wispy meal. We are the meat.

22

The Trumpets and the Drums

The description of Mary Toothaker's examination draws from the trial records ("Examination of Mary Toothaker," July 30, 1692, SWP No. 128.2 in the Salem Witch Trials Documentary Archive). No dialogue is direct quotation, as the records describe what Mary said without giving her precise words, but all dialogue is closely inferred from the records.

Salem Town
July 30, 1692

Word of what had happened to the Carrier boys didn't take long to spread. When Martha heard, she wretched up the contents of her stomach, bile and a little bread, into a damp corner of the cell until there was nothing left.

The next week was a haze, blank and terrible, her stomach qualmish and unable to settle. The night that the constables came to arrest her, Martha had thought she would be able to keep them safe if she went. Her boys. And where on God's earth was Thomas? He hadn't come to visit the jail since word came that the boys had been arrested, but she would have heard if they'd taken him, too. How could he have let them take her children?

She remembered Susannah Martin's question, posed quietly one night back when Martha still believed they might all make it out of the cell alive. *Will your husband speak for you, do you think?* She'd been snappish in return, offended by the implication. And here was the implication, made flesh.

She spent long hours watching Ann Foster and Mary Lacey Jr., gathered with the other confessors against the far wall, spat on the floor whenever one of them was taken past for questioning. Mary tried to stop her, the first few times, but eventually she gave up, averting her eyes. It made Martha furious. She ignored Mary in return. Rage roiled constantly in her stomach, heavy and clicking, like she'd swallowed stone after stone from a riverbed.

Some of the women had begun to hack with what was vulgarly called a churchyard cough, for it only led to one place. Martha shut her ears to them, listened as hard as she could to the noises from outside the jail—carts rattling in the street, jays and crows calling harshly to each. The noise of a world outside the wet, stinking boundary of their prison. Sometimes she imagined she could even hear the slap of waves against the hulls of ships in Salem harbor.

She didn't think of her hip bones, protruding like the wings of a bird, or the way her skin was chapped and flaking. Didn't think of the way her sister was retreating into herself, staring at the cell walls for hours at a time. Didn't think about the smell seeping from her own body, from all their bodies, the sourness of piss overlaying something dark and hard as iron. In the week after her sons were arrested, Martha tried very hard not to think of anything at all.

Morning, heat keeping them huddled against the cool stone walls. The jailer came to summon Mary for questioning. Martha roused herself to tell her sister she would watch Margaret while Mary was gone, but Mary hardly seemed to hear. Didn't make a sound when the jailer pulled off her shackle to reveal festering flesh beneath. Martha hissed through her teeth, but Mary didn't look at the rot in her own leg. She rose.

Later, remembering that moment, Martha would think, *she was already past the point of pain.*

* * *

Mary Toothaker stood in the Salem Town courthouse, twisting her fingers, thinking of her daughter.

"Did you not covenant with the devil?" Magistrate Hathorne asked her. It was the fifth time he had asked. All he did was ask the same questions over and over in different words: had she covenanted with the devil, who had she seen, who had she afflicted. Mary protested each time, telling him that she knew nothing of witchcraft, but the questions kept coming.

She couldn't turn her head, couldn't look away from Hathorne for a moment. If she turned and her gaze fell upon one of the afflicted girls who ringed the courtroom, they would shout and fall. She'd already struck down two by turning her eye upon them.

This newfound power terrified her. Mary knew that her sister thought the girls were liars, or madwomen at best, but Mary did not have the luxury of such dismissal. Mary knew there were those in the world with access to power. She'd spent years married to a man who claimed the sight, and some-times—not always, but sometimes—his predictions proved true.

When Roger had first drawn away from her, he'd said that he'd been called by God to do his work, and that she could not follow, that she was not fit to follow. Perhaps he'd been right, Mary thought. Perhaps her husband had seen something in her that was unfit. For here she stood, children scattering before her like rabbits.

The girls ringed her like they were preparing for one of the skipping games Mary's daughters used to play with their cousins, girls chanting as they jumped in and out of the hoop in the center of the circle. *Apples, peaches, pumpkin pie. How many years afore I die?*

Martha thought the afflicted girls were liars, but Martha had always thought she could do what she liked, *say* what she liked, and suffer no conse-quences. Mary was not her brash, dismissive younger sister, and she did not suffer from the same misconception.

"Wait," Mary Toothaker said, cutting across the magistrate's droning ques-tion. "Sir. I desire to tell the truth in this matter."

The girls quieted.

"This May last," Mary said slowly, "I was greatly discontented. I was—trou-bled with fear. Of the Indians. I used to dream of them, very often, that they would come, and I would have to fight. And—the devil—" She stopped. The word, passing her lips, sent a ripple through her whole body. Her chest felt sud-denly tight, her lungs shriveling like leaves. She tried to draw a deep breath.

"What was the devil's temptation?" Hathorne asked.

The breath wouldn't come. Mary gasped airlessly.

"Do you not wish to confess?"

"Look at her, she is afflicted—"

"I—I would—" The words came out squeezed, thin as winter air. She couldn't speak, couldn't *breathe* through the terrible pressure pushing down at her breast. *The devil,* Mary thought wildly, *it is the devil, it is* true—and panic spiked through her. She clutched at the neck of her dress, gasping for air.

"Pray with me," a voice said, and a man came into her field of vision. Through the dizzy fear she recognized him, vaguely, as the minister of Beverly. His voice was kind, his eyes worried. "Blessed be His incarnation and His holy light—"

Mary followed the words, her mouth shaping the prayer automatically. All at once, at the end of the third line, the pressure at her breast lessened.

She dragged in a deep draught of air, cool and sweet in her throat. The minister kept reciting, calm and steady, and by the time he finished the prayer, she was speaking it with him in a reedy voice.

"Thank you, sir," she said when she could manage it. Her voice was trembling. "I have—often prayed, but." She hiccupped. "Sometimes I have been—the worse for praying. The devil would—stop up my breath." She took another breath, and this one came more easily. "As just he did."

The minister nodded, as if her gasped words made perfect sense, and stepped aside. Slowly, still focusing on filling her lungs, Mary looked to the magistrates.

"Widow Toothaker," Hathorne said. "How long have you yielded to Satan?"

"I could not well tell how long," Mary answered him, still unsteady but speaking clearly. "But I think it has been not more than two years."

"As I came to my examination," Mary Toothaker told the court, "I promised myself twenty times that I should die upon the gallows and would not say anything but that I was innocent. But I fear it was a promise I made not to myself, but to the devil."

Not long ago, Mary confessed, she had been frightened by dreams that the Indians would come for her. She said the devil appeared to her in the shape of a tawny man and promised to keep her from them if she should serve him. If she agreed, he promised, she would have happy days with her son.

She confessed that she had signed the devil's book and agreed to serve the devil and to praise him with her whole heart. She had gone in her spirit to afflict the children—whichever children the magistrates named. Yes, she had been twice to witch meetings in Salem Village. (Twice more she was choked up but recovered. The devil is subtle, the court noted, and stops her when she would speak.)

Mary confessed that the dark minister George Burroughs had preached at the witches' sabbath, when all the witches spoke of pulling down the Kingdom of Christ and setting up the Kingdom of Satan in its place. She said that she had heard the sound of a trumpet, the beating of drums, the clarion call of war. And she said that when she went to the witches' meetings, her sister Martha came with her.

* * *

The cell door opened. Martha searched her sister's body for blood or rope marks, but there were no obvious signs of torture. She let out a breath and took her hand off Margaret's. "Go to your mother."

Margaret ran to Mary, who stood just inside the cell door. The jailer was locking it behind her, and Martha frowned, something bothering her, a tickle in the skull.

The jailer hadn't refastened Mary's shackle. He didn't, sometimes, for confessed witches, but never for—

Martha's heart began to thump, her body coming to the answer before her mind. "Mary," she said.

Mary ignored her. Instead, she crouched down before Margaret, taking both her daughter's hands in hers. There was something sharp about her movements, her chest rising and falling fast. She looked more awake than she had in days. "Listen," Mary said to Margaret, her voice low and hard. "Listen carefully. I have told the truth, Margaret. I have confessed. I have told them that I am a witch and your father told you how to kill a witch, and you must tell them, and we will go home—"

Margaret was staring at her mother, lips trembling. The shackle around Martha's ankle seemed to be shrinking, cutting off blood. She didn't think she could stand, but she struggled to her feet, throwing out a hand. "Mary, stop. Her father did no such thing. Do not poison the child's mind—"

"Silence!" Mary shrieked. She whipped around and her eyes were terrible, white at the edges but perfectly clear. "Do not speak to her. For once in your life, *hold your tongue.*"

A hole had opened in the cell floor, the kind of sinkhole that took ships, swallowed cities. "Mary," Martha said. Her lips were numb. "Mary."

Mary took her daughter by the wrist. Without a word, she turned away and towed Margaret to the other side of the cell, the confessors' side, where Martha, shackled, could not follow.

23

The Gauntlet

I didn't put a picture of Mary Toothaker up on the Murder Wall. I didn't have one, first of all. No drawings or pictures of her survive, if any were ever made, which is unlikely.

But she wasn't the villain I'd been looking for. And Mary was not, as it happened, allowed to enjoy the "happy days with her son" that she told the magistrates the devil had promised. Instead, three years after the trials, a group the Billerica town records identify only as "ye Indian enemy" attacked the town.[1] Mary Toothaker was killed. Margaret, then fifteen, disappeared.

I wonder if Mary remembered her confession to witchcraft before she died. If she remembered that she'd told the court she'd made a deal with the devil because he'd "promised to keep her from the Indians."[2] I wonder if she understood it as Satan's revenge, or just a simple, vicious irony.

* * *

No one can get under your skin like a sibling. The night before I turned in my thesis, I called my brother. I was outside the library, watching students smoking on the steps. Eli picked up somewhere with traffic in the background. "What's up?"

"You got a sec?"

"A sec, sure."

"My thesis is due tomorrow. I mean, it's due in a couple days but I'm submitting it tomorrow in case the internet goes down in the next forty-eight hours."

He snorted. "How's it feel?"

"Not. Done?"

A brief silence as he tried to figure out how much shit I was in. "I mean, it's *done*," I said. "Literally it's done, the whole thing's on paper, but it's not…" Someone was playing in the library's revolving door, going around and around. "It's like you said."

"Like *I* said?"

"You remember when I found that book? When I came to visit you at college when you were a freshman?"

"Vaguely."

"You remember what you said?"

"Definitely not."

"I asked who killed her and you said *the other villagers*. Like it was the most obvious thing in the world." I sighed and surrendered. "And you know what? You were right."

* * *

It was galling. I turned in the thesis and celebrated with the other seniors outside the library on an overcast day, the steps so wet with champagne I was afraid somebody was going to fall and crack their skull. I swigged from my bottle and ran over Martha's villains in my head, everyone I'd pinned to the Murder Wall: Putnam, Parris, Hathorne, Stoughton, Cotton Mather, Ann Foster, Goody Lacey, Mary Lacey Jr. I had their names. I knew the parts they'd played.

As if that was enough.

Let it go, I told myself. *Let* her *go.* It was over. Maybe the best thing I could do was put aside the shovel and stop trying to dig her a deeper grave.

Unhook the strings of the Murder Wall, take down the graphs and notes and trial records, pack up the books, schlep them out of the house and out of the state, far from Thomas's grave, hours from Salem, all the way home to New York.

Summer hit me like a wrench to the head. Freedom! Freedom! Get a job! I worked part-time selling medicinal hemp oil for dogs with arthritis and anxiety and kept turning around on subway platforms, thinking someone was calling my name. I couldn't help it: Salem's story was everywhere. On the subway, where the automated voice instructed me to watch my neighbors. On the news, where immigrant toddlers, seeking asylum at the southern border, were separated from their parents and made to appear in court. Prosecutors did everything but say that they saw yellow birds whispering on the kids' shoulders to make them seem demonic.

The youngest person to go to jail in Salem was five-year-old Dorothy (a.k.a. Dorcas) Good, Sarah Good's daughter. After Dorothy was released, she went mad. What do you call a tragedy that keeps repeating itself?

History is full of wounds. Wounds are portals.

I couldn't remember where I'd read that. Rubbed my eyes on the subway. The dregs of the evening commute stared dully back.

A few weeks into the summer, my mother and I went hiking on an island off the coast of Maine. Near the end of a seaside trail we came across a small graveyard nestled in an overgrown clearing. A handful of headstones in the local pitted granite, knobby roots curling through the dirt, and, incongruously, a large laminated sign like a museum plaque. I went toward it, tripped over a fallen headstone, and hopped the last yard, cursing. I found my footing just in time to read the sign and tripped again.

The sign read TOOTHAKER.

Under that:

Elijah Toothaker and his wife Elizabeth Daggett Toothaker came here some time before 1798. It is not known when or where they arrived in this country but Elijah's grandfather John and his wife Mary were accused of being witches in Salem in 1692. John died in jail before being tried; Mary was found guilty and later exonerated by the Massachusetts Supreme Court.

The long grass swayed in the breeze. Through numb lips I said, "His name was Roger. Not John. Roger."

The graves of Mary and Roger Toothaker's grandchildren stared at me like milky blind eyes. Martha's great-nieces and nephews.

I raised one incredulous hand and waved. "Hi, cousins."

I fled back to Brooklyn before the story could ambush me with more bodies. In a hipster coffee shop the note on the tip jar read: *Tip If You Want To Go Back In Time And Talk To Your Ancestors.* I tipped and left, and before I could cross the street, a truck with the words *SALEM SHIPPING* emblazoned on the side drove by, carving through a puddle and splashing my bare legs to the knee.

I cycled through incredulity and suspicion and landed on cool disdain, the kind usually reserved for listening to an acquaintance you don't particularly like telling an embellished but harmless story. I'd already been seduced and betrayed by a hollow headstone, after all; no truck or hipster tip jar could beat that. In comparison to finding the graves of Mary Toothaker's grandchildren, these little coincidences felt almost charmingly cheap. *Fool me once.*

So what if I was seeing Salem everywhere? We see our surroundings selectively; there's too much in the world, stimulus and detail, to take it all in. So we notice the pieces that connect back to whatever we're already thinking about, the same way that when you learn a new word everyone seems to start using it. Sometimes a coincidence is just a coincidence.

If Salem's story was everywhere, if the story didn't feel over, it was because I didn't *want* it to be over. I was still hoping to make it better, somehow, make it right. But that wasn't possible. I wasn't a questing bloodhound, just some little rat dog that doesn't know better once it's got its teeth sunk in.

You see the omens we look for, I told myself, walking home wet from the coffee shop. *You see the omens, you see the omens, you see the omens.*

Which raised the question, What wasn't I seeing, just because I wasn't looking for it?

The answer came in the shape of three things that happened that summer. The first was that I met a woman. She asked me not to reveal who she is, so I'll call her Liana. What's important is that she's also a descendant of Salem, and though Liana doesn't call herself a witch, other people might. She's a reiki practitioner, channeling energy through her hands into another person's body.

We got together at a bar on Third Avenue to talk about Salem. An hour turned into two, because it was nice to agonize over the trials with someone who was interested in them for her own sake, and Liana has a way of looking at you that makes you want to tell her about your childhood. We went from discussing the substance of Salem's story to how I was stuck on it, how it felt like there was some unfinished business, but I couldn't for the life of me figure out what it was.

I was a couple of whiskey cocktails in, feeling benevolent and glowy, when Liana said, "Would you like me to try to ask?"

"Ask?"

"I have guides. I can ask them, if you want me to."

"Guides," I repeated. Racked my brain, came up empty. Unless she meant— "Like, uh. Spirit guides?"

"They're higher beings. They've got a much bigger field of information to work with than we do. I can't promise that they'll be able to reach Martha, but there's no harm in trying."

I blinked for a few seconds, not wanting to offend, but her gaze was perfectly steady, her tone as solid as wood. It occurred to me that I couldn't offend her if I tried. She didn't care whether or not I believed her.

I took a different tack. "What if there *is* harm in trying?"

"What do you mean?"

"Any of—" I tried to find a word for what she was proposing and settled for waving a hand. "It makes me feel like—I mean, to be blunt, it makes me feel like I'm excusing the witch hunters. Martha wasn't a witch. If I do this, I'm validating their claims."

She shook her head dismissively. "You aren't. Martha wasn't a witch. And what I do certainly isn't witchcraft the way the Puritans thought of it. But that doesn't mean that there aren't things about this world that exist that we don't understand."

"Sure," I said. "But I'm honestly—look, I'm—okay. It actually doesn't matter to me whether or not magic exists. Okay? Witch hunts exist regardless, and they're purely human, and they pretty much exclusively happen to people who don't claim to be witches. Who don't do anything, quote, unquote, witchy at all. Magic is *irrelevant*."

Liana studied me. "Interesting," she said. "I agree."

"Thank you." I took a gulp of my drink.

"So," she said, "if magic is irrelevant, want to try this?" And she set her hand on the bar, palm up.

I snorted. She waited.

I took her hand.

"Now, I'm going to need you to take that handy skeptic of yours and put her in the other room for a minute, okay? Just send her off to debunk conspiracy theories or something. I need you here with me, and she'll get in our way."

"I'll try," I said, which was sort of true.

Liana eyed me knowingly, but she took a deep breath and closed her eyes. "Martha?" she murmured. "Are you there?"

A moment passed. Then she said, "Oh," in that solid, matter-of-fact tone. "She's here."

I raised my eyebrows. "Here?"

"Close." Her eyelids flickered. "Trying to come closer."

"What's stopping her?"

"You are. She can't come to you, not clearly."

"Why not?"

Her response was immediate. "Because you don't trust yourself."

Dragged by a ghost. Fair enough. I ate an almond from the dish on the table with my free hand. Probably eating was interrupting whatever we were doing, but I felt like I should maintain the appearance of normalcy for the bartender's sake. Though the bartender had probably seen far stranger things than an impromptu séance.

"She doesn't care about me," Liana said after a moment, amused. "She thinks I'm—beside the point. No, worse. She thinks I'm a softie."

"Why does she think you're a softie?"

"Oh, because I believe in the goodness of the world. I believe we can make the world fair, even if it isn't that way to begin with. She believes the world is inherently chaotic." Liana's lips curved. "She says, *pea brain.*"

"Sounds like her."

"But she cares about you."

I held the second almond but didn't eat it. "She does?"

"She knows you," she said, and she sounded like she was marveling at something. "She's been waiting for you. You know her name."

"Plenty of people know her name."

"Our names aren't just what others call us. They go deeper than that." She tilted her head, eyes still closed. "You've been calling out her name for a long time now."

A library, dust motes floating, a red book on a shelf.

"I don't understand how she's still there," Liana continued, frowning. "It's been so long. But—she says it's a blink. Time doesn't work the same way for her. And she's not…done here." Her eyes opened and focused on me. "She's tired."

Was I supposed to apologize for dredging up the story? "I'm sorry."

"She doesn't want your apologies."

"Then what does she want?"

"She didn't want any of this. She wanted to stay with Thomas, with her children—"

Her grip on my fingers tightened so swiftly that I flinched. "There was never any choice," Liana said. "That's what she's saying. She never really considered confessing because there was never any choice. It was the only way she could reassert control in the situation."

"It would have been a more interesting story if she had considered confessing," I muttered.

"She didn't die to be interesting." It was an admonishment, from at least one of them. "She didn't do it to be a hero. She had no special source of strength. She had no choice but to be strong."

"Okay," I said, "but what does she *want*?"

"She doesn't understand what happened. She doesn't get it. It all happened fast, and it was so—unreal." Liana's face twisted. "She wants to understand."

If *that* was all she wanted—"I can explain," I offered. That I could do; that was what I'd been learning to do for months.

But Liana said, with hollow finality, "No. They can see some things. She's heard the explanations and it doesn't make sense. It will never make sense."

"Then—"

Liana shook her head and let go of my hand. "She's gone."

I stared at her. Like the lights coming up in a movie theater, the rest of the bar filtered back in: laughter and chatter, slim thirtysomethings, candles flickering at intervals along the curved stone. My hand was aching; I didn't realize how hard she'd been gripping it. "Just like that?"

"They don't tend to hang around. She was already much more—present—than I'm used to." Liana flexed her hand. "You must have been calling very loudly for a very long time."

I pressed my knuckles against the bar. Now that it was over, whatever it had been, I wasn't willing to commit to anything. "Yeah," I said. "Maybe."

It occurred to me that even if I decided to take what Liana said as the truth, I had pretty much the same amount of actual information as before. She hadn't told me anything I couldn't have guessed. *It all happened fast. It was the only way to reassert control.*

I told Liana as much. She laughed. "Well," she said, "that's usually how it works. They can tell us some things, but most of it we have to figure out for ourselves."

I went home. Windy dark, humming city, the wide empty loading bays of Brooklyn's Fourth Avenue giving way to the crackle of cars on Fifth. Faint laughter through the windows where people sat eating burgers and Caribbean food, all of them blurry and insubstantial, on the other side of some impenetrable veil.

I wanted to believe her. Not because I wanted to believe in magic, or ghosts, or that people could talk to them, but because if she'd been telling the truth, it changed everything. It was the slack hand squeezing back. It was the lost radio wave, flying in from a dark corner of space long after you've given up on receiving an answer. It was recognition. I wanted to believe Liana because I wanted to believe that I mattered to Martha the same way she mattered to me.

But I tend to have trouble with belief; it makes desire look too much like truth. The prospect of what it would mean to accept what she had said stretched out, as enormous and daunting as the stack of books on my desk had been when I'd first started researching Martha's story. The prickling intimation, staring at them, that every answer would lead to another question. That it was mysteries, all the way down.

Second thing that happened that summer: my aunt Nadine came to visit. Nadine is the unofficial family historian; my uncle was the first to find Martha, but Nadine found everyone else. She brought an ancestry map with her, a sprawling paper half-moon she'd filled in by hand that tracked nine generations back. Her father's name was at the center in the lowest row, and his parents and their parents and their parents' parents fanned out to each side. Martha and Thomas were in the top row, as far back as Nadine had been able to go.

Something slid through me, sharp and gleaming. Across from Martha and Thomas's names, in the same generation but on the opposite side of the family, there was a name that I recognized.

"What does that say?" I asked, needing to confirm it, not quite willing to trust my own eyes.

"Herrick," Nadine said. "Why?"

"Because," I said, "he was Martha's jailer."

Joseph Herrick wasn't Martha's jailer in that he wasn't the jail *keeper*, but he was one of the primary law enforcement officers of the trials. He was the acting constable of Salem Village. When the very first accusations were leveled against Sarah Good and Sarah Osborne and Tituba, it was Joseph Herrick who took them into custody.

He seems to have been in the camp that believed in some accusations but not others. He testified against Sarah Good but signed the petition on Rebecca Nurse's behalf, affirming that he did not believe she was a witch. It's not clear what he thought about Martha, but many generations after the witch trials, a descendant of Joseph Herrick married a descendant of Andrew Carrier, and they had a child. That child was my great-grandfather.

I was not just the descendant of a woman who had been killed as a witch. I was the descendant of a man who had helped the hunters.

A Salem inheritance—a colonial inheritance—is inherently compromised. But more than once, eyeing the Murder Wall, I took a kind of comfort in Martha. Whatever else she represented, she had been on the right side of what happened there.

Joseph Herrick stripped away that easy righteousness. For every ancestor who had opposed Salem's injustice I had one who had supported it. Witch or witch hunter, accuser or accused, every faction of the trials was represented in my blood.

Oh, Martha, I thought, like she could hear me, like Liana was right and she was waiting to answer, if only I would let her. *Oh, Martha. Whatever it is that you want, are you sure that you want it from me?*

After Nadine showed me the ancestry map, things got weird. By which I mean aggressively normal. The coincidences evaporated. I stopped seeing Salem everywhere, mostly even stopped *thinking* of it, as if my access to Martha's story had been revoked with the revelation of my genetics. Herrick's arrival had turned the trials from an open question into a closed circle, shutting me out.

The truth is that being related to an accuser really shouldn't have surprised me. The trials were, in so many ways, a family affair. Magistrate John Hathorne, king of the preliminary hearings, was related by marriage to George Burroughs, the alleged King of Hell. Hathorne's counterpart, Magistrate Jonathan Corwin, was the uncle of Salem's sheriff, George Corwin, who arrested a number of accused witches and stole property from some of them. Thomas Putnam and his cousins filed more than a third of all the formal accusations of witchcraft.

I wondered if, when Martha's descendant married Joseph Herrick's descendant, they knew what their families had been to each other. If it had mattered to them, or would have mattered if they'd known.

A friend relayed a story about two families their grandfather had known, families who were good friends before they discovered that they both had connections to Salem. One family was descended from an executed witch, the other from one of the judges on the Court of Oyer and Terminer. The revelation ended the friendship.

Which seemed bizarre. I mused to my friend that my incredulity might stem from the fact that I was Jewish; if I cut ties with anyone whose ancestors had hated mine three hundred years ago, my social circle would be limited. But seriously, were those two families really going to give Salem so much power over them, centuries later? Did they really *care* so much? My friend pointed out that I was hardly one to talk.

Finally. Third thing.

On the night of the July full moon, I went walking along the edge of Prospect Park. The wind was warm and oily, sliding around the detritus of the day's barbecues and knots of teenagers hiding joints behind cupped hands. Mars hung low and golden on the horizon, barely visible through the layers of light pollution.

Mars, god of war. Battle-fever. Loss. The trees trembled in the darkness, dappling leaf shadows on the low stone wall that divided soil from concrete. I passed through a pool of streetlight and saw another shadow beside my own.

It wasn't late and the street wasn't empty. I looked over my shoulder to see who was walking behind me.

Low light, cars buzzing.

The closest people thirty feet away.

I took out my headphones, turning, and in that moment I came as close as I ever have to seeing them. They stretched out along the avenue, a line of shadowy women like ripples of dark heat, reaching back and back in an endless hall of mirrors. Women in the night, hundreds of them, and men, barely more than silhouettes, most of them forgotten and all of them dead.

But not all of them nameless. There she was, the closest shadow, just behind my shoulder, nothing more than moonlight and memory but there, still there.

We all have ghosts. How they manifest depends on what omens we look for, what we believe we might be able to see. What I saw—what I'd been showing myself—was that Martha was still here, after three centuries, and if it was only in my memory, then memory was enough. She wanted something from me, or I wanted to give her something, and there was no difference between those two desires that mattered.

And for the first time I thought I knew what it might be. I thought of Joseph Herrick, shutting me out of the past, shoving me firmly into the present. Thought of Liana by candlelight, saying, *she's heard the explanations. It will never make sense. But she wants to understand.*

The line between understanding and being understood is porous. Maybe I couldn't explain Salem in a way that would matter to the dead, but Martha had come to me. Forget ghosts—her *story* had come to me, had fallen into my hands, and a story is a truer ghost than almost any other kind.

I could tell it again. I knew her. It might be enough.

"Okay," I said aloud, alone on the street. A gauntlet thrown down in the low light of the war star. "I'm ready when you are."

24
The Trial

The official transcript of Martha's trial has been lost. Cotton Mather described the proceedings in his book Wonders of the Invisible World *(1692); though Mather himself was not in attendance, he used court records for his research and can presumably be trusted for the basic shape of things. The detail about the earthquake is from Marilynne K. Roach's* The Salem Witch Trials *(2004).*

Salem Town
August 3, 1692

When they came for her, Martha hadn't slept in two days. Even in the heat that blanketed the cell she felt cold, and there was no longer anyone beside her with whom to huddle for warmth. Mary and Margaret slept together on the opposite side of the cell. Martha slept alone, and after her second sleepless night she realized that she had a fever or something like it, her eyes hot and blurry, her throat aching.

She heard the jailer's slow footfalls first. His eyes appeared, glowing like dogs' eyes in the gloom. He undid the shackle and they hauled her up the stairs.

The brightness of day hurt. She sneezed until her eyes ran, and saw only the suggestion of people lining the roads as they hustled her to the courthouse. Crowds, come to watch the Queen of Hell brought to her trial.

Hands pushed her up a step, through a door, between sheaves of people. And then the hands withdrew and she was alone, standing on the sanded boards in the Salem Town courthouse.

Sun filtered through a leaded window, falling across the judges and gentlemen of the jury in a pale mantle. *Lambskin-men*, Thomas always called them, men draped in the law like it was finery. The one in the longest wig struck his hand upon the wooden desk and called out, but Martha couldn't seem to hear the words. The room swam.

She dug her fingernails into her palms until the pain cleared her head. Another voice was speaking now, sonorous and repetitive.

Slowly, she came to realize they were reading the charges against her.

It wasn't just fever making her sway on her feet but refusal. Each night she'd prayed for the judges to be released from their delusion, for the girls and their parents to be punished, for someone to speak against it. For God, who knew the truth, to come to her aid. But she was here now, and there was silence from God.

There was silence. She looked up into the pale faces of the judges, no longer speaking, and realized they had asked her a question.

The man with the longest wig opened his mouth, revealing two sets of teeth.

She blinked. One set of teeth. He was a man, just a man. But the question was real, had been asked, required an answer.

"How do you plead?"

She didn't want to answer. What she wanted to do was shake him senseless, make him explain. It was rage as much as fever that made her vision blurry, made her hands shake. *It doesn't make sense it doesn't make sense and I don't understand how this is what's happened, how this is what God planned and how the world has turned mad—*

You are not required to understand. Master yourself, girl.

The choice, when she came down to it, was simple. If she confessed she might be allowed to go home. All she had to do was lie, and say she had betrayed God for the devil, and that others had done it too, and give the court their names.

It might be possible to give the court only the names of those who had accused her in turn. Ann Foster. Goody Lacey. Mary Lacey. It was nothing they had not done to her.

But those were not the only confessors who had named her. If she began to confess, if she bowed to the court, they would make her name her sister. They would make her name her children.

For once in your life, Mary had screamed at her, *hold your tongue.*

And there wasn't really any guarantee they *would* let her go home, was there? For some confessors, perhaps, but not the Queen of Hell. They could decide to kill her anyway, if it suited them. She would have forsworn herself, told a lie thrice over, damned herself, for nothing.

For she *would* be damned. To confess would be to choose her own life, her own desires, over God's truth, and placing oneself before God was heresy. Martha would not pretend that she had never committed the sin of self-interest, but that transgression had been born of love, not fear, and she had not done it alone.

With that thought Martha turned, still moving in a daze, to look into the crowd of spectators for the first time. Their faces blurred and melted. Neighbors, strangers, enemies.

No one head and shoulders above the rest.

Thomas wasn't there.

In that endless breath between the asking of the judge's question and her answering, Martha understood two things.

The first was that Thomas had always been less trusting of authority than she. It didn't matter that he had not yet been accused; with his wife named as the Queen of Hell and his sons confessors, Thomas would assume that if he came within grabbing distance of the court, it would seize the opportunity. He was afraid that if he came to the jail, if he came to Martha's trial, he would leave in irons.

And there would be no one to look after the children.

Something in Martha was cracked and seeping. Thomas had not come to her trial because he knew what she was about to say. Of course he knew; they'd been married a long time, and he'd made his own choice that was no choice, once. She could still smell the shed in Billerica, conjure the way his voice had gone rough when he told her what he'd done to his king. She could even remember wondering how it must have felt—to be ready to die for something, and be told to kill for it instead.

And now she knew, and could not make the same choice. It had broken her husband fundamentally to kill his king, and Charles had only been a man. Martha's king was God. If she broke faith now, if she let the devil in, she would never get him out again, and she would know it for the rest of her life. She would know it each time she looked at her children.

And so Thomas could not come to her trial, because he knew that she would not be coming home.

To be known in that moment felt to Martha like a gift, translucent and rare as the wings of an infant bird. He knew. He understood. She could trust him to explain it to the children.

The judge repeated himself for the final time: "How do you plead?"

"Innocent," Martha said.

It began.

One by one, men and women that Martha knew and men and women she had never seen stood up and accused her of witchcraft. Her neighbor Benjamin Abbot recounted every fight they'd ever had, every curse and caustic word. Samuel Preston accused her of bewitching his cow, and John Roger did the same. Little Phoebe Chandler said she was a poisoner and that once Martha's voice had come from the trees all around her, shouting, when no one had been there at all. *I remember that,* Martha wanted to tell her, *I was there, I spoke to you in my own voice*—but she said nothing. They wouldn't hear. She let the accusations wash over her like a heavy rain, not caring if it soaked her through.

The court showed her one mercy. They did not bring in her sons to speak against her. Richard's and Andrew's confessions were read aloud for the jury to hear instead. Martha shut her ears to them, for if she listened she would imagine how they had been obtained, and she could not bear the imagining. But at least they were not made to stand up in front of the court, in front of their mother, and say it again.

Mary's confession was read aloud. The confessions of Ann Foster and Goody Lacey and Mary Lacey were read aloud. Martha was named the Queen of Hell. She didn't crack until one of the afflicted girls repeated the accusation that Martha had killed thirteen in Andover, the smallpox dead, her father and mother and brothers.

At that she couldn't hold it in. Martha twisted around, ready to bare her teeth and call the girl a liar.

But before Martha could open her mouth, the girl screamed. Another shriek followed, and a different girl jerked hard, her whole body in a spasm. "She hurts me! She wants to keep me from telling—" The girl broke off, bending over, clutching at her wrists.

"The prisoner did the same at her hearing," a man shouted from the watching crowd. "I saw her afflict my daughter until her neck was twisted almost round." He pushed forward, the crowd parting for him. "Goody Carrier, let her go! Have mercy on her!"

Mercy, Martha thought, an awful laugh bubbling up in her throat. She bared her teeth at him. "It is no matter to me at all if her neck had been twisted quite *off*."

The crowd roared, and then a scream sliced through the room. An older afflicted girl, one Martha recognized from her preliminary hearing—the one who had stood before the magistrates with preternatural stillness—was staggering forward. Someone shrieked, "Susannah!" as the girl collapsed on the floor, holding out her hands.

They were bound, Martha realized. A wheel band had been wrapped about the girl's wrists, tightly enough that her hands were turning bloodless. "Let me go," Susannah shrieked, her eyes shut tight, head thrashing back and forth. "Goody Carrier, I beg you!"

The bailiffs were already rushing forward to surround her. One of them pulled at the wheel band and shook his head, drawing a knife from his belt. "Hold her. It's too tight, I've got to cut her free."

The other man grasped the girl's elbows and the bailiff carefully sawed through the band. When the last strand parted with a snap, Susannah's eyes fluttered open. The audience cheered.

* * *

Half a day's ride away in the farmhouse in Andover, three-year-old Hannah Carrier pulled at her father's trousers, babbling a question.

Thomas lifted her, held her, but his mind was far away. It would be happening now, if it hadn't already. They would be passing judgment, and unless he was miraculously wrong, he knew what would come to pass.

He had spent the night praying he was wrong, but now, as they came down to it, he wasn't praying but planning. If there was some way to change her fate—pay or kill the jailer, break the lock, get her out, and the boys; they would have to leave Massachusetts, but he could take them through the woods. They could go south, all the way to the town of New York at the mouth of the Hudson River, still more Dutch than English in its sensibilities. It was rumored that Philip English, the merchant who had fled Salem Town, had found sanctuary there.

But Thomas was not Philip English, and had no way to get to New York even if, somehow, impossibly, he could break the iron bars of Martha's prison. He had no money. Those who had found sanctuary in New York were wealthy men. The rich might be accused of witchcraft but they did not die of it.

Thomas's ax hung over the door. He set his daughter down and went to it, took it in his hand, felt the heft. He could still swing it, but it was heavier than it used to be. He'd become an old man when he wasn't watching.

Sometimes Thomas wondered if this was his fault, his punishment. He'd brought an ax down once on an anointed king, which was a blow struck against God himself. This, perhaps, was the bill come due: his wife and sons accused of the heresy he had been the one to commit.

It made him want to walk into the court and give himself up. Offer them his confession. Bare his throat. He would trade places with her in an instant if it were permitted.

A dream was all it was. Thomas had known his share of bloodthirsty men; he did not delude himself into thinking they would accept a trade. He could not save her. All he could do was watch it moving toward them: the end of the road they had been walking together since he first saw her, too far out in a field at sundown, summer ripening around her without a thought for the coming fall.

The next day, when Thomas finally forced himself to go to Chandler's tavern to find out what had happened, he found it buzzing with other news entirely. An earthquake had hit Jamaica and most of the British colony of Port Royal had been cast into the sea, killing hundreds. The ministers were sure it was divine justice.

"And the trial?" Thomas had to raise his voice to make himself heard, leaning close to the innkeeper. "Do you know the verdict?"

Chandler wouldn't meet his eyes, which was answer enough. Thomas turned and walked out of that place, and heard Chandler say behind him, jumping back into the conversation as if Thomas had never there, "A quake like that? A child could read the signs. It *must* be the end of days."

Yes, Thomas thought as he walked outside. Blazing blue sky, grass rippling, just this side of scorched. Yes, it was.

25
Thirty Thousand

At the beginning of fall, nearly a year to the day since I'd begun to research Martha, a friend sent me information about a public lecture. Silvia Federici, the author of *Caliban and the Witch*, the economic analysis of the Great Witch Hunts of Europe, was about to give a talk at a leftist archive in my neighborhood.

It had been six weeks since I'd told Martha I was ready. I was still wary of reading too much into coincidence, but this was no half-interpreted sign; this was real. I went alone to the lecture. Inside a narrow room that smelled sweetly of crumbling paper, Silvia perched on a stool before ranks of folding chairs and began to speak. She was a small, birdlike woman with short gray hair, a habit of nodding for punctuation, and a gravelly Italian accent. The room was enthralled.

It was a long talk, and I took four or five pages of notes, but what I remember most clearly was a brief statistic near the end. Over the last thirty years, Silvia said, more than thirty thousand people around the world had been killed after being accused of witchcraft.

There was so little response from the hushed, attentive audience that at first I thought I'd misheard. I'd come across individual articles in the course of my research, sure—a woman accused of witchcraft and burned in Papua New Guinea, one stabbed in India, another beaten in Brazil—that had time-stamps of 2012, 2014, 2017. Two women had been killed in 2014 in New York City, only a few miles from where I grew up, by a man who believed they were bewitching him.[1] But I thought they were isolated tragedies. I'd even had a conversation with my mother once, offhandedly, about why hardly anyone writing about Salem mentioned that witch hunts were still happening. We'd concluded that it had to be an issue of scope; that compared to Salem or the Great Witch Hunts of Europe, there weren't enough people dying in witch hunts today.

Thirty thousand people in thirty years broke down to more than two people per day. It was a rate even higher than that of the Great Witch Hunts of Europe. It left Salem panting in the dust.

At the end of the talk, I approached Silvia. As she signed my copy of *Caliban*, I added, "An ancestor of mine was hanged in the Salem witch trials, and I—"

Her gaze snapped to mine. "Really? Where do you live?"

"Uh, here. Nearby. I mean, Brooklyn—"

"Wonderful! So do I. Here is my phone number. Give me a call and we will meet to talk about this. I am going to South America but call me when I return, okay?" She had me write down the number, the date she would return. "Good," she said, and sent me dazed from the archive out onto the street.

Laughter and traffic on the avenue, sneakers slapping at the concrete, all of it ringing at a higher decibel. Or maybe it was just that the nagging questions I'd been fending off for so long—*What do you do with a mystery when solving it doesn't matter, when it's over, when she's gone?*—all those questions were dissolving. It felt like my ears had cleared after being stuffed up for days with a cold.

The fact that I'd missed the reality of modern witch hunts revealed a major blind spot. Extensive discourse on the subject (from anthropologists, historians, sociologists, economists, not to mention groups organizing against witch hunts worldwide) isn't hard to find. I just hadn't been looking for it. I'd been so focused on the past, on how it was lost to me, that I'd missed the present, and the fact that Salem's story wasn't over for the simple reason that people were still living it.

* * *

I called Silvia when she got back from South America expecting her to have forgotten me. Instead she invited me over for coffee, which she made in an old moka pot in her apartment's slit of a kitchen. She set out almonds, apologized that there was no chocolate, and we sat in folding chairs in the living room. The walls were a mosaic of Mexican paintings and old posters, propped up by overstuffed bookshelves.

We talked for a while about Salem. Silvia nodded briskly as she listened, humming in her throat. I recounted Martha's pregnancy, the plague, the land disputes, her temperament, her tortured sons, her confessing daughter, her sister, all of it.

Then I asked her about the statistic from her talk. "That night, at the archive, did I—I can't have heard you right. Thirty thousand witch hunts in thirty years?"

"Oh, yes," Silvia said. "Maybe more. It is probably more. It is hard to tell because many are not reported."

The most comprehensive study on modern witch hunts worldwide, released in 2021 by the office of the United Nations Independent Expert on Albinism, reports that ten thousand people—and possibly as many as twenty thousand—were the victims of witch hunts between 2009 and 2019.[2] In ten years, as many as twenty thousand people were harmed, expelled from their homes, ostracized, or killed after being accused of being witches.

It didn't fully confirm Silvia's numbers; not all of the victims the UN counted were killed. But Silvia is right that many more attacks go unreported, and as it was, the study noted witch hunts in close to fifty countries, including Western countries. Every inhabited continent had seen at least one witchcraft accusation that led to harm. And witch hunts were taking place in communities in Africa, South Asia, and areas of Papua New Guinea that had *not* historically had them. They were spreading. In some places, experts think they may be on the rise.

In Silvia's apartment that afternoon, I didn't have a sense of the scope. All I could do was ask why.

"Well," Silvia said, making it a multisyllabic word. "Where to start?"

Because it was Silvia, we started with money. In the latter half of the twentieth century and into the twenty-first, governments and corporations acquired land across the Global South, for everything from mining to food crops to carbon credit schemes, from the mass production of palm oil to that of sugar cane for biofuel. This land, however, was not uniformly empty: people lived on it, used it, and as they lost access, many were no longer able to make a living.[3]

The ensuing displacement, Silvia argued, had been just as effective in destroying local economies as the enclosure of common fields and forests had been in Europe in the years before the Great Witch Hunts. The loss of common lands led to mass displacement. People fled, or if they stayed, they competed for newly limited resources. Inequality grew alongside resentment.

Meanwhile, beginning in the 1980s and 1990s, the International Monetary Fund and the World Bank offered loans to countries that wanted to kickstart their economies. These loans usually came with strict belt-tightening conditions, requiring governments to slash food subsidies, healthcare budgets, and education budgets. Poverty and mortality rates increased dramatically—and, Silvia argued, contributed directly to the increase in witchcraft accusations as people searched for an explanation for their hardships.

The processes she sketched out weren't a perfect mirror for the Great Witch Hunts of Europe, but they were familiar. The displacement of enclosure echoed in the displacement of corporate land acquisition. The sixteenth-century wage crisis refracted into the cut-away social safety nets. The context for the wave of witch hunting was, once again, increasing poverty and inequality during the transition to a globalized capitalist economy.

In both eras, witch hunts could be seen as part of a vicious cycle. The Great Witch Hunts took place as peasant rebellions spread across Europe, and they ruptured many of those rebelling communities, directing fear and violence inward rather than upward. The more that powerful economic actors fracture communities and local economies, the more witch hunts there tend to be. The more that witch hunts create distrust and fear within communities, the less people are able to present a united front against those same economic actors, which is to say against any multinational corporations that might want to acquire their land.

"Witch beliefs," Silvia said over a cooling cup of coffee, "are some of the most destructive of social solidarity. Capitalism rests on exclusion, and it requires the periodic assignment of people to be excluded on the basis of being not human, of being demonic. It was very useful in Europe when the peasants were rebelling against the aristocracy. And it must be useful now that communities are divided when they are facing privatization, mining corporations, Monsanto."

"Do you think the witch hunts are actually encouraged?"

"Not directly, no. No. But people do not hunt witches unless they feel safe killing them—unless they are backed by someone powerful. God. The police. And a community cannot fight back if they are looking for the witch. If a corporation wants to buy the land, and one person wants to sell but another does not—the person who wants to sell can point to the other person and say, this is the witch. It is possible."

Witch hunts still come down hardest upon women, Silvia noted, and particularly upon older women who are past childbearing age and are seen as unproductive in the monetary economy. These women prove especially susceptible to accusations when their families are displaced by the lack of jobs or land. Older women are not always the most likely to be *accused* of witchcraft; the gender breakdown of accusation varies by cultural context. But evidence suggests that even in places where men appear more likely to be accused, women are more likely to suffer violent consequences.[4]

Before I left, Silvia went on a search through her apartment, sifting through the folders and books and filing cabinets. Finally, she pulled something down from a stack by the window. "Here," she said, "take this. Yes, yes, take it with you, read it. It has some information on the witch hunts happening today. Read it and we will talk more."

She held out a red binder. And I know, *I know* we see the omens we look for, but the binder was stuffed so full that for a second I thought she was handing me a big red book.

I smiled. Took it, thanked her, and went home to start again.

26
The Sheriff and the Minister

For details on Sheriff Corwin's seizure of accused witches' goods, see Stacy Schiff's The Witches *(2015). For Mercy Lewis's history, see Benjamin Ray's* Satan & Salem *(2015). For details on Burroughs's conflict with the Putnam family, see Boyer and Nissenbaum's* Salem Possessed *(1976). The account of George Burroughs's trial comes from Cotton Mather's* Wonders of the Invisible World *(1692). The lines that Burroughs quotes in his own trial are from Thomas Ady's* A Candle in the Dark: Shewing the Divine Cause of the Distractions of the Whole Nation of England, and of the Christian World *(1655).*

Salem Town
August 10, 1692

A week had passed since the trial. Martha's fever had broken but she still felt weak and dizzy, hunger winning the long race. She spent less time inside the jail than inside her own mind, looking at no one and speaking not at all. Mary and Margaret were distant figures across the cell, and Thomas still had not come.

The cell door opened, and the jailer pushed a small, bedraggled figure inside. At first Martha thought she had fallen asleep without knowing it. Days and nights blended together in the jail, and she had seen this in her nightmares.

But then Sarah was rushing toward her, her face wet, and it was real, and Martha was on her feet, pinioned ankle stretched out behind her. She swung her daughter up into her arms and curled around her, sheltering her with her body, crawling back to sit against the wall with Sarah in her lap.

Sarah's story came out in gasps and sobs. Men had come to the farmhouse, men with muskets. They had waited until Thomas was out in the fields, trying to handle the harvest on his own—*the fields were overgrown, the summer passing without her, it was all going to ruin*—and they had taken Sarah and her ten-year-old brother Tom away, leaving baby Hannah wailing alone in the house. They had brought Sarah here, to this wet and stinking place, because she had been accused of witchcraft.

Martha knew her heart was beating, but it was as if an icy hand had reached directly into her chest and closed bony fingers around it. All of her children except the baby were somewhere in the jail. How could Thomas have let this happen? She wanted him here, now, to slap him and spit in his face. She wanted him here.

"Hush," Martha murmured, to Sarah and to herself, still holding the girl in her lap as if she could push her back into the womb, hidden and safe. "It's all right."

Sarah spent a while longer sniffling, her face pressed into Martha's armpit, but finally she straightened. Driven up for air, Martha suspected; she knew she was rank after two months without washing. She let her arms go loose, letting Sarah sit up, even if it hurt to do so.

Sarah was still taking shaky breaths, scrubbing snot and tears across her face, when she went still. "Margaret?"

Martha had almost forgotten about Mary and Margaret, sitting in their corner. Almost. Mary was still there, back straight as a musket, watching her daughter—who was standing halfway across the cell, twisting her fists in her smock. Watching Sarah, who had been her playmate, with an awful, hopeful uncertainty.

Martha did not want to let Sarah go to her cousin. She did not want to let Sarah go at all. But Sarah was twisting around, looking up at her with those enormous blue eyes, so like Thomas's, and Martha thought quite suddenly that it didn't matter whom Sarah spoke to. It would be hard enough, here in the jail. She would let Sarah do whatever was necessary to survive it.

"Go on," Martha whispered in her ear, taking another lungful of the sweet summer smell of her, and then Sarah was sliding out of her lap and darting into the center of the cell. She threw her skinny arms around Margaret, who clung to her.

Martha knew that Mary was watching the girls from her corner, too, but she didn't look over. She watched their daughters embracing instead, a kind of neutral ground, until her vision went blurry and she had to blink to clear it.

A few hours later, the jailer returned to fit a tiny shackle and long, light chain around Sarah's ankle. "This one'll cost," he said, driving the pin home. "Blacksmith had to make it special. Didn't have one small enough to fit."

* * *

With Sarah there things were worse and better. Martha was not alone. She felt awful for being grateful for it. But once Sarah had gotten over her initial shock and terror, she was as she'd always been: a clever, excitable child who was curious even when she was nervous. The jail was a horror, certainly, but it was a novelty, too. She had her mother there. She had her cousin. She was young enough that it made her feel safe.

Listening to Sarah chatter with her cousin, Martha felt more awake than she had in weeks, the last haziness of her fever falling away. She came out of the place she'd retreated to in the days after her trial.

She no longer believed any of the women were witches. The confessors were cowards, the accusers fools, malicious or out of their wits. Which was not to say there were no witches in the world; she would make no claim there. But she would stake her life—was staking her life—on the fact that there were no witches in the cell with her.

It helped, quite a bit, to take that attitude. There were no witches in the cell with her, only fools, and she knew how to handle fools.

She began to listen, once more, to the quiet, constant gossip of the other women in the cell. The night Sarah arrived, their target was George Corwin, the young sheriff of Salem Town. He'd served many of their warrants, but he'd done a little more than that for some, it seemed: Corwin had stripped the Procters' home bare when they were arrested. He'd even taken with him the stewpot in which Elizabeth had been cooking dinner.

Property could only be seized from convicted witches, not suspected ones. Elizabeth made a point of complaining about Corwin's actions regularly to the jailer, but received grunts in response. Both Procters had since been convicted; if their property had been seized early, no one was about to raise a stink. The sheriff came from a good family, after all. His uncle was none other than Magistrate Jonathan Corwin, who oversaw the accused witches' preliminary hearings along with Hathorne.

Corwin's best haul, one woman said, rather admiringly, had undoubtedly been the many-gabled mansion of Philip English in Salem Town. Once the merchant had fled—Martha remembered hearing about that, months ago, a lifetime ago, from Thomas, but she'd never heard what happened next— Corwin had gone to his house and taken whatever he could carry. Tableware, snuffboxes, furniture of polished oak and cherry, silver candlesticks, clocks with good glass faces. It was illegal, certainly, but if Philip English wanted to complain, he'd have to return and face the court. Martha hoped, rather grimly, that he wasn't fool enough to do so.

When the women tired of discussing the sheriff, they turned to George Burroughs, the minister who was said to be a wizard. The so-called ringleader of the coven had been convicted a few days after Martha. She remembered bringing home news of his accusation, back when the conspiracy of witches had felt real, dangerous, something that could threaten her children. Well. She'd been a fool herself, back then, but she'd been right in her own way, hadn't she?

The rumors scuttled across the jailhouse floor.

"They say he is a sorcerer with the strength of seven devils."

"They say when he fought the Indians in Wells, he fired a rifle three men could not lift."

"They say he baptized only the first of his children."

"And he doesn't take the Lord's Supper. Can you imagine one of our ministers refusing sacrament?"

"Perhaps he is a Baptist," a woman suggested.

"Perhaps the devil is a Baptist," came the retort, and in the heated debate that followed, Martha learned that much about George Burroughs was under dispute. Nearly ten years ago, he been the minister of Salem Village, and his tenure had not ended amicably. Martha remembered knowing this, vaguely, remembered listening to Deliverance Dane and some other Andover gossips in the churchyard, but she'd paid more attention to the fact that he'd been the minister of Casco Bay when the Indians attacked. She'd thought that what he'd done in Salem didn't matter.

The way one woman told it, Burroughs's stint as Salem's minister ended when he borrowed money from the Putnam family to pay for his own wife's funeral. When Salem Village failed to pay him his salary—a habit of theirs, someone added snidely—he was left unable to fulfill his debt. To encourage repayment, the Putnams had imprisoned their own minister for a night in Ingersoll's ordinary.

It took no little audacity to do a thing like that. Martha thought of Susannah Martin, whispering the story of the Putnam family's clash with the Nurse family, and Thomas Putnam's rivalry with his own half brother. It dawned on her that if she'd been a little more clear-eyed, she would have seen it weeks ago. Susannah had known. Susannah kept bringing the Putnam family up, while Martha had dithered about, wondering if the confessors might be telling the truth.

Susannah had known better, but then, Susannah had been from Salem. Of course she'd have been more likely than Martha to recognize the witches in her own town.

Burroughs, Martha thought—Burroughs had seen it, too. Had seen the Putnams for what they were. As soon as Burroughs was released, he left Salem Village for good. He traveled north, became minister of the settlement of Wells. He'd apparently taken to the frontier rather well.

"Well, of course he did," Goody Lacey was saying. "That is precisely where the devil's minister *would* thrive."

Martha had only been intending to listen, not speak, but Goody Lacey's prim voice clawed into her eardrums. "Don't be a fool," she snapped.

The conversation broke off like a branch. It was the first time that Martha had spoken to anyone but Sarah in—had to be days. She hadn't quite realized that. Most of the others were watching her with wariness, Goody Lacey with something darker. Martha cleared her throat, to make sure Lacey could hear her, and went on. "He'd lived there in the past, hadn't he? He was the minister at Casco Bay."

Someone sucked in a breath, but Elizabeth Procter—now halfway pregnant and still refusing to confess—favored her with a considering nod. "He was. And do you know who else was there that night when Casco burned?" She waited to make sure she had everyone's attention before saying, softly but clearly, "Mercy Lewis."

Martha stared at her. Mercy Lewis was Thomas Putnam's maid and a prolific accuser. But the massacre at Casco Bay had been nearly twenty years ago. "How is that possible?"

"She was a babe," Elizabeth said. "Most of her family died that night. But her parents made their way down to Salem Village, along with their minister."

"Burroughs."

"Yes, when he first came. They lived there a while. I knew them. Godly people."

"They no longer live in Salem?" Martha asked. Somehow the conversation had narrowed to her and Elizabeth. Sarah slid quietly from where she'd been crouching by Margaret and came to sit beside her mother, dragging her little shackle and its thin chain.

"They did not care for the village," Elizabeth answered. "They left, not long after Burroughs did, and returned to Casco. When it was attacked again, they were killed."

"And Mercy—"

"She came back to Salem when her parents died and took work in Putnam's house. Don't ask me how, I haven't an inkling. But she was a maid to Burroughs, too, for a while."

"I imagine she saw some things there," a woman Martha didn't know murmured to her neighbor.

"Like what?" Martha asked.

Again, her voice seemed to stop them, but Sarah, sitting cross-legged, echoed, "Yes, what?" and it was enough to coax out an answer.

"Well, he is a murderer," the woman said gently—to Sarah, not Martha. "He is said to have bewitched many soldiers at the eastward when the Indians attacked Casco. And Mercy says he even killed his own wives with witchcraft."

"He'd got more than one wife?" Sarah asked.

The woman smiled wanly. "Not at the same time, child. He was twice a widower, that man. He's said to have been ... " She hesitated. "Rather harsh."

"One of those wives," Elizabeth Procter said lightly, as if it didn't matter, "was the widow of John Hathorne's brother."

Her eyes met Martha's. John Hathorne, hardfisted magistrate of the preliminary hearings, the man who had sent each of them to jail. His sister-in-law had married the king of the witches. And died in his house.

"I see," Martha said.

Mary Easty leaned forward. She and Martha had spoken at length when she'd first been brought in, for Easty, too, had refused to confess. She had even joined in some of the discussions of scripture that Martha and Mary used to coax out of Margaret. "At his trial," Mary Easty said softly, "Ann Putnam testified that the spirits of his dead wives came to her. They told her that their husband had misused them and killed them."

In that moment, Martha decided, unequivocally, that George Burroughs was innocent. He might have been harsh to his wives, but he wasn't a witch. It was a decision born of reaction: Ann Putnam had accused him, and Martha would not believe her.

"That's horrid," Sarah said.

"It would be horrid if it were true," Martha corrected.

"It is true, Goody Carrier," someone called. "They found him guilty."

Martha ignored her. "What else did Burroughs do?"

What George Burroughs did, the women said, was walk into his trial with confidence. He was a Harvard-educated minister, after all—although, the gossip was, he'd never been officially *ordained* as a minister. And he had Baptists for friends. And he had neglected to baptize his children at their births, just as the Baptists did, believing it better to wait for a child to be old enough to choose baptism. Some of the women insisted that Burroughs was a Baptist in all but name.

But perhaps he had been hoping on personal connections to save him. A number of the judges in the courtroom had been his classmates at Harvard. What was more, Burroughs had spent ten years living at the edge of the world. He had faced deadly winters and nighttime raids, Indian fire arrows and French guns, and the massacre of almost his entire congregation in Casco Bay. George Burroughs had lived through it all. He wasn't frightened of little girls.

He should have been. The afflicted girls had screamed and thrashed when he tried to speak. His former classmates had watched with increasing doubt.

Finally, Burroughs had taken a piece of paper from his pocket to give to the jury, the contents of which had raced through the jail's gossip network. It had read: "There neither are, nor ever were witches, that having made a compact with the devil can send a devil to torment other people at a distance."

In other words, witches could not send specters to afflict people. And to make matters worse, one of the women whispered, it hadn't taken the judges long to place the quotation. It was the work of one Thomas Ady, an English writer. Ady, it seemed, was infamous for arguing that while witches *might* exist, they were extremely rare. He'd once written that spiritual affliction was most often an excuse made up by a physician out of his depth. And he thought that the Bible, in its treatment of witches, was largely *allegorical*.

"That's heresy," Martha said sharply when this particular piece of information came to light. "Sarah, don't mind that. The Bible is no allegory."

"Surely not," Mary Easty agreed. "And the court was inclined to agree."

Martha paused. To agree with anything the court said was intolerable—but the Bible was the Bible. She decided to put the issue aside for a moment, in favor of a more pressing matter. The court had condemned George Burroughs to death. If they would condemn a minister, they would condemn anyone.

And so that night, in the lost hours when the rats ran free and the women slept, Martha woke Sarah and she told her daughter, softly but in no uncertain terms, what needed to happen next.

27
The Devil in the Ground

In a book about Salem published soon after World War II, Marion L. Starkey recounted that after the trials were over, people in Salem Village shunned parcels of land that had belonged to the executed witches. "For a century or more," she wrote, "some places would be shunned. It was as if people feared to break the devil from the ground."[1]

I think she was right. The devil is in the ground. Just not quite how Marion Starkey meant it.

When I first opened Silvia's red binder, I found a hodgepodge gold mine. Academic papers, news clippings, a pamphlet she'd been given in Tanzania that advised that there could, indeed, be witches in your community, and you needed to learn how to identify them. (The pamphlet's provenance was unclear, but the name of the Evangelical group printed on the back was headquartered in Louisiana.) I started trawling the internet, setting up alerts for news articles about witch hunts, which I fed into a spreadsheet. It contained the following:

- Date and location of the attack
- Victim's name, age, gender; the accusation made against them
- Preexisting feud between accuser and accused, if noted
- Number of accusers and their relation to the victim
- Court process, formal or informal (y/n)
- Presence of a "witch finder" (y/n)
- Outcome (injury/death)

My spreadsheet did not suddenly illuminate a universal model for witch hunts. There is no single kind of hunt, and no single explanation, in any era. But there are trends. There are layers of real-world forces and interests beneath the lacquer of belief. There are policies.

I found my way to the website of the Witchcraft and Human Rights Information Network, run by a British man named Gary Foxcroft. The original network is no longer active, but at the time it connected researchers and organizers all over the world. I cold-emailed Foxcroft, and he helpfully provided a short list of people who were studying, publicizing, or protesting against witch hunts.

One of the first people I got in touch with was Leo Igwe, founder of the Nigeria-based group Advocacy for Alleged Witches (AfAW). AfAW provides aid to victims of witch hunts in Nigeria and some surrounding nations, does outreach and education work, and lobbies the government to investigate instances of vigilante witch hunting. Igwe, who has a PhD in religious studies and studied witchcraft accusation in Ghana, told me that he'd started AfAW because he felt that the Nigerian government was treating witch hunts with kid gloves. There were few consequences for witch hunting, he said, and bystander intervention was rare. "What you'll see when people are accused of witchcraft," he said, "is instead of people trying to stop the violence, they'll film it."[2]

This is what happened to Akua Denteh, a ninety-year-old woman killed in Ghana in July 2020. According to news reports, she was accused by a witch finder of causing "certain strange happenings in the area including limiting the progress of the town."[3] She was beaten to death by a mob while someone filmed. Denteh's death actually broke the norm of invisibility: the video of her killing swept the internet and produced a public outcry in Ghana from civic and political groups. Members of Parliament called for an investigation.

But if the response to Denteh's death was unusual, the accusation leveled against her—that she had "limited the town's progress"—was not. This kind of economic accusation crops up often. Igwe described a recent case in southern Nigeria in which a man had been accused of "holding hostage the futures of young people in the community" through witchcraft.[4]

Samuel Parris would have understood both these accusations intimately. When Betty and Abigail started screaming, Parris thought their futures were being held hostage as punishment for his attempts to create a pure Salem Village church. But in addition to being a punishment, the witches were also understood to be part of the original problem: their existence in a Puritan community angered God, undermined the church, and limited the progress of both Salem Village and the Puritan project as a whole.

"When people get alarmed," Leo Igwe told me about twenty-first-century witch hunts, "there's always a tendency to take flight into the spiritual, into the supernatural. Witch persecution is a hydra. It has economic issues, political issues, issues of belief, issues of law." But the hostage-taking accusations he's seen were often explicitly linked to economics. He echoed Silvia, describing how the pressures of economic dispossession increase the likelihood of a witch hunt. "There are no unemployment benefits, no loans, no subsidies. There's despair, hopelessness, limited chances. So people embrace other hopes, and other ways of understanding. It creates an atmosphere for promoters of witchcraft to say, 'Hey, some people are holding your destiny hostage.'"[5]

If Samuel Parris thought Salem's witches were limiting the village's future, Thomas Putnam believed they were holding his own personal destiny hostage. Stealing his inheritance, stripping away his prestige, his wealth, his hope that things could change. This framework, too, endures. Berrie Holtzhausen, another anti-witch-hunting activist I spoke with, described how uneven economic development has helped spur similar accusations in his area of Namibia. He noted that the newly wealthy will often hide their assets when visiting poorer family members to avoid accusations of witchcraft. "When people achieve work, house, a car in the city, they'll travel back to the rural area without the car, because they say: 'people will think I got rich through killing people with magical powers.' The so-called 'development' is part of the increase in witch hunts."[6]

The decisions that make or break economies are often made far away from the people they affect, in halls of power and banks in distant cities and different languages. When prices and prospects rise and fall apparently without explanation, it's not surprising that people might wonder if there are arcane forces at play—especially if some people successfully manipulate the market while others cannot. The Puritans, for example, believed that being a witch could make you wealthy, but also that witches would use their power to keep *other* people from becoming wealthy. The phenomenon they were describing wasn't entirely made up: people absolutely used an arcane force to become wealthy, and that same force concentrated wealth in the hands of relatively few people. But the culprit wasn't the devil. It was the market economy, growing fast.

Igwe told me, "As long as there is inequality—if a few people are rich, but others are very poor—people will say that the rich people used witchcraft to get there."[7] I asked if he meant that we had to solve inequality to stop witch hunting. His answer, in a word, was yes, but he is also fundamentally trying to change how people see witch hunting. His position is categorical: "Witchcraft is superstition, and those accused of it are innocent." This has gotten him into trouble more than once—with church leaders, he says, who decline to disavow the possibility that Satan could recruit witches, but also with international aid groups. Western scholars, Igwe feels, are too reluctant to condemn witch hunting. They "try to say, 'Oh, you shouldn't offend the traditional sentiments of Africa.' So you think we should live with this? They are trying to be respectful of African beliefs, but in a misguided way, and this leads them to say witchcraft is superstition in the West but in Africa it's something else."

When I asked him what groups like AfAW wanted, Igwe's answer was simple. "Noise," he said. "I want the world to know where we stand. Why is it that universities overseas are ready to amplify the voices of Africans who believe in witchcraft, but not the voices of those Africans who don't? Don't get me wrong—witchcraft belief is a phenomenon that manifests. But if we want to understand it, we have to understand it in its contexts, and with its resistances."

The next person I spoke with was Miranda Forsyth, and she led me back to Martha. Forsyth is a professor at Australian National University and a leader in the university's Sorcery Accusation Related Violence (SARV) project.

The SARV project analyzed more than 1,500 accusations of witchcraft in Papua New Guinea between 2016 and 2020. The researchers found that community disputes often preceded a witch hunt—which makes sense—but also that the single most common kind of dispute to precipitate a witch hunt was over land.[8]

The cases that the SARV researchers studied showed that nearly 35 percent of *all* witchcraft accusations were between parties who had a preexisting land dispute. Land disputes were more common than disputes over money, movable property, sex, tribal conflict, or any other kind of grievance.

This is what I mean when I say that Marion Starkey was right and the devil is in the ground. In an agrarian culture, like areas of Papua New Guinea—like Salem—land isn't just property, it's life. An enemy in a land dispute can be seen as more dangerous than any other kind. The witch who threatens your land is the harbinger of a unique evil. She holds your future hostage.

Some witch hunts today that involve an explicit land grab take place within families, for obvious reasons: you can't inherit a stranger's land, but you might be able to inherit your aunt's—or your father's. The Kaya Godoma Rescue Center is a sanctuary for elderly people at risk of being accused of witchcraft in Kilifi County, Kenya. An estimated four hundred-plus elders in Kilifi are killed after being accused of witchcraft every year.[9] By 2020, Kaya Godoma had provided sanctuary for one hundred elderly people, nearly all of whom were men. "Most of them are here due to family differences," Emmanuel Katana, the head of Kaya Godoma, told the Kenyan newspaper the *Star*. "Some were accused after refusing to sell their land or cede part of their land to family members."[10]

To be a woman who inherits land after the deaths of several male relatives can be as dangerous today as it was when Martha did it. "When my father died, then shortly after his brother and my nephew [also died], my mother was accused of being a witch," a Ugandan woman named Fortune Izama told a journalist with *Global Press Journal* in 2019. "My uncles said she killed them all and wanted to take the property."[11]

Izama's mother's house was set on fire while she slept. She escaped but was driven out of town. "It is hard to clear your name," Izama said, "when you have nothing and no one on your side."

28
Forever and Ever and Amen

Much of the dialogue in Sarah's examination is direct quotation from the trial record ("Examination of Sarah Carrier," August 11, 1692, SWP No. 26.2 in the Salem Witch Trials Documentary Archive). The description of Thomas Jr.'s examination comes from the trial records ("Examination of Thomas Carrier, Jr.," August 10, 1692, SWP No. 27.1 in the Salem Witch Trials Documentary Archive).

Salem Town
August 11, 1692

The jailer unlocked the door of their cell and came straight for Martha. At the last second, he swerved to unlock Sarah's shackle, seizing her by the arm.

"Wait—Sarah—" Martha grabbed for her daughter, but the jailer hauled her out of reach. "Let go of her!"

"She's wanted for questioning." The jailer dragged the squirming child across the cell.

"Remember what we spoke of—Sarah!" Martha was on her feet, calling after her, the chain stretched as far as it could go. Sarah gave a single white-faced nod and disappeared around the corner.

Martha sank down. She thought she might be sick but had nothing to vomit. She'd given Sarah her dinner.

"What you spoke of?" Mary Easty murmured, leaning over.

Martha dug her fingers into her thighs, watching the cell door. She whispered, "I am already condemned."

* * *

Magistrate John Hathorne began, as was his custom, with the presumption of guilt. "How long hast thou been a witch?"

Sarah Carrier looked up at the tall, bewigged, stern-faced men, and she answered, quite clearly, "Ever since I was six years old."

Hathorne blinked, taken aback. "How old are you now?"

"Near eight years old, brother Richard says. I shall be eight years old in November next."

"Who made you a witch?"

Sarah swallowed. She had blubbered, in the early morning darkness of the cell, but it hadn't swayed Martha. Blubbering never did.

And now she was here, and they were asking her the questions her mother had predicted they would, and she knew what she was supposed to tell them. She knew what she was supposed to say. But she didn't *want* to. It went against everything she'd ever been taught, particularly by her mother, who hated liars.

Not this time, child, Martha had whispered. *Here is what you will say.*

"My mother," Sarah said. "She made me set my hand to a book."

A rustle went through the men, reminding Sarah of nothing much as a dog shaking fleas from its fur. "How did you set your hand to it?" one asked.

"I touched it with my fingers," she said. "The book was red. The paper of it was white."

"Did you ever see the black man?"

"No." Her mother had been clear on this, too. "No, there was no black man."

"You did not see him?"

She shook her head. They exchanged a look among themselves. One said, "Where did it happen?"

"Andrew Foster's pasture."

"And who was there? Besides you and your mother."

She didn't want to say it. She hadn't wanted to say it as soon as her mother had whispered it, fiercely. Sarah had tried to protest, and Martha had taken her thin shoulders in her big hands and said, *It will help them believe. You must do this.*

"My—my aunt," Sarah said now. "My aunt Mary. And my cousin."

"Your aunt Goody Toothaker."

She couldn't speak, but they seemed satisfied with her nod. A man in the corner was scribbling. Sarah twisted her fingers.

"What did they promise to give you?"

"A black dog."

"Did the dog ever come to you?"

"No. But I saw a cat once."

"What did the cat say to you?"

Sarah stuttered. She almost told the magistrate *cats don't talk*, but her mother had told her not to contradict them. She grabbed at one of Martha's favorite curses. "It said it would tear me in pieces, if I would not set my hand to the book."

The man in the corner scribbled. "And it was your mother who baptized you?" the magistrate asked.

"Yes."

"And the devil was there?"

He'd already asked her this. Sarah realized, all at once, that this man with the wobbly skin under his chin was trying to catch her in a lie. She bristled. "Not as I saw. Only my mother."

"What did your mother say to you when she baptized you?"

"Thou art mine forever and ever and amen."

Those words were easy. Her mother liked to reuse Biblical phrases, and she used to say that one when Sarah was very young and frightened of the wolves that howled in the woods. *Don't fret, child,* Martha would say, *I shan't let them in, thou art mine, not food for any overgrown dogs. Thou art mine forever and ever.* And she would tickle Sarah's ribs until Sarah was overcome with laughter instead of terror.

"How did you afflict folk?"

Sarah told them that she pinched to afflict, the way she pinched her older brothers. No, she had no poppets; she went in spirit to the people to pinch them. No, she did not know how she had done it. Her mother had carried her.

"How did your mother carry you," another magistrate, not the wobbly chinned one, interrupted, "when she was in prison?"

Sarah shrugged. "She came like a black cat."

"How did you know that it was your mother?"

"The cat told me so, that she was my mother."

"And who have you afflicted?"

They listed some names and she agreed to all of them. They listed some other witches who might have helped her, and she agreed to those names, too. And as she spoke, Sarah found herself warming, a little, to the telling, the way she did when her older brothers told her stories at bedtime, chiming in with suggestions until sleep took her. This was just like that; it was just a story. Yes, she had a wooden spear, about as long as her finger, that she used to afflict people. Yes, she'd gotten it from Elizabeth Johnson. Yes, it could have originally come from the devil, but she hadn't seen him. No, she had never been to the witches' sabbath in Salem Village. Yes, she was certain of it. She had hardly ever been to Salem Village at all. No, that was all she knew. Wouldn't they please let her go home?

* * *

The day before Sarah's confession, her brother Thomas Jr. was interrogated by Dudley Bradstreet, the Andover Justice of the Peace. Thomas Jr. confessed that he was a witch—and had been one for the sum total of a week. His mother, he said, had appeared to him as a yellow bird and had instructed him to set his hand to a book. She had threatened to tear him in pieces if he did not.

Once he had agreed to her demands, she dipped him naked in the stream that ran between the Carrier and Foster lands in a demonic baptism. Thomas Jr. maintained that he had never actually *done* any witchcraft, only been primed for the practice by his mother.

It was enough.

* * *

It was night when the footfalls sounded in the corridor. They were heavier than the jailer's—all the women knew his tread by now—and Martha watched the grate warily along with the others.

Then Sarah, unshackled since her confession, squealed and threw herself at the bars.

By the time Martha made it there, Thomas was kneeling, holding on to his daughter. Sarah had thrust her hands through the grate and she was clinging to his shirtsleeves so tightly she threatened to rip the fabric, crying as her father murmured to her.

The jailer stuck his head around the corner. "'Til sundown only," he snapped, and his footsteps receded.

Thomas looked up at Martha without a word.

To keep herself from reaching out to him Martha smoothed a hand down Sarah's back. The girl bawled louder. Martha said, "Has something happened to Hannah?"

"She's all right. Captain Danforth's girl is watching her."

Martha blinked. Captain Danforth was a man of no small stature in Billerica, and in her own life. It was in the shed behind his barn that she had taught Thomas to read, and where other things had happened.

"Danforth was asked to testify against you for the court," Thomas said. "For the trial. He would not go."

"Wouldn't he," Martha said, and she wasn't sure what it sounded like, but Thomas reached out to her through the bars, still cupping the back of Sarah's head with his other hand, and Martha was moving before she had consciously decided to do so. It was like coughing when there was water in the lungs, a commandment of the body. Thomas held out his hand, and she took it. She said, "I thought you would not come."

His face crumpled. "Forgive me. I did not want—"

"I know," she said. "Tom. I know." He still looked wretched. She tried for the levity that had always been his gift, not hers. "What did you pay the jailer to let you in?"

He didn't smile. "More than we can afford."

"Thomas—"

"What would you have me do?" he asked. His voice was rough, wrung out. "Martha. What would you have me do?"

He held her gaze, and she knew that he wasn't speaking of bribing the jailer. Sarah was shuddering under Martha's hand, and she wanted to send the girl away, didn't want her to hear what had to be said, but she couldn't bring herself to do it. Sarah was being held by both her parents, and Martha would not cut short what would very likely be the last time.

The words broke in her mouth. She made herself say them anyway. "I would have you leave," she said. "I would have you take them away."

Thomas opened his mouth to speak, and Martha fumbled onward before he could say something to change her mind. Nearly anything would do it. "No, Tom, listen to me. They have not sent any confessors to the noose. It may take some time, but I believe the children will be allowed to come home, and when they do, you must be there. Thomas. You must not leave them."

"*You* must not leave them."

It's too late, Martha said, or tried to say, but her throat was too tight. She let go of Sarah, just for a moment, and held on to Thomas with both hands.

Distantly, a bell tolled. It would be sundown soon.

There were a thousand things Martha wanted to say, and time for only one. She pressed a hand to Thomas's cheek. "If the Lord is kind," she said, very softly, "we will see each other again."

Thomas turned his face into her palm with a shuddering breath. He didn't say *he is not kind*, though she saw the thought pass over his face. But he didn't say it, and she couldn't be angry with him for thinking it, not now. Wouldn't waste her breath. Instead they stood there, holding on to each other, their daughter between them, until the last of the light faded and the night came rushing on.

29
The Witch Finder

Of all the confessions in Salem, there is only one that I want to be true. Or, more accurately, one that I want to make real. It came from an Andover man named William Barker at the end of the summer of 1692. Like others before him, Barker confessed that the aim of the witches in Salem and Andover was to tear down the Puritan project in New England, to destroy the government and the churches, and to set up the devil's kingdom.

But Barker went a step further. He described to his interrogators what kind of place the devil's kingdom would be. It would be a land in which all "should live bravely, that all persons should be equal, that there should be no day of resurrection or of judgment, and neither punishment nor shame for sin."[1]

This was the devil's kingdom: a land of courage. A land without resurrection, where the only life you got was the one you were living. A land without judgment, shame, or punishment for sin—which was a challenge to having a theocracy at all. (What was government for, the Puritans wondered, if not to outlaw sin?) This was the devil's kingdom: a land with equality for all.

This is what the Puritans were so afraid of. This is what they accused Martha of trying to create.

* * *

Once I turned my attention to the witch hunts of the present, Salem loosened its hold. But every so often, when I opened my weekly alert for articles on witch hunts, something would surge up. This happened most frequently, I discovered, when my alert delivered accounts of witch hunts that had involved a witch finder.

Broadly defined, witch finders are people who are believed by others to have the ability to identify a witch. Some witch finders also offer to cure affliction or fight off witches, but identification is the core power. Witch finders may be engaged directly by an individual who is experiencing some kind of affliction, or they may act as part of an informal legal or community process. Witch finders can be local or can be brought in specifically to provide services. They add legitimacy to an accusation of witchcraft, especially if it's against a more respected member of the community. By professionalizing accusation, witch finders act as a kind of insurance, a way to be sure you have the right person.

In the wake of added legitimacy comes increased violence. Of the nearly 1,500 cases of witchcraft accusation in Papua New Guinea studied by Miranda Forsyth and her colleagues, almost a third involved a witch diviner, a kind of witch finder.[2] The researchers found that witch diviners were much more likely to be involved in cases where accusations led to violence than in cases where accusations were made but not acted upon.

As in Salem, witch finders have various motivations, including the genuine desire to protect their community from harm. That said, witch finding can be a lucrative business. In many of the cases documented by the researchers in Papua New Guinea, the witch diviner was paid; sometimes they were paid more than the equivalent of $500.[3] (The average income in Papua New Guinea in 2023 was $275/month.[4]) And while witch diviners have existed in Papua New Guinea for a long time, Forsyth notes, paying them for their services is new.

In Salem, the primary witch finders—the afflicted girls—did not profit monetarily. That benefit went to someone else. It was legal for the state to confiscate a condemned prisoner's belongings and movable goods in Puritan Massachusetts, though it was *not* legal to do so before conviction, a law that seems to have been broken in the case of John Procter.[5] Nor was it legal for the confiscating officer to sell off belongings for cash, though the twenty-five-year-old sheriff George Corwin, nephew of Magistrate Jonathan Corwin, seized items from the homes of accused witches and apparently sold them for his own profit.[6] According to a complaint made years later, Corwin also seems to have demanded that Thomas Carrier pay him fifty shillings,[7] or about five hundred dollars.[8] It's unclear what was promised or threatened in return for that money, but Thomas paid.

Monetary compensation isn't the only benefit available to witch finders. There's real power in becoming one. Jean La Fontaine, a professor emeritus at the London School of Economics, studies how traditional allegations of witchcraft have evolved in modern Africa, expanding to include a belief in child-witches. Her work shows that many modern witch finders are Evangelical and Pentecostal pastors who offer to identify and exorcise witches for their constituents. "The 'finding' of witches and their exorcism afterwards is a very attractive source of income for pastors," La Fontaine told me, and it doubles as "a 'proof' of the power given them by God."[9]

Many of the African Evangelical churches La Fontaine studied hold the belief, as the Puritans did, that material success could be a mark of God's favor, while a lack of material success could be due to witchcraft.[10] If a family is struggling, La Fontaine told me, they might ask their trusted pastor to help them pinpoint the witch who is poisoning their success. It's becoming more and more common for families to specifically inquire whether or not their own children are witches, a cultural shift that La Fontaine attributes to the fusing of some traditional beliefs with Evangelical theories of original sin. Not only are children (as inheritors of original sin) not *exempt* from evil, but some strains of Evangelical thought suggest that children may be particularly easy to for the devil to possess.[11]

If a pastor agrees that a child is a witch, they may offer the parents an exorcism—usually for a fee. I asked La Fontaine how many pastors she thought moonlighted as witch finders. She told me, "I would almost say that the majority of pastors are willing to 'find' witches or to 'identify' a child-witch."[12] A paucity of data makes it impossible to tally a full count, but a 2022 African Child Policy Forum report noted that hundreds of children are abused and abandoned in Malawi each year after being accused of witchcraft, and thousands more accused child-witches have been made homeless in the capital of the Democratic Republic of the Congo.[13]

Berrie Holtzhausen, who has been an anti-witch-hunting activist for eleven years, is a former pastor himself. He's also the founder of Alzheimer's Dementia Namibia, a group that defends elderly people with dementia from accusations of witchcraft. The symptoms of dementia are sometimes seen as evidence that someone is a witch, redirecting accusations from children to the elderly. But here, too, Holtzhausen said, he was inclined to credit Christian churches with the prevalence of witch hunts in Namibia. "The European concept of witchcraft mixed with traditional African beliefs in evil spirits," he explained, and the combination produced "the 'witch in your community you have to find.'"[14] He recounted a time when he had attempted to defend a man from a witchcraft accusation. Another man stood up to tell Holtzhausen, who is white, "Your ancestors brought Christianity to us. They made us Christians. And in your Bible, it says there are witches and they must be killed."

Samuel Parris would understand; Cotton Mather would understand. But Holtzhausen has his doubts as to how many of the witch finders and witch doctors actually believe it. "I'm convinced that a lot of them—both the authorities and the witch doctors—don't really believe in witchcraft," Holtzhausen told me. "They see it as a very powerful weapon because everyone else believes in it, and they use the fear to control people. They say, 'all your misfortunes are because of witchcraft. I am the only one with the magic, I am the only one who can see the witch. So you have to come to me.'"[15]

To be a witch finder imparts power, but it also takes power. It takes a kind of authority, real or presumed, which is given to the finder by the community and reinforced by looking or acting the part. Like *the witch* itself, the witch finder is a social role.

This means it's often easier to be a witch finder if society is already willing to grant you some power. Not always—the afflicted girls in Salem had very little power before becoming witch finders—but the afflicted girls only managed to *become* witch finders because they were backed up by people with more social power, like Thomas Putnam and Samuel Parris. And the afflicted girls were not, in fact, the only witch finders in Salem. They were the primary witch finders, but there is someone else who played the role of a witch finder specifically for Martha and the others who were with her the day that she was taken to Gallows Hill. The last witch finder in Martha's story is Cotton Mather.

Mather had plenty of social power. He was well educated, well-to-do, practically Puritan royalty. Not yet thirty, he was already preaching at Boston's North Church, where he gave fire and brimstone sermons with a cerebral poeticism. A number of judges on the Court of Oyer and Terminer, not to mention members of the Massachusetts legislature, were family friends or members of Mather's church.

Mather wrote extensively on the Salem witch trials. He didn't agree with every action the Court of Oyer and Terminer took—he had cautioned the judges against relying on spectral evidence more than once and urged them to move carefully—but he fundamentally supported them, because he believed the devil's aim was to tear down the Puritan project. "It may be fear'd," he wrote late in the summer of 1692, that "the design of the Devil is to sink that Happy Settlement of Government."[16] This was, of course, speculation on Mather's part; he hadn't spoken to any accused witches in person, nor attended a single courtroom session. Mather didn't actually go to Salem at all that year—until he went to Gallows Hill in August, on the day Martha was to be hanged.

He went that day because he wanted to witness the execution of George Burroughs, the alleged leader of the coven. Mather may well have been frightened that the devil's aim was to create a land like the one William Barker would go on to describe, a land with equality for all. George Burroughs—a minister who had never been officially ordained, who had Baptist friends and neglected to take part in some Puritan sacraments—was the threat incarnate.

But I think it was personal, too. In the struggle between Good and Evil that was always playing out in Cotton Mather's mind, Burroughs must have seemed like his foil, the dark minister to his light, the man trying to tear down everything he hoped to build. If this framing seems a little self-centered on Mather's part, he was verifiably obsessed with how the state of Massachusetts Puritanism reflected on him personally. In his diary, Mather mused whether the witchcraft outbreak might have been his own fault for being such a good minister. Could it be, he wrote, that the afflictions were "intended by hell, as a particular defiance, unto my poor endeavors, to bring the souls of men into heaven?"[17]

He kept writing himself into the story. I don't think he could help it. So that day on the hill, when the call for a witch finder went out one last time, Cotton Mather answered, and wrote himself into Salem's story forever.

30
The Hill

*The account of what happened on the hill is drawn from Thomas
Brattle's 1692 account and Robert Calef's book* More Wonders
of the Invisible World *(1700), both later republished in George
Lincoln Burr's* Narratives of the Witchcraft Cases *(1914). We
do not have the text of the speeches that George Burroughs and
Cotton Mather made, but we know that Burroughs proclaimed
his innocence from the ladder and concluded by saying the Lord's
Prayer, and that the speech drew tears from the crowd to the point
that it seemed like people might protest. We know the substance
of Mather's speech as described by Calef.*

Salem Town
August 19, 1692

Martha was acutely aware of the earth under her feet.

She stood barefoot in the street outside the jail. She'd lost her shoes at
some point in the last three months, couldn't remember when, and her feet
were unrecognizable lumps of flesh attached to her ankles, mottled with
scabs and bruises and dirt. But they were hers, and she was moving them,
one after another, stirring the street dust and placing them back down on the
ground.

She felt like a babe walking for the first time, unsteady, pressed up too
close to the world. Not feverish, as she'd been when they'd taken her to trial,
but excruciatingly sensitive to the feeling of the earth under her feet, the feeling of breathing. *This is the world,* her body seemed to be saying. *This is what
it is.*

The rest was out of reach. Thomas was gone, and she'd told him not to
come back. Her children were beyond her, in a wet hole in the ground. When
the jailer had come, Martha had gone to Mary for the first time in weeks,
and Mary, for the first time in weeks, had stood to meet her. They did not
embrace, but Martha had pushed Sarah into Mary's arms and kissed her and
told her to have courage. Mary had taken the girl and held her tightly.

Now, outside the jail, Martha couldn't hear Sarah screaming anymore. A small mercy.

Another: the sky was a cloudless, aching blue, and a quiet wind was blowing in from the sea, clean and sharp. It shouldn't have mattered but it did. She was glad she would die in the sunlight.

"Up you go." The sheriff, Corwin, hooked his hand around her arm and pushed her into the cart. He bound her hands to a slat at waist-height in the far corner. She didn't fight him, let him rustle with his ropes and binds.

Once she was secured, they brought out the men. Old George Jacobs stamped out first, taking each step as if the ground offended him. He was a thickset man with pale eyes glittering in the folds of his face, and he looked windburned, even after the jail, as some old farmers managed to do. In his trial, Martha had heard, he'd told the court that he was no more a wizard than he was a buzzard.

Then came John Willard, a constable who had brought accused witches to jail before attempting to flee his own accusation. John Procter, Elizabeth's husband, followed Willard. He would never see his baby, Martha thought, turning away from the sky to blink at him. She wanted to tell him Elizabeth was well, but she would not lie, not now.

Last they brought out George Burroughs, her supposed consort and partner in crime. He was shorter than she'd expected, hardly taller than Martha herself, but broad, with a barrel chest and capable hands. His face would have been handsome if not for the dark straggle of his prison beard.

Martha was the only woman among them. She wondered vaguely if she should be honored or insulted.

The sheriff swung up on his mount and the cart-driver clicked his tongue. The horses, shying away from the stench of the jail, were only too happy to oblige, and they jerked into motion.

Before they'd clattered a cart length, George Burroughs spoke. "We must try to persuade them."

He said it quietly but Martha still startled. His voice was shockingly deep, and still warm and rich despite his long imprisonment. He continued, "I have something prepared, but you must all stand with me. We must persuade them of their folly."

George Jacobs spat out through the cart slats and shot Willard a bitter look. "Aye, an' what does he think we been doing all these days in the prison?"

"I mean no disrespect, sir," Burroughs said, low and fierce, "but we must not give in to despair. We must act."

"What do you propose?" John Procter bent down so that he could match Burroughs's volume, though neither the cart-driver nor the sheriff showed any sign of listening.

"If this day goes as I think it will," Burroughs said, "there will be a great gathering on the hill. There will be men who were not present at our trials. We speak to *them*. We proclaim our innocence and pray that the Lord opens their hearts."

"*Pray*," George Jacobs said with disgust, and hawked another gob of spit, but this time it didn't make it through the slats of the cart, and swung back by a line of spittle to slap onto his shoulder.

Martha grimaced. Tied as she was, she managed to clip the old man's arm with her elbow. "Have some dignity. Or will you surrender that, as well?"

All four men turned toward her with varying degrees of surprise and, on the part of Jacobs, indignation. Martha ignored him. She met Burroughs's gaze for the first time and said, "I will call out."

Her voice sounded strange in the open air, harsh and thin, but it made her feel more like her old self to hear it. More awake. She added, "Though they will not listen."

"You are Goodwife Carrier?" Burroughs said, rather cautiously. "I have heard of you."

"And I you," she said. "Next time you hold a witches' sabbath, sir, I would be obliged if you'd forget my invitation."

Burroughs stared at her, and George Jacobs let out a rough, humorless snort. A small smile cracked across Burroughs's face. "If only all our invitations had been lost."

"Look," Procter said lowly, and he motioned with a jerk of his chin. Martha turned to see that Burroughs had been right. A crowd was beginning to form, folk of all ages trailing the cart, in farmer's homespun and in richer town dresses and cloaks of serge, and more already lining the road ahead.

Burroughs took a quick breath and Martha followed his gaze to see a fine white horse prancing halfway up the hill. The rider was young and dressed in the black suit of a minister. "Cotton Mather," Burroughs said when she caught his eye. "He may aid us. He has cautioned the court against spectral evidence." He nodded to himself, then straightened, surveying the crowd with narrowed eyes. "I had thought to wait until we reached the hill, but I think there are enough of them now."

The man who had once been Salem's minister sucked a breath into his barrel chest. "Listen!" George Burroughs roared. *"Listen to me!"*

The people nearest to the cart jerked back like he'd splashed them with a well bucket. Ahead, a man holding a child on his shoulders retreated a few steps and a plump woman in a gray dress pressed her hand to her mouth. The sheriff twisted around on his horse. "Quiet," he growled.

Burroughs ignored him entirely. "We are wronged!" he shouted. "We are innocent! We have known nothing of the devil!"

"I said *quiet*." The sheriff urged his horse toward Burroughs, coming around the side of the cart.

Martha was tethered on the other side. "We are innocent!" she cried, and saw the sheriff's head snap her way, snarling. She snarled back, "The devil is a liar. It is a *shameful thing* that you do this day!"

The sheriff was before her, raising his riding crop. Martha flinched, but before he could bring it down John Procter broke in hoarsely, sincerely, to say that he forgave the jury and judges their trespasses but begged them to come to their senses. "Our most fervent prayer," he finished, "is that our blood might be the last innocent blood shed on this account."

John Willard echoed him, and then Burroughs took up the cry once more. The sheriff looked between them, crop still raised, unsure where to strike first. Martha and the men kept shouting and finally the sheriff dropped back, hand clenched on his crop. He plunged ahead and urged the driver grimly upward.

When they were in earshot of the young minister on his white horse, Burroughs called out for him to pray with them. The minister startled at being addressed, but before he could answer, George Jacobs heaved himself up. The old farmer stood as straight as his bent spine and bound hands and the rattling cart would allow and said, with awful dignity, "I forgive 'em. My accusers. I forgive my granddaughter who has spoken against me. I forgive 'em all."

Something hot rushed through Martha. She did not forgive her accusers, or the judges, or the jury, or the people on the road. God would, or wouldn't; she did not. "We are wronged!" she bellowed. "We are innocent!"

The cart crested the last rise with a jerk. She saw the tree, and five nooses waiting.

They set the rope around Burroughs's neck first, but he had one last plan. From the steps of the ladder, George Burroughs did what he knew best. He gave a sermon.

He called on God to deliver the people of Massachusetts from evil. He prayed that no more innocent blood would be spilled. He asked the people to consider the evidence, asking them not to rely on the words of those who might be deceived by the devil—for the devil was endlessly conniving—but instead to remember that he was a minister. He was sworn to God. He had led the congregation in Salem, once. "You know me," George Burroughs told the crowd on the hilltop. "*You know me.* And you know that I am not now, nor have I ever been, a witch."

Martha could see women in the crowd openly weeping. Burroughs paused, raising his bound hands, and began to recite the Lord's Prayer.

She was so caught up that it took her a moment to realize why mouths were opening, men turning to their neighbors, why a red-faced woman near the front of the crowd looked like she'd been slapped. It wasn't until George Jacobs let out a strangled grunt beside her that Martha understood.

A witch, it was thought, could not say the blessed words of the Lord's Prayer. This was part of what had convicted Jacobs: he had been ordered to recite the prayer at his trial and had fumbled the words. When Martha had heard that, she'd been a little resentful, in truth; she knew the prayer perfectly, only she'd never been asked.

George Jacobs was shuddering, mouthing the words along with Burroughs. For Burroughs was doing it—he was speaking the unspeakable—

Had done it. He finished without a single hesitation or stumble, and he was *crying*, which was shocking in its own right, since it was widely thought that witches could only shed three tears from the left eye. Burroughs was weeping from both.

A wave of muttering swept up and over the crowd. Something was shifting, souring, raising the hair on Martha's neck.

"It is the devil!" a voice called, a girl's voice, and Martha recognized one of the afflicted girls who had spoken at her trial. She stood white-faced, stabbing a finger up at Burroughs. "It is the devil dictating what he says!"

"It can't be," someone else snapped, a woman Martha didn't know. "Satan himself cannot say the Lord's Prayer. The words would burn his lips."

In answer the girl screamed, hard, and fell to her knees, but it didn't have the effect that it did in the courtroom. Here, she hit the soft earth without a sound, disappearing into the ranks of spectators. Other girls, scattered in the crowd, mirrored her—but even as people knelt to aid them, more were looking up at Burroughs with what was, unmistakably, doubt.

Martha was hardly breathing. She had always understood doubt to be a kind of arrogance, the enemy of faith, the province of heretics and Jews, but there on the hill she decided that she had been wrong. Wrong entirely. Her hands were twisting hard against the rope. She had been willing to die for God but she didn't want to, Lord help her, she didn't want to. She looked out at the people and found herself mouthing the prayer. *Deliver us from evil.*

A horse whinnied, and a new voice snapped like a whip over the hill. "Be not deceived!"

The crowd parted. The young minister on his white horse rode forward.

Cotton Mather did not look to the prisoners. He looked instead into the faces of the people that he passed, riding slowly, the horse tossing its head as its master held it tightly in check. Held them all in check. Mather's voice was higher than Burroughs's, but he spoke with the same minister's cadence. A man accustomed to being heard.

"This unsettling of your hearts and minds is the devil's work, make no mistake," Mather told the crowd. "This is no true minister. This man has not been ordained. Yes, you hear me truly! He has not been ordained, nor does he practice the offices of a minister. He declines sacrament and *defies* Christ Jesus."

Mather jerked his horse to a halt. The animal tossed its beautiful head, snorting, and its rider stood in the stirrups. He lifted a hand, pointing to the minister tethered to the tree.

"This is the agent who means to tear down our work in this country!" Mather cried. "The work for which we have strived so long and hold so very dear! My brothers and sisters, be not deceived. Be not swayed in holy purpose. Remain vigilant, and I swear to you, the time of the devil's rule in this land will come to an end."

Burroughs's throat was working, silently, as if his voice had failed him. He stared down at the young minister, and Cotton Mather gazed back at him with what looked, horribly, like sorrow.

"The speech that this man has given is the devil's speech," Mather said, more softly now. "You must not be deceived. The devil has often been transformed into an angel of light, but it makes him no less a devil."

Both men had gone blurry in Martha's sight. She blinked, felt furious tears slip free. Mather's words did not explain, she thought, how Burroughs had managed to say the prayer. But they were certain. They were permission.

And he wasn't wrong. What better disguise for the devil could there be than a minister, bearing conviction, draped in morning sunlight?

George Burroughs's cheeks were still wet when he died.

The other men were next. One by one, they mounted the ladder, upright, proclaiming their innocence, and one by one, they fell.

Martha was last. By the time her turn came, the wind had stopped. In the quiet she ascended the ladder one rung at a time. She felt again as she had coming out of the jail, capable only of sensation, the wooden rungs under her palms and the soles of her feet, the sun on her face.

The hangman checked the bindings on her hands and at her throat, and stepped away.

The young minister nudged his horse forward. "Goody Carrier," he called. "There is time still to save your immortal soul. Will you not confess, even now?"

Martha looked down at him. Swallowed, felt the rope. "Never," she said. "I am no witch."

She turned her gaze away then and looked past him, past the crowd of neighbors and strangers, out over the hill and its high-crowned trees to Salem harbor, where gulls rose and fell above the glinting sea. God's earth. Hers, too, for a while.

She said the words that would commend her soul to God's hands. She kept her eyes open.

31
Burial

For a long time, Gallows Hill was lost.

It didn't take long for Salem Village and Salem Town to flinch away from what had happened. In 1698, just six years after the trials, Samuel Sewall, a judge who had served on the Court of Oyer and Terminer, issued a public apology for his part in the witch hunt. So did multiple members of the jury, who said they had been deceived by Satan—that Prince of Lies. The ministers of Massachusetts eventually did a complete about-face: they concluded that the witch trials had not been a case of witches invading the colony but of Satan successfully deceiving the Puritans into killing innocents as witches. The trials became, and would remain, a source of shame. Less than a hundred years later, John Adams would call them a "stain upon this country."[1]

Adams wrote those words in 1775, at the beginning of the American Revolution. Only three years earlier, Sarah Carrier had died in Connecticut. She was nearly ninety years old. Archivist Richard Hite writes that Sarah was, by the time she died, "almost certainly the last survivor of those accused of witchcraft in 1692."[2]

When Sarah died, she took the final living memory of that summer in the jail with her. Salem Town had changed unrecognizably in her lifetime, and would soon become known not for witches but as a whaling center and a trading port. Salem Village, which finally achieved independence from Salem Town in 1752, changed its name to Danvers, eschewing all relationship with the trials. It tried to leave the story behind.

But stories, unlike bodies, do not decompose when buried. They wait to be unearthed. In the second half of the twentieth century, Arthur Miller wrote *The Crucible* and witch shops started cropping up in Salem—which used to be called Salem Town but is now the only Salem left. Eventually tourists started filing in wanting to see where the witches had died.

The work of forgetting had been done too well. While the rise known as Gallows Hill is still there, it's rather large, and no one was sure, anymore, where exactly the hangings had taken place. City officials picked a spot on the hill to stick a sign in, but scholars realized pretty quickly that it wasn't the right one.

In 2016, the Gallows Hill Project confirmed the site of execution. Martha and the others were hanged on a sharp rise of land tucked behind a Walgreens parking lot, known locally as Proctor's Ledge.

There's a memorial on Proctor's Ledge now, but when I went there was nothing to mark it, and most tourists still made their way to the official Gallows Hill, so I had the place to myself.

It was evening and I was discontented. I'd spent the afternoon wandering Salem, poking my head into shops selling crystals and coyote teeth and sage smudges, into witch museums that made liberal use of blood-red lighting. Salem has a flourishing tourism industry these days, much of it witch-based, bringing in around a hundred million dollars annually.[3] One of the attractions is a re-creation of the Salem Town jail, marked by two plaques: The first plaque proclaims that you are standing at the spot of the original jail, in which the accused witches were imprisoned. The second plaque, much smaller, clarifies that the first plaque was taken from another building—you aren't at the site of the witch jail at all.

Walking around what had once been Salem Town, I felt no connection to Martha at all. She had been there, certainly, but it was hard to say where, and harder to say if it mattered. Salem wasn't her home. It was only the place she died.

So that's where I went. I picked a bad route to climb up Gallows Hill and had to grab at thorny bushes to pull myself onto the ridge. By the time I reached the top, a narrow spine of earth capped with a grove of thin trees, my palms were stinging.

The Walgreens sign flinched on in the parking lot below, bathing the pavement in neon green. I made my way through the grove and stopped beneath a tree with diamond-patterned bark like the skin of a snake. Wind clicked through the branches, carrying the scent of pine and fast food.

There was a flash of black wings in the pale sky. A crow perched in the snake tree, creak-cawing. Cotton Mather would call it an omen. Depending on which mythology you look at, crows can be messengers between worlds, harbingers of death, living incarnations of thought and memory, tricksters, or lost souls.

When the bodies of the executed witches were cut down, they were tossed into shallow graves right there on the hill. Martha was buried in a pit

with George Burroughs and John Willard, and the shoveling job was so hap-
hazard that someone's arm and leg remained visible in the dirt.[4] She wasn't
in the hill by the time I got there. A radar analysis by a geologist at Salem
State University in 2015 revealed that there are no human remains in the top-
soil of Proctor's Ledge.[5] Where they went is an open question. Legend has it
that some families, like the Nurses, came by night to retrieve and rebury the
bodies of their loved ones. Maybe Thomas came for Martha. Maybe she was
washed away by the next three centuries, the deluge of time and progress. But
she had been there once, in the soil underneath me, not the Queen of Hell
but of the Hill.

I explained all this to the crow. It fixed me with a stereotypically gimlet eye
and flew away.

We know that as the cart climbed the hill to the gallows, "all of them said
they were innocent, Carrier and all."[6] Those words were written in the diary
of Samuel Sewall, the judge on the witchcraft court who would later make
a public apology for his actions. The specific callout of Martha ("Carrier and
all") probably reflects Sewall's astonishment that a woman so guilty—the
chief witch of Andover, the Queen of Hell—should maintain her innocence.
Or maybe she said something particularly striking. In his account of her
trial, Cotton Mather described Martha as a "rampant hag."[7] As far as history
records, he only saw her once, and it wasn't at her trial. He would have had to
form that opinion on the day she died. *Hag* is easy: it meant an old witch.[8] But
rampant? In the 1600s, the word already meant fierce, raging, uncontrollable.
A woman on the attack.

There's no way to know what might have happened if Mather hadn't
intervened that day on the hill after Burroughs gave his sermon. Perhaps
nothing: some historians speculate that Burroughs was actually already dead
when Mather began speaking, that the hangman had already pushed him.[9] In
this line of thinking, Mather's speech was not intended to ensure Burroughs's
death but to keep the crowd from becoming a mob by reassuring them that
they hadn't just murdered a minister. This theory charges Mather with crowd
control rather than incitement to riot.

But if his intention was to control the crowd, he was a few months too
late, and I personally doubt that a sermon that moved listeners to tears would
have had no effect at all on the hangman. If the crowd had begun to doubt

that Burroughs was a witch, would the hangman have forged ahead without hesitation? Or would he have waited for encouragement, for permission, for certainty?

"The Boston merchant Robert Calef (who, in fairness, hated Mather) later wrote that Mather's speech on the hill "did somewhat appease the People, and the Executions went on."[10]

Eleven months after Burroughs and Mather gave their competing sermons, and Mather won, and Burroughs died, Mather did something strange. He officiated the remarriage of George Burroughs's widow.[11] Nothing points to why she might have wanted him to. But Burroughs was known for being harsh to his wives. The accusation was witchcraft; the insinuation under it was domestic violence. There's a possibility—and this is strictly conjecture— that George Burroughs's wife was *happy* about what Cotton Mather did that day on the hill.

And Martha was, what, caught in the crossfire? *You're reaching,* I told myself. *Grasping.*

The dregs of dusk glowed cold blue. I leaned down and pressed my palm to the earth. There'd been scant signs of Martha in modern-day Salem, but any of the trees growing on the ridge might have put down roots that fed on nutrients in the dirt that had once been the flesh and blood of a woman. If Martha was in the hill, then she was all around me, in the soft-rough bark of the snake tree, in the sap and the fallen leaves.

A stick cracked. I whirled upright to see a woman coming through the woods.

She was definitely alive and from the twenty-first century, wearing a blue jacket and trailed by a man and two boys. "Excuse me," she asked, "is this Gallows Hill?"

"Oh, uh." I wiped my dirty hand on my jeans. "Yeah."

Her boys ran off to explore. The woman smiled. "You must be from around here?"

"No, I'm from New York."

"Oh," she said, politely surprised. "Do you have family here, then?"

I couldn't help it. "No," I said, "not anymore."

* * *

Driving away from Gallows Hill that night, pressing down hard on the gas, I thought, *There is no other ending to this story. I cannot tell it any other way.* It is what happened, it is fact, and it is one of only two things I knew about Martha from the beginning, when I found the red book in the library: she was related to me and she was dead.

I wrote the story anyway, because this is Salem's promise: if you find the right words you can change the ending. This was the operating principle of the afflicted girls, of Samuel Parris with his sermons, of Thomas Putnam with his well-deployed pen, writing the trials into existence. It is what William Stoughton did in Rebecca Nurse's trial when he told the jury to go out and deliberate again, and it is what George Burroughs tried and failed to do on the hill. It was the chance offered to Mary and Margaret and Richard and Andrew and Sarah and every accused person who stood before the Court of Oyer and Terminer, the dangling possibility that speaking the right words will change everything.

It's my story too. When I was young, I experienced a lot of what you might call unpredictable death—deaths from plane crashes, from falling trees, the kind that comes sudden and rips the illusion of safety away at the quick. The kind of death that would have made me look for witches if I believed in them. Not only to find out who had been responsible but to know that there had *been* a reason, and to know that this kind of loss could be prevented from happening again.

I don't believe things happen for a reason. The crops fail, the child sickens, the branch breaks. There is no witch and you are not safe.

But that isn't the whole story; if that was the whole story I never would have written this. After those years of unpredictable death, I spent a lot of time with the specter of a more predictable kind of death, talking friends off ledges, and I don't know if that's where I got the idea that words can stave off death but it might be. However it happened, I think I embarked on Martha's story still carrying the hope that the right words can be more powerful even than the pull of the abyss. The hope that if you stand at the mouth of the underworld and tell the right story, death itself might loosen its hold.

It is the same as hoping that if you tell the story one more time, the ending will be different. A kind of magical thinking, to be sure. But what is a spell but the right words, in the right order, reshaping the world we thought we knew?

Belief in a witch restores the illusion of safety, imposes order on a random, ruinous world. So does narrative. Salem began as, and has remained, a story of stories, and not all of them are true. The witch trials are widely seen as a hysteria, which implies they were uncontrollable; I would call this propaganda. Salem was neither random nor unstoppable.

When I first saw *The Crucible*, one line stuck with me. Not when John Procter shouts, *because it is my name!* or when Abigail Williams says she's seen Goody Procter with the devil. The line wedged in me is when Procter says: *I have known her.* Miller wrote it to be a euphemism, the confession of Procter and Abigail's sexual relationship, but it isn't a euphemism. Leaving aside that Procter and Abigail did not, in fact, know each other, most of the players in Salem *did.* The ones in Salem Village, the ones who started it—*they all knew each other.* They were neighbors, sisters, cousins, friends, master and servant, husband and wife, enslaver and enslaved. They were people living in a society with one another. Some of them—not all—would have said they were trying to live in community with one another.

They failed. And it wasn't because of some sudden illness, some hysteria, a weakness that came upon them or to them. They built it themselves, story by story. The Salem witch trials are a ledger of the responsibility of belief—not the belief in witches or in magic but the other stories we tell about what we, and others, deserve. The trials are the earliest American record of the way that injustice is seen as legitimate as long as it targets the marginalized, and only when it attacks a higher stratum of society is cruelty finally understood, by its perpetrators, as demonic. The Salem witch trials happened because the Puritans built a society in which some people were marked as disposable, their humanity on sufferance, from the beginning. They created a system that rested upon injustice for some, and so, taken to its own illogical extreme, it allowed for injustice for all.

When I found the red book in the library, when I got hooked on Salem, I wondered if it might be an instruction manual instead of a cautionary tale. The truth is that it's both, and it's William Barker who gave us the instructions, back in 1692, when he described how to create what the Puritans feared most. A land of equality, without fear, without shame, where the Puritan project would be cast down once and for all. That's Salem's instruction. It isn't the reason we tell the story again and again, but it could be.

I have known her.

Yes, I thought, driving away from the hill that night. *I have.* I knew Martha as well as I could, had made her as knowable as was permitted. It wasn't enough. *There is no other ending to this story.*

I drove further and further from the place where she'd died. Ahead, where the highway curved in the darkness, the road signs seemed to float, green and luminous.

And at the sight of one of those signs a thought came into my head fully formed, as sharp and startling as someone slamming a book down on a table. If there was no other ending to Martha's story, the only possibility for a new ending was in mine.

I drove to Andover. The Historical Societies of Andover and North Andover have a good map of what the town would have looked like in 1692, and even after three centuries the land holds enough of its shape to overlay the 1692 map on a modern one. The Salem Witch Museum in modern-day Salem has also worked through a couple possible locations for the old Allen farm. It was enough to work off, to triangulate the rough area where Martha's parents had made their farm and where she had grown up.

Off Interstate 93, past compounds of warehouses the size of towns and the river that Martha's son Thomas confessed she'd baptized him in, I parked on the side of the road. I took an old red backpack and a gardening spade to use as a shovel from the trunk.

After a few minutes of walking, I left the road and its colonial houses, heading down into a muddy gully. I wasn't entirely sure what I was looking for, but figured I'd know it when it came.

The gully had the feeling of a shipwreck, half-submerged. There was a flash of color among the green and brown and gray—a tree stump, about four feet tall, with a pink plastic tie wrapped around it and knotted in a bow. It was the same fluorescent pink as the tie that had been wrapped around Thomas's gravestone.

I went over the trunk with hands and eyes. The bark was wet and came off easily. The ground around it was undisturbed, patches of wet emerald moss at the base. When I pulled at the bow, it turned out to be so old the plastic tore like paper, and the whole thing came off in my muddy hands. By all appearances, the tree stump was ordinary, and it had nothing in common with Thomas's grave except that both were hollow, and both were marked.

Long before she became known as the Queen of Hell, before she was made into a curio and a ghost story and a souvenir, Martha had been here. She'd lived here before she became defined by the thing that killed her. When she was a woman, nothing more and nothing less.

I'd been looking for the right words, the spell to stave off death. In the end the only thing I said was her name. Because it was her name; because she would not have another in her life; because she had died rather than sign it to a false confession; because it was here that it had been given to her; because the old tales are true after all. There's power in a name.

Then I hefted the spade and started digging at the base of the hollow stump.

When the hole was deep enough, I extracted the tin from my backpack and flipped it open. It was full of dirt and a few fragments of bark. Half of the soil was pale and crumbly, taken from the base of Thomas's grave. The rest was darker and wetter. That dirt, and the bark, was from Gallows Hill.

I poured it all into the hole. Martha had spent time in the hill. If what had once been her body had served as nourishment to that tree and strengthened its bark, then some part of her would be together with the earth where Thomas was buried, in the land where they had lived.

The tin was warm in my hands, light as a bird. I nestled it in the hole. It looked out of place there, an empty Altoids tin long bereft of mints, but it felt wrong to keep. Sometimes a thing's second life should be its last.

An Incomplete List

35 Years After Salem

Her name: Janet Horne.

Age: Elderly, showing signs of dementia.

The story told about her: Her daughter had a deformity. Her neighbors said that Janet had attempted to transform her daughter into a pony to ride.

Janet and her daughter were arrested. After a quick trial, they were sentenced to death. The daughter managed to escape, but Janet was stripped, tortured, and burned to death.

The place: Dornoch, Scotland.

The year: 1727.[1]

90 Years After Salem

Her name: Anna Göldi.

Age: 48.

The story told about her: She had children out of wedlock, one of whom died in infancy. She was accused of murdering her baby. Later, she was accused of using magic to harm other people's children.

She worked as a maid and was fired after needles were found in her employer's daughter's milk. A few weeks later, the girl said she had vomited some kind of metallic object. Anna's former employer accused her of bewitching the child. She was arrested and confessed to witchcraft under torture. She recanted her confession once the torture stopped but was found guilty—officially of poisoning, unofficially of witchcraft. She was beheaded. By some reports, she was accused because she had had a relationship with her former employer and threatened to reveal as much when he fired her.

The place: Glarus, Switzerland.

The year: 1782.[2]

144 Years After Salem

Her name: Krystyna Ceynowa.

Age: Unknown; adult woman.

The story told about her: She cast a spell on a fisherman.

She was not legally tried for witchcraft, as witch trials were no longer legal. However, a number of her neighbors decided to determine whether she was a witch by "ordeal," in which a person is subjected to tests believed to show innocence or guilt. Krystyna was thrown into the Baltic Sea. When she did not immediately drown—she floated for a time, her skirts possibly acting as a buoy—her captors decided she was a true witch. (It was believed that water, being pure, would not accept a witch's body, causing her to float.) She was brought back aboard and subsequently stabbed to death.

The place: Chałupy, Poland.

The year: 1836.[3]

165 Years After Salem

Their names: Numerous. At least fifty-nine people, mostly women.

Age: Adults.

The story told about them: They were witches who had killed children, caused fevers, or otherwise harmed the community.

Beginning in 1857, as resistance grew against the British colonizers in India, there was a surge of witch hunting among the tribal communities of Singhbhum and Santhal Pargana, where witch beliefs were long founded and witches seen as extremely dangerous. Some scholars argue that these witch hunts are best understood as an act of resistance against the British, who had banned witch hunting. This theory is supported by the fact that the hunts took place within a matrix of other forms of uprising against British rule. Others note that communities may have believed that the British ban on witch hunts allowed witches to flourish, thus necessitating larger hunts. The hunts were performed by mob and informal community adjudication processes, and individual accusations are largely unknown. Some hunts also had a practical mechanism. "Witch-hunts were systematically incorporated into the mobilisation strategies of the anti-colonial adivasi movements in Chhotanagpur," writes researcher Shashank Sinha.[4] During one rebellion, "to secure recognition of the clan brotherhood's right to the forest they had settled in, women were denounced as witches and killed."

The place: Chhotanagpur, India.

The year: 1857–1858.[5]

203 Years After Salem

Her name: Bridget Cleary.

Age: 26.

The story told about her: She had been abducted by fairies and replaced with a changeling.

Cleary apparently became ill. At some point, her husband became convinced that she was a fairy. He menaced her with a piece of burning wood; her dress caught fire, and he threw kerosene on her. He was found guilty of manslaughter and served fifteen years in prison. The case gained significant attention at the time; papers in London used it as an excuse to criticize occupied Ireland as rural and backward.

The place: County Tipperary, Ireland.

The year: 1895.[6]

239 Years After Salem

Her name: Mwaiki.

Age: Unknown.

The story told about her: She had bewitched a neighbor.

She was accused of having bewitched the wife of a man named Kumwaka. Kumwaka and a group of men seized Mwaiki. Mwaiki said that she had removed part of the spell. The next morning, she attempted to flee. She was chased and beaten to death, an act that flew in the face of traditional Kamba law and custom, which required evidence against accused witches to be reviewed by elders. The case against the men who had killed her, Rex v. Kumwaka s/o of Mulumbi and 69 Others, became the most high-profile witch-hunting case of the colonial era, a flashpoint for clashes of British and Kenyan law.

The place: Kenya.

The year: 1931.[7]

302 Years After Salem

Her name: Chhutni Mahato.

Age: 26.

The story told about her: She bewitched her relative to make her ill.

Her brother-in-law's daughter fell ill. Mahato was accused of witchcraft. She was attacked and beaten, forced to go partly naked through the village, and some of her teeth were knocked out. She survived and left the village. Since then, she has dedicated herself to assisting accused witches, providing support and pressuring community leaders and police on behalf of witch-hunt victims. She has helped more than 150 women.

The place: Jharkhand, India.

The year: 1994.[8]

305 Years After Salem

Her name: Tanya Tarasova.

Age: 22.

The story told about her: She used black magic to send ruination. Also, she was said to have a lazy eye and enjoyed solitude.

Two men, an uncle and nephew, believed that Tanya had cast a curse on the nephew after going on a few dates with him. They broke into her house at night with hammers and knives, in what they later said was an attempt to kill her entire family. They allegedly killed Tanya's mother and injured three of her siblings. Tanya herself suffered multiple hammer blows to the head but survived.

The place: Terekhovo, Russia.

The year: 1997.[9]

321 Years After Salem

Her name: Kepari Leniata.

Age: 20.

The story told about her: She used witchcraft to kill a neighbor's son.

The boy's family members reportedly stripped her and tortured her with a hot iron rod. She was burned to death on a pile of car tires in front of hundreds of people.

The place: Mount Hagen, Papua New Guinea.

The year: 2013.[10]

322 Years After Salem

Her name: Fabiane Maria de Jesus.

Age: 33.

The story told about her: She abducted children to use their organs in black magic rituals.

A Facebook page known for publishing news posted a police sketch of a kidnapper. A rumor began to circulate that a woman was abducting children for use in witchcraft rituals. De Jesus, who reportedly suffered from bipolar disorder, was seized by a group of some hundred people, her hands bound with wire, and beaten for two hours. She died two days later.

The place: Guarujá, Brazil.

The year: 2014.[11]

325 Years After Salem

Her name: Vilma Trujillo Garcia.

Age: 25.

The story told about her: She was possessed by demons.

An evangelical pastor and four other people performed an exorcism that ended up with Trujillo Garcia naked, tied to a tree trunk, and burned in a fire for five hours. She suffered severe burns and died a few days later. The pastor denied that he threw her into the fire, claiming that she fell into the fire and a demon exited her body, but all five people were later found guilty of homicide. A women's rights advocate advising the family noted that Trujillo Garcia had mental health problems and that in some areas of the country, "pastors and religious leaders dominate the community with apocalyptic ideologies that the devil will come."[12]

The place: El Cortezal, Nicaragua.

The year: 2017.[13]

326 Years After Salem

Her name: Seti Maya Layo Magar.

Age: 73.

The story told about her: She was accused of practicing witchcraft to inflict chest pain.

Four men, three of them local witch finders and one of them a member of the Nepali military, allegedly seized her and tortured her, forcing her to eat human feces. She survived and eventually reported the attack to authorities. The *Kathmandu Post* spoke with her granddaughter, who claimed that after the attack, Magar was pressured by local political leaders not to report what had happened.

The place: Dhading, Nepal.

The year: 2018.[14]

327 Years After Salem

His name: Killo Jayaram.

Age: 55.

The story told about him: He had killed a young girl with witchcraft and infected another.

A girl in his community died after an illness; soon, another young girl showed signs of illness. Jayaram was accused of having used black magic to kill them. At a village convening to discuss the issue, the sick girl's family members blamed him for her illness. A group of her relatives reportedly attacked him, allegedly beating him and his family and burning him alive.

The place: Andhra Pradesh, India.

The year: 2019.[15]

328 Years After Salem

Their names:

Benard Kekong

Rita Abang

Margaret Akan

Edward Kekong

John Otu

Mama Delia Kubua

Rose Obi

Patricia Obi

Kaka Olum

Mary Ada Otu

Martina Maurice

Serah Kepua Odu

Paulina Owan

Sussana Bisong

One other, unidentified.

Age: Adults.

The story told about them: They were suspected of witchcraft.

Thomas Obi Tawo, also known as General Iron, a special adviser on forest security to the governor of Cross River State, allegedly led a team of men into the district of Boki, where his mother lived. According to an eyewitness who spoke with Advocacy for Alleged Witches, Tawo had a list of names of suspected witches. The accused, including his mother, were allegedly dragged from their homes and beaten, and some were thrown into a fire. Three people reportedly died of their wounds. Tawo was eventually dismissed from his government post.[16] He was killed the following year in an unrelated shoot-out.[17]

The place: Boki LGA, Nigeria.

The year: 2020.[18]

329 Years After Salem

Her name: Silvia Banda and her daughter.

Age: Elderly woman and adult daughter.

The story told about her: She had killed a young boy with witchcraft.

A twelve-year-old boy became sick. His parents took him to a traditional healer and then to a hospital, where he was diagnosed with malaria. He died in the hospital. According to police, the traditional healer told the boy's family that Banda had bewitched him. Three of the boy's relatives then allegedly attacked Banda and her pregnant daughter with sharp weapons, and Banda was killed.

The place: Dedza, Malawi.

The year: 2021.[19]

331 Years After Salem

Their names: Sibal Ganhju and Bavni Devi, a married couple.

Age: 70 and 65.

The story told about them: They were adversely affecting the village through black magic.

A panchayat, a village council, claimed that their black magic was responsible for the village's ills. The couple was reportedly beaten to death.

The place: Jharkhand, India.

The year: 2023.[20]

Epilogue

Even after I buried Martha, she lingered in my life. That was all right; this wasn't an exorcism. If anything it was a long shiva, and getting to the end just meant uncovering the mirrors and seeing what they reflected.

In the last few years, my spreadsheet of witch hunts has only grown. But so has the work people are doing to combat witch hunting. In 2021, after years of agitation by a mix of witch hunt survivors, organizers, academics, and the Witchcraft and Human Rights Information Network, the United Nations passed a resolution recognizing that witch hunting is an ongoing problem around the world today. The resolution recognizes that the *belief* in witchcraft is not at issue, and it does not attempt to curtail beliefs or specific cultural practices. Instead, it holds that accusing people of witchcraft continues to lead to human rights violations, including:

> *Killings, mutilation, burning, coercion in trafficking of persons, torture and other cruel, inhuman or degrading treatment and stigmatization, particularly for persons in vulnerable situations, including women, children, persons with disabilities, older persons and persons with albinism, and that these forms of violence are often committed with impunity.*[1]

The resolution urges all member states to combat witchcraft-accusation-related harms wherever they appear. Easier said than done. But there are people working against witch hunts around the world, to stop them before they start. Advocacy for Alleged Witches remains in constant motion, providing direct aid to victims of witch hunting. Sashiprava Bindhani, the former state information commissioner of Odisha—a state with one of the highest rates of witch hunting in India—is on a one-woman crusade to make people take witch hunting seriously. The Stop Sorcery Violence project in Papua New Guinea creates resources for policymakers and community leaders, and directs victims of attacks to aid.

In 2022, I joined the working committee of the International Network Against Accusations of Witchcraft and Associated Harmful Practices. The

network (TINAAWAHP) connects organizers, academics, and others working on and against violent witch hunts. We gather and share information to
educate the public and policymakers. Part of our aim is to figure out what
practices work to stop a witch hunt and to disseminate that information as
widely as possible. You can find more resources about witch hunts today at
TheInternationalNetwork.org.

Martha lingered, but Salem doesn't haunt me anymore. Let me tell you how
it ended.

On September 22, 1692, eight people were hanged in the largest and last
execution of witches in the Salem witch trials. The court had started back
in June by hanging one woman, Bridget Bishop, who had already suffered a
witchcraft accusation earlier in her life. In July they hanged five women, one
of whom was highly respected. Next up, in August, were four men, including a minister—a man both more and less vulnerable than the others—and
one woman, accused of being the Queen of Hell. In September they hanged
eight, men and women both.

A test of the waters each time. If you start with eight, there will be an
uproar. If you work up to it, a few women at a time, you can get away with
it, assuming there are people like William Stoughton and Cotton Mather on
hand to rile up the crowd when they lose their nerve.

To rile up the crowd and write down the story. By the end of that long
summer of 1692, Cotton Mather was preparing to publish a book that he
would call *Wonders of the Invisible World*, which was both explanation of and
justification for the trials. The book was endorsed by Chief Justice William
Stoughton, who seems to have known that the Court of Oyer and Terminer
would need to explain itself to an audience of learned Puritans; they were
becoming increasingly voluble in their criticisms of spectral evidence. Stoughton was scrambling to own the narrative, to maintain power.

He failed. Two weeks after the September executions, Increase Mather,
Cotton's father, published a paper denouncing spectral evidence. "I would
rather judge a witch to be an honest woman," he wrote, "than judge an honest woman as a witch."[2] Eight heavy hitters in the Puritan clergy (though
not his son Cotton) signed their support to Increase's paper. Anonymous

letters and publications began circulating in Boston that questioned the Court of Oyer and Terminer's methods, implicitly critiquing Governor Phips and Stoughton. Phips wrote to ministers in New York for an outside opinion, and they advised him spectral evidence was insufficient for a conviction. Plus, the logistics of the trials were becoming untenable: so many had been accused of witchcraft that the jails were overcrowded, and when winter came, they would be basically uninhabitable.

Meanwhile, in early October, Governor Phips's wife, Lady Mary Phips, ordered the release of a woman who had been accused of witchcraft.[3] According to some historians, she may have known the accused personally. In response, an afflicted girl—there is no record of which one—accused Lady Phips of witchcraft.

With his own wife named as a witch, the clergymen speaking out against the use of spectral evidence, and anonymous papers questioning his judgment and authority, Governor Phips had had enough. He decided to halt all court proceedings on October 12, 1692.

We know this because he wrote to England, begging for the king's guidance—saying that until he received instruction, there would be no more arrests besides those that were unavoidable, no further trials, and no more "discourses," the circulating papers that questioned the court he had authorized.[4] (There would certainly be no warrant issued for his wife.) But he did not share the contents of this letter with anyone in Massachusetts, and the accused witches remained in prison.

The whole conceit of a letter to the Crown was a smokescreen. Communication between the colonies and the court took months, and it was already rolling toward winter in Massachusetts. When the cold set in, the overcrowded jails would become a death trap. Phips can't have actually thought he would be able to wait until he heard back from England before deciding what to do with the accused. Most likely he was trying to cover his tracks, separating his legacy from what he had belatedly realized was a disaster.[5]

Even a man so warlike as Samuel Parris apparently began to see the writing on the wall. At the end of October, a few weeks after Increase Mather published his paper denouncing spectral evidence, Parris gave a sermon that was a radical departure from his usual martial exhortations. Instead, he preached community and forgiveness: "Oh, be reconciled to me, and give me a kiss of reconciliation."[6] Before, one assumes, the Salem villagers decided to take revenge for what he'd wrought. Or the Andover townspeople, twenty-four of whom submitted a petition to the court the very next day, calling the afflicted girls "distempered persons" and protesting their influence.[7]

Finally, on October 29, responding to the growing pressure, Governor Phips publicly dissolved the Court of Oyer and Terminer. It would not be sitting a few days later, as scheduled, to try witchcraft cases.

But the trials weren't over yet. A problem remained: the legions of accused witches in jail, some of whom were confessors. They couldn't simply be released.

On January 3, 1693, almost a year after Abigail and Betty began having fits, a special session of the Superior Court was held to hear the remaining cases.

At first it promised to be the Court of Oyer and Terminer reborn. The new court comprised almost all the same judges who had served on the first court, including William Stoughton as chief justice. But this time, Governor Phips instructed, the judges and jury were *not* to accept any spectral evidence.

Without it—without the girls' afflictions, the witches' sabbath, the devil's book—the cases against the accused melted like snow in hard rain. The new court heard fifty-two witchcraft cases over the next two weeks. They dismissed thirty of those cases as having insufficient evidence. Nineteen people were found innocent, including confessors who explained they had been frightened or confused into their confessions.

Only three people were found guilty: three women who seem to have been unable to convince the court that their previous confessions were invalid. William Stoughton quickly signed warrants for their executions, as well as for the executions of five other women who had been convicted over the summer and had been given temporary reprieves (including Elizabeth Procter).

But Phips, tired of his critics and witch hunting alike, overturned Stoughton's warrant. The hangings would not take place. He was done.

The Salem witch trials were over.

When Stoughton found out, he was furious. "We were in a way to have cleared the land of these [witches]!" he raged.[8] "Who it is obstructs the cause of justice I know not, but thereby the Kingdom of Satan is advanced. The Lord have mercy on this country." He stormed off the bench, resigning his post as chief justice and leaving Massachusetts to a kind of mercy, after all.

Four years after the trials, Samuel Parris's contract as Salem Village minister expired. To absolutely no one's surprise, it was not renewed. Soon, Parris and his family moved so that he could become the minister of another town. He lasted only one year there before getting into a fight about his salary.[9]

In 1706, fourteen years after the trials, twenty-six-year-old Ann Putnam Jr. formally apologized. As part of her testimony to become a full church member, the most prolific accuser in Salem stood before the village church and said:

> *I desire to be humbled before God for that sad and humbling providence that befell my father's family in the year about '92; that I, then being in my childhood, should, by such a providence of God, be made an instrument for the accusing of several persons of a grievous crime, whereby their lives were taken away from them, whom now I have just grounds and reason to believe they were innocent ... It was a great delusion of Satan that deceived me ... I did it not out of any anger, malice, or ill-will ... and particularly as I was a chief instrument of accusing of Goodwife Nurse and her two sisters, I desire to lie in the dust and to be humbled for it, in that I was a cause, with others, of so sad a calamity.*[10]

With others. Her parents, Thomas Putnam Jr. and Ann Putnam Sr., had both died in 1699, unable to see the new century.

In 1710, the Massachusetts legislature established a committee to process monetary claims filed by trial survivors. By this point, it was widely understood that the trials had convicted and executed people who were innocent of any crime. One such claim was filed by Thomas Carrier, who was living with his children in Connecticut. His claim reads:

> *To the Honorable Committee Sitting at Salem this 13 day of Sept. 1710*
> *These are to Inform your Honours that my wife Martha Carrier was condemned upon an Accusation of witchcraft, and Suffered Death at Salem in the year 1692.*
> *I payd to the Sherriff upon his Demand fifty Shillings.*

I payd the prisonkeeper upon his demand for prison fees, for my wife and four children four pounds Sixteen Shillings.

My humble request is that the Attainder may be taken off; and that I may be considered as to the loss and dammage I Sustained in my Estate.

Totall 7-6-0.

Thomas Carrier.

Below his signature, it reads, *"I found my wife and children provision during their imprisonment."*[11]

The court paid Thomas seven pounds and six shillings,[12] approximately $1,400. It also complied with his request to remove the attainder—the record of Martha's guilt. In 1711, nearly twenty years after her death, Martha was exonerated.

Martha's Memorial Stone in Salem Today

Afterword

Why is it important to return to the issue of witch hunting, an issue that to many seems to belong to a different age? Witch hunting is not about superstition or a rehearsal of archaic forms of being. Nor is it a resurgence of hatred or misogyny in the abstract. On the contrary, witch hunting is connected with profound social and economic transformations that have produced new forms of dispossession and marginalization.

Witch hunting today has many roots. It connects with the use of religion to support new forms of colonization. It is a means of undermining women's autonomy and exerting control over the family. And witch hunting is often a product of the intensification of social conflict in the aftermath of economic structural adjustment programs. It is deeply linked with processes of land privatization, and with the destruction of the commons and of other collective forms of agriculture.

As these processes of land privatization and dispossession are central to the political economy of large parts of the world today, so is witch hunting, undoubtedly one of the most misogynist and destructive attacks on women. The struggle against it, then, should be understood as an opening into a whole world of injustice, manifesting in different forms but always connecting with economic relations. The woman who is accused of witchcraft and exiled, mutilated, or stripped naked and doused with gasoline and burned, is, in a sense, the graphic expression of the violence produced by the neoliberalization of the world economy.

As in the past, witch hunts today have profound roots in the expansion of capitalist relations. Our task, then, is to build broad resistance movements that theoretically and practically show and denounce this connection and the ways in which the charge of witchcraft functions as a means of control.

One model for resistance is the Campaña por la Memoria de las Brujas, based in Spain. The Campaña examines the history of witch hunting, past and present, and strives to make it a key issue in both feminists organizing internationally and in ecological movements against corporate land acquisition. We must also understand that witch hunts are part of the surge of violence taking place in many contexts against women, sexual dissidents, and other dissenting bodies and organize accordingly.

Finally, we must foreground the political reality of witch hunting, as Alice Markham-Cantor does in this book. By re-examining the Salem trials and connecting them with the present, she contributes to the historical grounding of the persecution of women in the name of witchcraft and denounces its folklorization—in no place more evident than in Salem. As the direct descendant of Martha Carrier, Markham-Cantor has a special relationship to the story she tells and the woman she brings to life. Yet her work is, in some ways, iconic of the approach that feminist historians have taken to the study of witch persecution, and it is an important contribution to the project of reclaiming and reconstructing from below the history of the women condemned as witches.

—Silvia Federici, 2023

Acknowledgments

Any book on Salem stands on the shoulders of giants (i.e., those who have done the research before you). In the case of this book, those giants are particularly Stacy Schiff, Marilynne K. Roach, Paul Boyer and Stephen Nissenbaum, Mary Beth Norton, and Benjamin Ray. Their invaluable research and thoughtful examination of the Salem witch trials shaped and guided so much of my thinking. My view of the past would be very different without them.

My understanding of witch hunts in the present has been deeply informed by Miranda Forsyth, Samantha Spence, Charlotte Baker, Muluka-Anne Miti-Drummond, and the rest of TINAAWAHP, as well as Leo Igwe, Sashiprava Bindhani, Berrie Holtzhausen, Jean La Fontaine, and Gary Foxcroft. They shared time, work, and resources with generosity, and are unwaveringly committed to resisting easy narratives of witch hunting.

I'm so grateful to Rebecca Traister, both for her trademark razor-sharp thoughtfulness and for being excited about this story even before she knew we were very distant cousins. And I'm grateful, as always, for Silvia Federici, who is an inspiration, a friend, and a tireless voice in the struggle. In so many ways, this book would not exist without her.

I owe enormous thanks to my agents, Jennifer Lyons and Mikaela Bender. And I am endlessly grateful to my insightful editor Elysia Gallo, who made the book much better, and my hawk-eyed production editor Marysa Storm, as well as the entire team at Llewellyn.

My early readers were indispensable: Elliot M. Komisar, Isaiah Back-Gaal, Hannah Henderson-Charnow, Isabel Benincasa Reade, Anna Fox, Rachel Sobelsohn, Liz Boyd, and Beck Zegans, who not only read the book but lived with it. My thanks also to Michael Hamburger, who answered all my questions about rocks; Ron, Rebecca, and Noam, who opened their homes; the women of the Feminist Research on Violence Collective and the Campaña por la Memoria de las Brujas; and Charles Barber, who told me to write the damn thing years ago and has been a mentor ever since. Not to mention Eli, who also always wants the answers.

There's always more to say, but in Silvia's words, sometimes you have to cut the cheese with the big knife. So I'll end with these last words of gratitude:

271

to Brackets Kaplan, who supported me throughout, including letting me put up a Murder Wall in our house. To Deldar Golchehreh, who somehow always manages to understand what it is I'm trying to say. To my father, for his relentless and keen editing eye (and for helping me avoid many needless words). And to my mother, who inherited so much of Martha's spirit.

Notes

Introduction

[1] Charles Taylor, *A Secular Age* (Cambridge: Harvard University Press, 2009), 29.

1. The Red Book

[1] Marion L. Starkey, *The Devil in Massachusetts: A Modern Enquiry into the Salem Witch Trials* (New York: Anchor Books Editions, 1969), 18.

3. The Witch Question

[1] Ronald Hutton, *The Witch: A History of Fear, from Ancient Times to the Present* (New Haven: Yale University Press, 2017), 14.

[2] John Winthrop, "A Model of Christian Charity," in *A Library of American Literature: Early Colonial Literature, 1607–1675*, ed. Edmund Clarence Stedman and Ellen Mackay Hutchinson, (New York: C. L. Webster, 1892), 304–7.

[3] Cotton Mather, *On Witchcraft: Being the Wonders of the Invisible World, First Published at Boston in Octr. 1692 and Now Reprinted, with Additional Matter and Old Wood-Cuts* (New York: Bell Publishing, 1974), 42.

[4] John McWilliams, "Indian John and the Northern Tawnies," *New England Quarterly* 69, no. 4 (December 1996): 580–604.

[5] Alfred A. Cave, "New England Puritan Misperceptions of Native American Shamanism," *International Social Science Review* 67, no. 1 (Winter 1992): 15–27. Also see Isaac Reed, "Why Salem Made Sense: Culture, Gender, and the Puritan Persecution of Witchcraft," *Cultural Sociology* 1, no. 2 (2007): 225, https://doi.org/10.1177/1749975507078188.

[6] Pierre de Lancre, *On the Inconstancy of Witches: Pierre de Lancre's "Tableau De L'inconstance Des Mauvais Anges Et démons."* *(1612)*, ed. Gerhild Scholz

Williams (Tempe, AZ: Arizona Center for Medieval and Renaissance Studies, 2006), 50–60.

7 "Examination of Martha Carrier," SWP No. 24.3 in the Salem Witch Trials Documentary Archive, accessed May 13, 2023, https://salem.lib .virginia.edu/n24.html.

5. The Surveillance Age

1 Henry A. Hazen, *History of Billerica, Massachusetts, with a Genealogical Register* (Boston: A. Williams, 1883), 22.

2 Bill Dalton, "Repost of Previous Bill Dalton Column on Thomas Carrier," *Andover Townsman*, February 10, 2011, www.andovertownsman .com/community/repost-of-previous-bill-dalton-column-on-thomas -carrier/article_0a9a7c5e-5d54-5bfb-ac15-95fd9877fd57.html. Again, as a fact-checker, this is not what I would call hard evidence. Bill Dalton tells this story, quoting Goffe, in the local *Andover Townsmen* paper, and it appears on several Carrier family genealogy sites, apparently drawn from a "Carrier Genealogy, 1974–1976" by one Carl W. Carrier. I've been unable to track down the diary or Carl Carrier, and unable to reach Dalton to see if he still has a copy of it. Take this as part of Thomas Carrier's legend, rather than cold, hard fact. There's also no certainty which "Morgan" Goffe meant.

3 Sarah Loring Bailey, *Historical Sketches of Andover, Massachusetts: Comprising the Present Towns of North Andover and Andover* (Boston: Houghton, Mifflin and Company, 1880), 203.

4 Hazen, *History of Billerica, Massachusetts*, 22.

5 "Five Ways to Compute the Relative Value of a UK Pound Amount, 1270 to Present," Measuring Worth, accessed August 7, 2023, https://www .measuringworth.com/calculators/ukcompare/.

6 Hazen, *History of Billerica, Massachusetts*, 193.

7 Hazen, *History of Billerica, Massachusetts*, 190.

[8] Ruth Wallis Herndon, *Unwelcome Americans: Living on the Margin in Early New England* (Philadelphia: University of Pennsylvania Press, 2001), 5.

[9] Sidney Perley, *The History of Salem, Massachusetts*, vol. 2 (Bloomington, IN: Indiana University, 1924), 165.

[10] "Middlesex County, MA: Abstracts of Court Files, 1649–1675" (AmericanAncestors, New England Historic Genealogical Society, 2003), vol. II, 192. Unpublished abstracts by Thomas Bellows Wyman, "Abstract of Middlesex Court Files from 1649," n.d., https://www.americanancestors.org/DB432/rd/12381/192/138357655.

[11] Betty B. Rosenbaum, "Sociological Basis of the Laws Relating to Women Sex Offenders in Massachusetts (1620–1860)," *Journal of Criminal Law and Criminology* 28, no. 6 (March–April 1938): 815.

[12] Ryan Wheeler, "Cutshamache and Cochichawick," *Robert S. Peabody Institute of Archaeology* (blog), Phillips Academy Andover, May 13, 2021, https://peabody.andover.edu/2021/05/13/cutshamache-and-cochichawick/.

[13] Hazen, *History of Billerica, Massachusetts*, 22.

7. The Murder Wall

[1] Carol F. Karlsen, *The Devil in the Shape of a Woman: Witchcraft in Colonial New England* (New York: W.W. Norton, 1987), 47.

[2] Robin Briggs, *Witches and Neighbors: The Social and Cultural Context of European Witchcraft* (New York: Penguin, 1998), 8.

[3] Elspeth Whitney, "The Witch 'She'/the Historian 'He': Gender and the Historiography of the European Witch-Hunts," *Journal of Women's History* 7, no. 3 (Fall 1995): 77–101, https://doi.org/10.1353/jowh.2010.0511.

[4] Isaac Reed, "Why Salem Made Sense: Culture, Gender, and the Puritan Persecution of Witchcraft," *Cultural Sociology* 1, no. 2 (2007): 225, https://doi.org/10.1177/1749975507078188.

[5] Heinrich Kramer and Jacob Sprenger, *Malleus Maleficarum* (Speier: Peter Drach, 1487; New York: Dover Publications, 1971), 43, 46, 47, 77. Citations refer to Dover edition.

[6] Joseph Klaits, *Servants of Satan: The Age of the Witch Hunts* (Bloomington, IN: University of Indiana Press, 1985), 65.

[7] Whitney, "The Witch 'She'/the Historian 'He,'" 87.

[8] Whitney, "The Witch 'She'/the Historian 'He,'" 88–89.

[9] Reed, "Why Salem Made Sense," 223.

[10] Karlsen, *The Devil in the Shape of a Woman*, 103.

[11] Karlsen, *The Devil in the Shape of a Woman*, 101.

[12] Benjamin C. Ray, *Satan and Salem: The Witch-Hunt Crisis of 1692* (Charlottesville: University of Virginia Press, 2015), 15.

[13] "Testimony of Benjamin Abbott v. Martha Carrier," SWP No. 24.8 in the Salem Witch Trials Documentary Archive, accessed May 14, 2023, salem.lib.virginia.edu/n24.html.

[14] Ray, *Satan and Salem*, 21.

[15] Ray, *Satan and Salem*, 24.

9. Follow the Money

[1] Silvia Federici, *Caliban and the Witch: Women, the Body and Primitive Accumulation* (New York: Autonomedia, 2004), 166.

[2] Juan Cruz López Rasch and Lucio B. Mir, "Collective Rights and Enclosures in 13th-Century England: An Interpretative Approach around the Statute of Merton (1236)," *Merton Historical Society Bulletin* no. 176 (December 2010).

[3] E. B. Fryde, *Peasants and Landlords in Later Medieval England* (New York: St. Martin's Press, 1996), 186.

[4] Federici, *Caliban and the Witch*, 76.

[5] Merry E. Wiesner, *Working Women in Renaissance Germany* (New Brunswick, NJ: Rutgers University Press, 1952), 174–82.

[6] Federici, *Caliban and the Witch*, 89.

[7] Federici, *Caliban and the Witch*, 100.

[8] Federici, *Caliban and the Witch*, 91.

[9] Federici, *Caliban and the Witch*, 173–4.

[10] Keith Thomas, *Religion and the Decline of Magic: Studies in Popular Beliefs in Sixteenth- and Seventeenth-Century England* (United Kingdom, London: 1971), 565.

[11] Elaine Forman Crane, *Ebb Tide in New England: Women, Seaports, and Social Change, 1630–1800* (Boston: Northeastern University Press, 1998).

[12] Bernard Rosenthal et al., *Records of the Salem Witch-Hunt* (Cambridge: Cambridge University Press, 2009), 204.

[13] Cotton Mather, *Durable Riches: Two Brief Discourses* (Boston: John Allen, 1695), Ann Arbor: Text Creation Partnership, 2011, http://name.umdl.umich.edu/N00592.0001.001, 1–12.

[14] Mather, *Durable Riches*, 18.

[15] Samuel Parris, *The Sermon Notebook of Samuel Parris, 1689–1694*, ed. James F. Cooper and Kenneth P. Minkema (*Publications of The Colonial Society of Massachusetts*, vol. 66, 1993, distributed by the University Press of Virginia), "February 14, 1692," https://www.colonialsociety.org/node/1188#dlheads01.

11. Under an Evil Hand

[1] Nicholas P. Spanos and Jack Gottlieb, "Ergotism and the Salem Village Witch Trials," *Science* 194, no. 4272 (December 1976): 1390–94, https://doi.org/10.1126/science.795029.

[2] Spanos and Gottlieb, "Ergotism and the Salem Witch Trials," 1390.

[3] Charles W. Upham, *Salem Witchcraft*, vol. II (Boston: Wiggin and Lunt, 1867), ii.3.

[4] Elaine G. Breslaw, "Tituba's Confession: The Multicultural Dimensions of the 1692 Salem Witch-Hunt," *Ethnohistory* 44, no. 3 (Summer 1997): 537, https://www.jstor.org/stable/483035.

[5] Stacy Schiff, *The Witches: Suspicion, Betrayal, and Hysteria in 1692 Salem* (New York: Little, Brown, 2015), 289–91.

[6] Richard Godbeer, *The Devil's Dominion: Magic and Religion in Early New England* (Cambridge: Cambridge University Press, 1992), 31.

[7] Schiff, *The Witches*, 330–31.

[8] David Wayne Price, "Cotton Mather's Cosmology and the 1692 Salem Witch Trials," (PhD diss., University of North London, 2001), 118–19.

[9] Samuel Parris, *The Sermon Notebook of Samuel Parris, 1689–1694*, ed. James F. Cooper and Kenneth P. Minkema (*Publications of The Colonial Society of Massachusetts*, vol. 66, 1993, distributed by the University Press of Virginia), "14. Feb. 1691," https://www.colonialsociety.org/node/1188 #dlheads01.

[10] Parris, *The Sermon Notebook of Samuel Parris*, "24. 9. 1689."

13. Prophets and Puppeteers

[1] Elaine G. Breslaw, "Tituba's Confession: The Multicultural Dimensions of the 1692 Salem Witch-Hunt," *Ethnohistory* 44, no. 3 (Summer 1997), 535–56, https://www.jstor.org/stable/483035.

[2] John Hale, *A Modest Enquiry into the Nature of Witchcraft, and How Persons Guilty of That Crime May Be Convicted: And the Means Used for the Discovery Discussed, Both Negatively and Affirmatively, According to Scripture and Experience* (Boston: B. Green and J. Allen, 1702), 415.

[3] Robert Calef, *More Wonders of the Invisible World: Or, The Wonders of the Invisible World, Displayed in Five Parts* (London: Nath. Hillar and Joseph Collyer, 1700), in *Narratives of the Witchcraft Cases, 1648–1706*, ed. George Lincoln Burr (New York: Charles Scribner's Sons, 1914), 343.

[4] Hale, *A Modest Enquiry into the Nature of Witchcraft*, 132–33.

5 Azeen Ghorayshi, "How Teens Recovered from the 'TikTok Tics'," *New York Times*, February 13, 2023, https://www.nytimes.com/2023/02/13/health/tiktok-tics-gender-tourettes.html.

6 Samuel Parris, *The Sermon Notebook of Samuel Parris, 1689–1694*, ed. James F. Cooper and Kenneth P. Minkema (*Publications of The Colonial Society of Massachusetts*, vol. 66, 1993, distributed by the University Press of Virginia), "Christ Knows How Many Devils There Are, March 27, 1691/92," https://www.colonialsociety.org/node/1188#dlheads01.

7 Examination of Martha Corey (SWP No. 38.2), Salem Witch Trials Documentary Archive, https://salem.lib.virginia.edu/n38.html.

8 Parris, *The Sermon Notebook of Samuel Parris*, "Christ Knows How Many Devils There Are, March 27, 1691/92."

9 Benjamin C. Ray, *Satan and Salem: The Witch-Hunt Crisis of 1692* (Charlottesville: University of Virginia Press, 2015), 94.

10 Peter Grund, Merja Kytö, Matti Rissanen, "Editing the Salem Witchcraft Records: An Exploration of a Linguistic Treasury," *American Speech* 79, no. 2 (Summer 2004):146–66, https://doi.org/10.1215/00031283-79-2-146.

11 Stacy Schiff, *The Witches: Suspicion, Betrayal, and Hysteria in 1692 Salem* (New York: Little, Brown and Company, 2015), 96.

12 Direct quote from the "Testimony of Daniel Elliott for Elizabeth Procter," SWP No. 106.8, in the Salem Witch Trials Documentary Archive, accessed May 13, 2023, https://salem.lib.virginia.edu/n106.html.

17. Naming Names

1 Samuel Drake, *The Witchcraft Delusion in New England* (Roxbury, MA: Printed for W. E. Woodward, 1866), 24.

2 Stacy Schiff, *The Witches: Suspicion, Betrayal, and Hysteria in 1692 Salem* (New York: Little, Brown, 2015), 283.

[3] Edward Randolph and Robert Noxon Toppan, *Edward Randolph: Including His Letters and Official Papers from the New England, Middle, and Southern Colonies in America, with Other Documents Relating Chiefly to the Vacating of the Royal Charter of the Colony of Massachusetts Bay, 1676–1703* (Boston: Prince Society, 1967), 85–86.

[4] David Levin and the Massachusetts Historical Society, "Cotton Mather's letter to John Richards, May 31, 1692," the Salem Witchcraft Documentary Archive, accessed May 13, 2023, https://salem.lib.virginia.edu/letters/to_richards1.html.

[5] Levin and the Massachusetts Historical Society, "Cotton Mather's letter to John Richards, May 31, 1692."

[6] Virginia Bernhard, "Cotton Mather and the Doing of Good: A Puritan Gospel of Wealth," *New England Quarterly* 49, no. 2 (June 1976), 230, https://doi.org/10.2307/364500.

[7] Cotton Mather, *A Midnight Cry: An Essay for Our Awakening Out of That Sinful Sleep* (Boston: John Allen, 1692), Early English Books Online Text Creation Partnership, accessed May 13, 2023, http://name.umdl.umich.edu/N00498.0001.001.

[8] Mather, *A Midnight Cry.*

[9] Mather, *A Midnight Cry.*

[10] David Wayne Price, "Cotton Mather's Cosmology and the 1692 Salem Witch Trials," (PhD diss., University of North London, 2001), 10–48.

[11] Paul Boyer and Stephen Nissenbaum, *Salem Possessed: The Social Origins of Witchcraft* (Cambridge: Harvard University Press, 1976), 26.

[12] Benjamin C. Ray, *Satan and Salem: The Witch-Hunt Crisis of 1692* (Charlottesville: University of Virginia Press, 2015), 118.

[13] Victor S. Navasky, *Naming Names* (New York: Viking Press, 1980), 28–29.

[14] Cotton Mather, *On Witchcraft: Being the Wonders of the Invisible World, First Published at Boston in Octr. 1692 and Now Reprinted, with Additional Matter and Old Wood-Cuts* (New York, Bell Publishing, 1974), 158–59.

19. No Return

[1] *Increase Mather and Deodat Lawson, A Further Account of the Tryals of the New-England Witches: With the Observations of a Person Who Was upon the Place Several Days When the Suspected Witches Were First Taken into Examination: To Which Is Added, Cases of Conscience Concerning Witchcrafts and Evil Spirits Personating Men.* London: Printed for J. Dunton, 1693. Ann Arbor: Text Creation Partnership, 2011, http://name.umdl.umich.edu/A70086 .0001.001

[2] John McWilliams, "Indian John and the Northern Tawnies," *New England Quarterly* 69, no. 4 (December 1996), 584.

[3] Direct quote from the "Testimony of Sarah Nurse Regarding Sarah Bibber, in Support of Rebecca Nurse," SWP No. 12.4 the Salem Witch Trials Documentary Archive, accessed May 14, 2023, https://salem.lib.virginia .edu/n12.html.

[4] Mary Beth Norton, *In the Devil's Snare: The Salem Witchcraft Crisis of 1692* (United Kingdom: Knopf Doubleday Publishing, 2007), 226.

[5] Direct quote from the "Declaration of Thomas Fisk, Juryman," SWP No. 94.32 in the Salem Witch Trials Documentary Archive, accessed May 14, 2023, https://salem.lib.virginia.edu/n94.html.

[6] "Declaration of Thomas Fisk, Juryman," SWP No. 94.32 in the Salem Witch Trials Documentary Archive.

[7] Roach, Marilynne K. *The Salem Witch Trials: A Day-by-Day Chronicle of a Community under Siege*, (Maryland: Taylor Trade Publishing, 2004), 193.

[8] David Wayne Price, "Cotton Mather's Cosmology and the 1692 Salem Witch Trials," (PhD diss., University of North London, 2001), 169–70.

[9] Stacy Schiff, *The Witches: Suspicion, Betrayal, and Hysteria in 1692 Salem* (New York: Little, Brown, 2015), 230.

[10] Schiff, *The Witches*, 228.

[11] Schiff, *The Witches*, 230.

[12] Marilynne K. Roach, *The Salem Witch Trials: A Day-by-Day Chronicle of a Community under Siege* (Lanham, MD: Taylor Trade Publishing, 2004), 196.

[13] Roach, *The Salem Witch Trials*, 198.

[14] All quotes come directly from Ann Foster's confession. "Examinations of Ann Foster," SWP No. 59.1 in the Salem Witch Trials Documentary Archive, accessed May 21, 2023, https://salem.lib.virginia.edu/n59.html.

21. The Grave

[1] Marilynne K. Roach, *The Salem Witch Trials: A Day-by-Day Chronicle of a Community under Siege* (Lanham, MD: Taylor Trade Publishing, 2004), 209.

[2] Salem Witch Museum, "Martha and Thomas Carrier," quoting the *New England Journal* from June 9, 1735, accessed August 5, 2023, https://salemwitchmuseum.com/locations/martha-thomas-carrier-widow-allen-home-site-of/.

[3] WikiTree, "Thomas Carrier (abt. 1626-1735)," accessed February 17, 2023, https://www.wikitree.com/wiki/Carrier-2, citing unavailable article by Pierre Comtois, "Billerica Family's 323-Year Exile Ends," *Lowell Sun Newspaper*, March 16, 1999.

23. The Gauntlet

[1] F. Apthrop Foster, ed., *Vital Records of Billerica, Massachusetts, to the Year 1850* (Boston: New England Historic Genealogical Society at the Charge of the Eddy Town-Record Fund, 1908), eBook, Section "400 Billerica Deaths."

[2] "Examination of Mary Toothaker," SWP No. 128.2 in the Salem Witch Trials Documentary Archive, accessed May 21, 2023, https://salem.lib.virginia.edu/n128.html.

25. Thirty Thousand

[1] Michael Schwirtz, "Man Admits Killing 2 Women with Hammer, Officials Say," *New York Times*, January 29, 2014, www.nytimes.com/2014/01/30 /nyregion/suspect-arrested-after-2-women-were-found-beaten-to-death -in-queens.html.

[2] This number comes from a Concept Note published in 2020 by the United Nations Independent Expert on the Enjoyment of Human Rights by Persons with Albinism, in collaboration with the Witchcraft and Human Rights Information Network (WHRIN). The note's data shows that twenty thousand people from 2009 to 2019 were the victims of witch hunts *or* "ritual attacks." (Ritual attacks are when a person is attacked as part of a magic ritual. It often takes the shape of attacks against albino people for the use of their body parts, which are seen as having magical properties in some parts of the world.) Upon contacting one of the Note's authors, Miranda Forsyth, she clarified that their data doesn't break down any further; in other words, we can't say for certain how many ritual attacks there were and how many witch hunts. In Forsyth's estimation, though, witch hunts had heavily outweighed ritual attacks. Therefore, we can assume that the full count of witch hunt victims is over ten thousand.

From United Nations Independent Expert on the Enjoyment of Human Rights by Persons with Albinism, "Concept Note & Preliminary Data: Elimination of Harmful Practices: Accusations of Witchcraft and Ritual Attacks," in collaboration with the Witchcraft and Human Rights Information Network and its member-networks: Under the Same Sun, National FGM Centre, UK, Doughty Street Chambers, UK, Australia National University, Divine Word University, Papua New Guinea, Lancaster University, Staffordshire University, the Centre for Human Rights of the University of Pretoria and the International Human Rights Program of the University of Toronto, March 2020, available for download at https://www.ohchr.org /en/documents/tools-and-resources/concept-note-elimination-harmful -practices-related-witchcraft.

[3] Liz Alden Wily, "The Global Land Grab: The New Enclosures," in *The Wealth of the Commons: A World Beyond Market and State*, ed. David Bollier and Silke Helfrich (Amherst, MA: Levellers Press, 2012).

[4] Miranda Forsyth, interview with the author, June 2022.

27. The Devil in the Ground

[1] Marion L. Starkey, *The Devil in Massachusetts: A Modern Enquiry into the Salem Witch Trials* (New York: Anchor Books Editions, 1969), 255.

[2] Leo Igwe, interview with author, June 10, 2022.

[3] "CSOs Demand Justice for Old Woman Killed for Alleged Witchcraft," *Ghana Business News*, July 25, 2020, www.ghanabusinessnews.com/2020/07/25/csos-demand-justice-for-old-woman-killed-for-alleged-witchcraft/.

[4] Igwe, interview.

[5] Igwe, interview.

[6] Berrie Holtzhausen, interview with author, December 3, 2020.

[7] Igwe, interview.

[8] SARV Project Incident Dataset, Australian National University, shared with author by Miranda Forsyth, 2022.

[9] Alphonce Gari, "Agony of Kilifi Elders Murdered for 'Witchcraft' in Land Grab." *Star*, May 29, 2021, https://www.the-star.co.ke/news/big-read/2021-05-29-agony-of-kilifi-elders-murdered-for-witchcraft-in-land-grab/.

[10] Elias Yaa, "Kaya Godoma Marks 10th Year Hosting Elderly," *Star*, January 20, 2020, https://www.the-star.co.ke/counties/coast/2020-01-20-kaya-godoma-marks-10th-year-hosting-elderly/.

[11] Patricia Lindrio, "When Land Ownership Is in Doubt, Some Ugandans Face Witchcraft Accusations and Eviction by Mobs," *Land Portal*, December 11, 2019, https://landportal.org/node/89154.

29. The Witch Finder

[1] "Examination of William Barker, Sr." SWP No. 9.2 in the Salem Witch Trials Documentary Archive, accessed June 14, 2023, https://salem.lib.virginia.edu/n9.html.

[2] Miranda Forsyth et al., "Sorcery Accusation–Related Violence in Papua New Guinea: The Role of *Glasman/Glasmeri* as Catalysts of Accusation and Violence," *Issues Paper 36* (July 2021): 3, https://pngnri.org/images/Publications/Issues_Paper_No_36.pdf.

[3] Forsyth, "Sorcery Accusation-Related Violence in Papua New Guinea," 5.

[4] "Papua New Guinea Minimum Wage Rate 2023," Minimum-Wage, accessed June 20, 2023, www.minimum-wage.org/international/papua-new-guinea.

[5] "Petition of John Proctor from Prison," SWP No. 107.19 in the Salem Witch Trials Documentary Archive, https://salem.lib.virginia.edu/n107.html, accessed Jan 28, 2024.

[6] Stacy Schiff, *The Witches: Suspicion, Betrayal, and Hysteria in 1692 Salem* (New York: Little, Brown, 2015), 306.

[7] "Petition of Thomas Carrier for Restitution for Martha Carrier," SWP No. 173.10 in the Salem Witch Trials Documentary Archive, accessed May 22, 2023, https://salem.lib.virginia.edu/n173.html.

[8] "Five Ways to Compute the Relative Value of a UK Pound Amount, 1270 to Present," Measuring Worth, accessed August 7, 2023, https://www.measuringworth.com/calculators/ukcompare/.

[9] Jean La Fontaine, email to author, November 22, 2020.

[10] Jean La Fontaine, *Witches and Demons: A Comparative Perspective on Witchcraft and Satanism* (Oxford: Berghahn, 2016), 77–78.

[11] La Fontaine, *Witches and Demons,* 85.

[12] La Fontaine, email to author.

[13] African Child Policy Forum, "Uncovering our Hidden Shame: Addressing Witchcraft Accusations and Ritual Attacks in Africa" (Addis Ababa,

Ethiopia: African Child Policy Forum [ACPF], 2022), 10, https://
africanchildforum.org/index.php/en/sobipro?sid=276.

[14] Berrie Holtzhausen, interview with author, December 3, 2020.

[15] Holtzhausen, interview.

[16] Cotton Mather, *On Witchcraft: Being the Wonders of the Invisible World,
First Published at Boston in Octr. 1692 and Now Reprinted, with Additional
Matter and Old Wood-Cuts* (New York: Bell Publishing, 1974), 20.

[17] David Wayne Price, "Cotton Mather's Cosmology and the 1682 Salem
Witch Trials," (PhD diss., University of North London, 2001), 139.

31. Burial

[1] Gretchen A. Adams, "Mysteries, Memories, and Metaphors: The Salem
Witchcraft Trials in the American Imagination," *American Antiquarian
Society* (2003): 261, https://www.americanantiquarian.org/proceedings
/44539515.pdf.

[2] Richard Hite, *In the Shadow of Salem: The Andover Witch Hunt of 1692*
(Yardley, PA: Westholme, 2018), 187.

[3] Ann Matica, "I Visited Salem and Toured a Haunted Airbnb, Got a Psychic Reading, and Met a Practicing Witch," *Business Insider*, October 26,
2022, www.businessinsider.com/i-toured-salem-massachusetts-halloween
-visited-psychic-witch-haunted-airbnb-2022-10.

[4] Robert Calef, *More Wonders of the Invisible World: Or, The Wonders of the
Invisible World, Displayed in Five Parts* (London: Nath. Hillar and Joseph
Collyer, 1700), in *Narratives of the Witchcraft Cases, 1648–1706*, ed. George
Lincoln Burr (New York: Charles Scribner's Sons, 1914), 213.

[5] Caroline Newman, "With UVA's Help, Salem Finally Discovers Where Its
'Witches' Were Execute," *UVA Today*, University of Virginia, January 19,
2016, news.virginia.edu/content/uvas-help-salem-finally-discovers-where
-its-witches-were-executed.

[6] Samuel Sewall, *The Diary of Samuel Sewall, 1674–1729* (New York: Farrar,
Straus and Giroux, 1973), 363.

[7] Cotton Mather, *On Witchcraft: Being the Wonders of the Invisible World, First Published at Boston in Octr. 1692 and Now Reprinted, with Additional Matter and Old Wood-Cuts* (New York, Bell Publishing, 1974), 128.

[8] *The First English Dictionary of Slang, 1699*, introduction by John Simpson (Oxford: Bodleian Library, 2010), 84.

[9] This idea comes from a note in Robert Calef's *More Wonders* that Cotton Mather began speaking "as soon as [Burroughs] was turned off." The line is quoted in George Lincoln Burr's *Narratives of the Witchcraft Cases, 1648-1706* (New York: Charles Scribner's Sons, 1914), 361.

[10] Calef, *More Wonders,* in Burr, *Narratives,* 361.

[11] Boston Record Commissioners Report, *Boston Births, Baptisms, Marriages and Deaths, 1630–1699* (Boston: Rockwell and Churchill City Printers, 1883), 210, Library of Congress, accessed August 6, 2023, https://tile.loc .gov/storage-services/public/gdcmassbookdig/bostonbirthsbapt00bost /bostonbirthsbapt00bost.pdf.

An Incomplete List

[1] "'Janet Horne' by Edwin Morgan," National Library of Scotland, accessed May 22, 2023, www.nls.uk/learning-zone/literature-and-language /themes-in-focus/witches/source-6/.

[2] Ben Panko, "Last Person Executed as a Witch in Europe Gets a Museum," *Smithsonian,* August 29, 2017, www.smithsonianmag.com/smart-news /last-witch-executed-europe-gets-museum-180964633/.

[3] Krzysztof Józwiak, "Procesy Czarownic w Rzeczypospolitej Obojga Narodów," *Rzeczpospolita,* October 16, 2016, www.rp.pl/historia /art3217791-procesy-czarownic-w-rzeczypospolitej-obojga-narodow.

[4] Shashank Sinha, "Witch-Hunts, Adivasis, and the Uprising in Chhotanag-pur," *Economic and Political Weekly* 42, no. 19 (May 2007): 1675, www.jstor .org/stable/4419566.

[5] Sinha, "Witch-Hunts, Adivasis, and the Uprising in Chhotanagpur," 1672.

6 Dean Ruxton, "The Story of the Last 'Witch' Burned Alive in Ireland," *Irish Times*, November 24, 2016, https://www.irishtimes.com/news /offbeat/the-story-of-the-last-witch-burned-alive-in-ireland-1.2880691.

7 Katherine Luongo, "The Wakamba Witch Trials," in *Witchcraft and Colonial Rule in Kenya, 1900–1955* (Cambridge: Cambridge University Press, 2011), 98–128, doi:10.1017/CBO9780511997914.005; Richard D. Waller, "Witchcraft and Colonial Law in Kenya," *Past & Present*, 180 (August 2003): 241–75, https://www.jstor.org/stable/3600744.

8 Animesh Bisoee, "Witch-Hunt Survivor to Padma Shri Glory," *Telegraph*, January 28, 2021, https://www.telegraphindia.com/jharkhand/witch -hunt-survivor-to-padma-shri-glory/cid/1804901; Suhasini Raj, "India Struggles to Eradicate an Old Scourge: Witch Hunting," *New York Times,* May 13, 2023, https://www.nytimes.com/2023/05/13/world/asia/india -witch-hunting.html.

9 Michael Specter, "In Modern Russia, A Fatal Medieval Witch Hunt," *New York Times,* April 5, 1997, https://www.nytimes.com/1997/04/05/world /in-modern-russia-a-fatal-medieval-witch-hunt.html.

10 "Woman Burned Alive for 'Sorcery' in Papua New Guinea," BBC News, February 7, 2013, https://www.bbc.com/news/world-asia-21363894; AP, "2 Charged in Papua New Guinea 'Witch' Killing,' February 18, 2013, https://apnews.com/article/c4375969422e4d28a20cb16683693593.

11 Fernanda Canofre, "Driven by Facebook Rumors, Violent Mob Murders Brazilian Woman," *Global Voices*, May 27, 2014, https:// globalvoices.org/2014/05/27/how-an-internet-rumor-in-brazil -killed-fabiane-maria-de-jesus/.

12 Samantha Schmidt, "'She Was Demonized': Nicaraguan Woman Dies after Being Thrown into Fire in Exorcism Ritual," *Washington Post*, March 1, 2017, https://www.washingtonpost.com/news/morning-mix /wp/2017/03/01/she-was-demonized-nicaraguan-woman-dies-after -being-thrown-into-fire-in-exorcism-ritual/.

13 "Nicaragua: Pastor, 4 Church Members Convicted of Young Woman's Exorcism Death," NBC News, May 10, 2017, https://www.nbcnews

.com/news/latino/nicaragua-pastor-4-church-members
-convicted-young-woman-s-exorcism-n757311.

14 "Woman, 73, Tortured over Witchcraft Allegation," *Kathmandu Post*,
November 18, 2018, kathmandupost.com/national/2018/11/19
/woman-73-beaten-fed-feces-on-witchcraft-charges-in-dhading; Keshav
Adhikari, "Single, Elderly Woman Tortured on Witchcraft Charge,"
Himalayan Times, November 18, 2018, https://thehimalayantimes
.com/nepal/single-elderly-woman-tortured-on-witchcraft-charge.

15 "Man Burnt Alive on Suspicion of Witchcraft in Visakhapatnam," *Times
of India*, September 26, 2019, timesofindia.indiatimes
.com/city/visakhapatnam/man-accused-of-using-black-magic-killed
/articleshow/71300981.cms.

16 John Owen Nwachukwu, "Witch Group Rejoices over Sack of Cross
River Forest Boss, Tawo," *Daily Post*, August 6, 2021, dailypost
.ng/2021/08/06/witch-group-rejoices-over-sack-of-cross-river
-forest-boss-tawo/.

17 Ada Wodu, "Suspected Mob Leader 'General Iron' Shot Dead in Cross
River," *Punch Newspapers*, August 27, 2021, punchng
.com/suspected-mob-leader-general-iron-shot-dead-in-cross-river/.

18 Leo Igwe, "Boki: Justice for Victims of Witch-Hunt," *Modern Ghana*,
June 11, 2020, www.modernghana.com/news/1008460/boki-justice
-for-victims-of-witch-hunt.html.

19 Russell Kondowe, "Woman Killed over Witchcraft Accusations,"
Malawi24, January 5, 2021, malawi24.com/2021/01/05
/woman-killed-over-witchcraft-accusations/; Owen Khamula, "Police
Arrest Traditional Healer over Murder," *Nyasa Times,* January 17, 2021,
https://www.nyasatimes.com/police-arrest-traditional-healer
-over-murder/.

20 "Jharkhand: Couple Beaten to Death over Witchcraft Suspicion in Latehar," *Free Press Journal*, May 3, 2023, www.freepressjournal.in/india
/jharkhand-couple-beaten-to-death-over-witchcraft-suspicion-in-latehar;
"Elderly Jharkhand Couple Beaten to Death over Witchcraft Suspicion:

Cops," *India News,* May 3, 2023, https://www.ndtv.com/india-news
/elderly-jharkhand-couple-beaten-to-death-over-witchcraft-suspicion
-cops-4002000.

Epilogue

[1] UN General Assembly, Resolution 47/8, Elimination of Harmful Practices Related to Accusations of Witchcraft and Ritual Attacks, A/HRC
/RES/47/8, 2 (July 12, 2021).

[2] Increase Mather and Deodat Lawson, *A Further Account of the Tryals of the
New-England Witches: With the Observations of a Person Who Was upon the
Place Several Days When the Suspected Witches Were First Taken into Examina-
tion: To Which Is Added, Cases of Conscience Concerning Witchcrafts and Evil
Spirits Personating Men* (London: Printed for J. Dunton, 1693; Ann Arbor:
Text Creation Partnership, 2011), http://name.umdl.umich.edu/A70086
.0001.001.

[3] Marilynne K. Roach, *The Salem Witch Trials: A Day-by-Day Chronicle of a
Community under Siege* (Lanham, MD: Taylor Trade Publishing, 2004), 304.

[4] Letters of Governor Phips to the Home Government, in *Narratives of
the Witchcraft Cases, 1648–1706* (New York: Charles Scribner's Sons, 1914),
196–99.

[5] Stacy Schiff, *The Witches: Suspicion, Betrayal, and Hysteria in 1692 Salem*
(New York: Little, Brown, 2015), 340–41.

[6] Samuel Parris, *The Sermon Notebook of Samuel Parris, 1689–1694,* ed. James
F. Cooper and Kenneth P. Minkema (*Publications of The Colonial Society of
Massachusetts,* vol. 66, 1993, distributed by the University Press of Virginia), "23. Octob. 1692," https://www.colonialsociety.org/node
/1997#ch34.

[7] Robert Calef, *More Wonders of the Invisible World: Or, The Wonders of the
Invisible World, Displayed in Five Parts* (London: Nath. Hillar and Joseph
Collyer, 1700), in *Narratives of the Witchcraft Cases, 1648–1706,* ed. George
Lincoln Burr (New York: Charles Scribner's Sons, 1914), 382–83.

[8] Paul Boyer and Stephen Nissenbaum, *Salem Possessed: The Social Origins of Witchcraft* (Cambridge: Harvard University Press, 1976), 78–79.

[9] Charles W. Upham, *Salem Witchcraft*, vol. II (Boston: Wiggin and Lunt, 1867), 486.

[10] "Petition of Thomas Carrier for Restitutiion for Martha Carrier," SWP No. 173 in the Salem Witch Trials Documentary Archive, accessed May 22, 2023, https://salem.lib.virginia.edu/n173.html.

[11] Henry A. Hazen, *Billerica, Massachusetts, with a Genealogical Register* (Boston: A. Williams, 1883), 197.

[12] "Five Ways to Compute the Relative Value of a UK Pound Amount, 1270 to Present," Measuring Worth, accessed August 7, 2023, https://www.measuringworth.com/calculators/ukcompare/.

Bibliography

Court records in the Salem Witch Trials Documentary Archive. Benjamin C. Ray and the University of Virginia, 2018. https://salem.lib.virginia.edu/home.html.

Cited or referenced:
- **SWP No. 9.2** (Examination of William Barker, Sr.)
- **SWP No. 12.4** (Testimony of Sarah Nurse Regarding Sarah Bibber, in Support of Rebecca Nurse)
- **SWP No. 13.20** (Physical Examination of Bridget Bishop, Rebecca Nurse, Elizabeth Proctor, Alice Parker, Susannah Martin, and Sarah Good, No. 1)
- **SWP No. 24.3** (Examination of Martha Carrier)
- **SWP No. 24.8** (Testimony of Benjamin Abbott v. Martha Carrier)
- **SWP No. 24.10** (Deposition of Phoebe Chandler and Testimony of [Bridget] Chandler v. Martha Carrier)
- **SWP No. 24.11** (Deposition of Allen Toothaker)
- **SWP No. 25.2** (Examinations of Richard Carrier, Mary Lacey Sr., Mary Lacey Jr., & Andrew Carrier, Copy)
- **SWP No. 26.2** (Examination of Sarah Carrier)
- **SWP No. 27.1** (Examination of Thomas Carrier, Jr.,)
- **SWP No. 59.1** (Examinations of Ann Foster)
- **SWP No. 63.2** (Examination of Sarah Good, as Recorded by Ezekiell Cheever)
- **SWP No. 63.4** (Examination of Sarah Good, Written by Jonathan Corwin)
- **SWP No. 87.2** (Examinations of Mary Lacey, Jr., Mary Lacey, Sr., Ann Foster, Richard Carrier, and Andrew Carrier, Copy)
- **SWP No. 94.32** (Declaration of Thomas Fisk, Juryman)
- **SWP No. 94.33** (Appeal of Rebecca Nurse)
- **SWP No. 95.2** (Examinations of Sarah Osborne and Tituba, as Recorded by Ezekiel Cheevers)
- **SWP No. 106.8** (Testimony of Daniel Elliott for Elizabeth Proctor)

- SWP No. 107.19 (Petition of John Proctor from Prison)
- SWP No. 125.3 (Examination of Tituba, as recorded by Ezekiell Chevers)
- SWP No. 125.4 (Examination of Tituba, as recorded by magistrate Jonathan Corwin)
- SWP No. 128.2 (Examination of Mary Toothaker)
- SWP No. 125.5 (Second Examination of Tituba, as recorded by magistrate Jonathan Corwin)
- SWP No. 173.10 (Petition of Thomas Carrier for Restitution for Martha Carrier)

Other Sources

"2 Charged in Papua New Guinea 'Witch' Killing." *AP*. February 18, 2013. https://apnews.com/article/c4375969422e4d28a20cb16683693593.

Adams, Gretchen A. "Mysteries, Memories, and Metaphors: The Salem Witchcraft Trials in the American Imagination." *American Antiquarian Society* (2003). https://www.americanantiquarian.org/proceedings/44539515.pdf.

Adhikari, Keshav. "Single, Elderly Woman Tortured on Witchcraft Charge." *Himalayan Times*, November 18, 2018. https://thehimalayantimes.com/nepal/single-elderly-woman-tortured-on-witchcraft-charge.

Ady, Thomas. *A Candle in the Dark: Shewing the Divine Cause of the Distractions of the Whole Nation of England, and of the Christian World*. London: Printed for Robert Ibbitson, 1655.

African Child Policy Forum. "Uncovering Our Hidden Shame: Addressing Witchcraft Accusations and Ritual Attacks in Africa." Addis Ababa, Ethiopia: African Child Policy Forum (ACPF), 2022. https://africanchildforum.org/index.php/en/sobipro?sid=276.

Alden Wily, Liz. "The Global Land Grab: The New Enclosures." In *The Wealth of the Commons: A World Beyond Market and State*, edited by David Bollier and Silke Helfrich, 132–40. Amherst, MA: Levellers Press, 2012.

Avalos, Nayda, Veronica Gonzales Stuva, Adam Heal, Kaoru Lida, and Naohito Okazoe. "Papua New Guinea and the Natural Resource Curse." *Comparative Economic Studies* 57, no. 2 (March 19, 2015): 345–60. https://doi.org/10.1057/ces.2015.1.

Bailey, Sarah Loring. *Historical Sketches of Andover, Massachusetts: Comprising the Present Towns of North Andover and Andover.* Boston: Houghton, Mifflin and Company, 1880.

Benton, Josiah H. *Warning Out in New England, 1656–1817.* Boston: W. B. Clarke, 1911.

Bernhard, Virginia. "Cotton Mather and the Doing of Good: A Puritan Gospel of Wealth." *New England Quarterly* 49, no. 2 (June 1976), 225–41. https://doi.org/10.2307/364500.

Bisoee, Animesh. "Witch-Hunt Survivor to Padma Shri Glory." *Telegraph*, January 28, 2021. https://www.telegraphindia.com/jharkhand/witch-hunt-survivor-to-padma-shri-glory/cid/1804901.

Boeck, Filip De, and Alcinda Honwana, eds. *Makers and Breakers: Children and Youth in Postcolonial Africa.* United Kingdom: James Currey, 2005.

Boston Record Commissioners Report. *Boston Births, Baptisms, Marriages, and Deaths, 1630–1699.* Boston: Rockwell and Churchill City Printers, 1883. https://tile.loc.gov/storage-services/public/gdcmassbookdig/bostonbirthsbapt00bost/bostonbirthsbapt00bost.pdf.

Boyer, Paul, and Stephen Nissenbaum. *Salem Possessed: The Social Origins of Witchcraft.* Cambridge: Harvard University Press, 1976.

Brain, Robert. "Child-Witches." In *Witchcraft, Confessions & Accusations*, edited by Mary Douglas, 161–82. London: Routledge, 2004.

Breslaw, Elaine G. "Tituba's Confession: The Multicultural Dimensions of the 1692 Salem Witch-Hunt." *Ethnohistory* 44, no. 3 (Summer 1997): 535–56. https://www.jstor.org/stable/483035.

Briggs, Robin. *Witches and Neighbors: The Social and Cultural Context of European Witchcraft.* New York: Penguin, 1998.

Brown, David C. "The Forfeitures at Salem, 1692." *William and Mary Quarterly* 50, no. 1 (January 1993): 85–111. https://doi.org/10.2307/2947237.

Burr, George Lincoln. *Narratives of the Witchcraft Cases, 1648–1706*. New York: Charles Scribner's Sons, 1914.

Calef, Robert. *More Wonders of the Invisible World: Or, The Wonders of the Invisible World, Displayed in Five Parts*. London: Nath. Hillar and Joseph Collyer, 1700. Reprinted in *Narratives of the Witchcraft Cases, 1648–1706* edited by George Lincoln Burr. New York: Charles Scribner's Sons, 1914.

Canofre, Fernanda. "Driven by Facebook Rumors, Violent Mob Murders Brazilian Woman." *Global Voices*, May 27, 2014. https://globalvoices.org/2014/05/27/how-an-internet-rumor-in-brazil-killed-fabiane-maria-de-jesus/.

Caporael, Linnda R. "Ergotism: The Satan Loosed in Salem?" *Science* 192, no. 4234 (April 2, 1976): 21–26. https://www.science.org/doi/10.1126/science.769159.

Cave, Alfred A. "New England Puritan Misperceptions of Native American Shamanism." *International Social Science Review* 67, no. 1 (Winter 1992): 15–27. http://www.jstor.org/stable/41882032.

Chandran, Rina. "Witches Beaten, Buried, Burned for Land in Princely Indian State." *Reuters*, October 4, 2017. https://jp.reuters.com/article/india-landrights-women-idINKCN1C90EL.

Crane, Elaine Forman. *Ebb Tide in New England: Women, Seaports, and Social Change, 1630–1800*. Boston: Northeastern University Press, 1998.

"CSOs Demand Justice for Old Woman Killed for Alleged Witchcraft." *Ghana Business News*, July 25, 2020. www.ghanabusinessnews.com/2020/07/25/csos-demand-justice-for-old-woman-killed-for-alleged-witchcraft/.

Dalton, Bill. "Repost of Previous Bill Dalton Column on Thomas Carrier." *Andover Townsman*, February 10, 2011. www.andovertownsman.com/community/repost-of-previous-bill-dalton-column-on-thomas-carrier/article_0a9a7c5e-5d54-5bfb-ac15-95fd9877fd57.html.

Demos, John. *Entertaining Satan: Witchcraft and the Culture of Early New England*. Oxford: Oxford University Press, 2004.

Dowden, Robert. "Small 'Witches' of Kinshasa." *Guardian*, March 3, 2006. https://www.theguardian.com/world/2006/mar/03/outlook.development.

Drake, Samuel. *The Witchcraft Delusion in New England*. Roxbury, MA: Printed for W. E. Woodward, 1866.

"Elderly Jharkhand Couple Beaten to Death Over Witchcraft Suspicion: Cops." *India News*, May 3, 2023. https://www.ndtv.com/india-news/elderly-jharkhand-couple-beaten-to-death-over-witchcraft-suspicion-cops-4002000.

Faber, Eli. "Puritan Criminals: The Economic, Social, and Intellectual Background to Crime in Seventeenth-Century Massachusetts." *Perspectives in American History* 11 (1978): 83–144.

Federici, Silvia. *Caliban and the Witch: Women, the Body and Primitive Accumulation*. New York: Autonomedia, 2004.

———. *Women, Witches, and Witch-Hunting*. New York: PM Press, 2018.

The First English Dictionary of Slang, 1699. With an introduction by John Simpson. Oxford: Bodleian Library, 2010.

"Five Ways to Compute the Relative Value of a UK Pound Amount, 1270 to Present." Measuring Worth. Accessed August 7, 2023. https://www.measuringworth.com/calculators/ukcompare/.

Flaherty, David. "Law and the Enforcement of Morals in Early America." *Perspectives in American* History 5 (1971): 203–53.

Forsyth, Miranda, William Kipongi, Anton Lutz, Philip Gibbs, Fiona Hukula, and Ibolya Losoncz. "Sorcery Accusation–Related Violence in Papua New Guinea: The Role of *Glasman/Glasmeri* as Catalysts of Accusation and Violence." *Issues Paper* 36 (July 2021): 1–11. https://pngnri.org/images/Publications/Issues_Paper_No_36.pdf.

Foster, F. Apthrop, ed. *Vital Records of Billerica, Massachusetts, to the Year 1850.* Boston: New England Historic Genealogical Society at the Charge of the Eddy Town-Record Fund, 1908.

Fryde, E. B. *Peasants and Landlords in Later Medieval England.* New York: St. Martin's Press, 1996.

Gari, Alphonce. "Agony of Kilifi Elders Murdered for 'Witchcraft' in Land Grab." *Star* (Kenya), May 29, 2021. https://www.the-star.co.ke/news /big-read/2021-05-29-agony-of-kilifi-elders-murdered-for-witchcraft-in -land-grab/.

Ghorayshi, Azeen. "How Teens Recovered from the 'TikTok Tics'." *New York Times.* February 1, 2023. https://www.nytimes.com/2023/02/13/health /tiktok-tics-gender-tourettes.html.

Godbeer, Richard. *The Devil's Dominion: Magic and Religion in Early New England.* Cambridge: Cambridge University Press, 1992.

Grund, Peter, Merja Kytö, Matti Rissanen. "Editing the Salem Witchcraft Records: An Exploration of a Linguistic Treasury." *American Speech* 79, no. 2 (Summer 2004): 146–66. https://doi.org/10.1215/00031283-79-2-146.

Hale, John. *A Modest Enquiry into the Nature of Witchcraft, and How Persons Guilty of That Crime May Be Convicted: And the Means Used for the Discovery Discussed, Both Negatively and Affirmatively, According to Scripture and Experience.* Boston: B. Green and J. Allen, 1702.

Hazen, Henry A. *History of Billerica, Massachusetts, with a Genealogical Register.* Boston: A. Williams, 1883.

Herndon, Ruth Wallis. *Unwelcome Americans: Living on the Margin in Early New England.* Philadelphia: University of Pennsylvania Press, 2001.

Holman, Mary Lovering. *Ancestry of Charles Stinson Pillsbury and John Sargent Pillsbury, Compiled for Helen Pendleton (Winston) Pillsbury.* Vol. 2. Rumford, 1938.

Hite, Richard. *In the Shadow of Salem: The Andover Witch Hunt of 1692.* Yardley, PA: Westholme, 2018.

Hutton, Ronald. *The Triumph of the Moon: A History of Modern Pagan Witch-craft*. Oxford: Oxford University Press, 1999.

———. *The Witch: A History of Fear, from Ancient Times to the Present*. New Haven: Yale University Press, 2017.

Igwe, Leo. "Boki: Justice for Victims of Witch-Hunt." *Modern Ghana*, June 11, 2020. www.modernghana.com/news/1008460/boki-justice-for -victims-of-witch-hunt.html.

"'Janet Horne' by Edwin Morgan." National Library of Scotland. Accessed May 22, 2023. www.nls.uk/learning-zone/literature-and-language /themes-in-focus/witches/source-6/.

"Jharkhand: Couple Beaten to Death over Witchcraft Suspicion in Latehar." *Free Press Journal* (Mumbai), May 3, 2023. www.freepressjournal.in/india /jharkhand-couple-beaten-to-death-over-witchcraft-suspicion-in-latehar.

Józwiak, Krzysztof. "Procesy Czarownic w Rzeczypospolitej Obojga Narodów." *Rzeczpospolita* (Warsaw), October 16, 2016. www.rp.pl /historia/art3217791-procesy-czarownic-w-rzeczypospolitej-obojga -narodow.

Karlsen, Carol F. *The Devil in the Shape of a Woman: Witchcraft in Colonial New England*. New York: W.W. Norton, 1987.

Khamula, Owen. "Police Arrest Traditional Healer over Murder." *Nyasa Times*, January 17, 2021. https://www.nyasatimes.com/police-arrest -traditional-healer-over-murder/.

Klaits, Joseph. *Servants of Satan: The Age of the Witch Hunts*. Bloomington, IN: University of Indiana Press, 1985.

Kondowe, Russell. "Woman Killed over Witchcraft Accusations." *Malawi24*, January 5, 2021. https://malawi24.com/2021/01/05/woman-killed -over-witchcraft-accusations/.

Kramer, Heinrich, and Jacob Sprenger. *Malleus Maleficarum*. Speier: Peter Drach, 1487; New York: Dover Publications, 1971.

La Fontaine, Jean. *Witches and Demons: A Comparative Perspective on Witchcraft and Satanism*. Oxford: Berghahn, 2016.

Lancre, Pierre de. *On the Inconstancy of Witches: Pierre de Lancre's "Tableau De L'inconstance Des Mauvais Anges Et demons" (1612)*. Edited by Gerhild Scholz Williams. Tempe, AZ: ACMRS (Arizona Center for Medieval and Renaissance Studies), 2006.

Larner, Christina. *Enemies of God: The Witch-Hunt in Scotland*. London: Chatto and Windus, 1981.

Lawson, Deodat. *Christ's Fidelity: The Only Shield against Satan's Malignity*. Boston: Printed by B. Harris, 1693.

Levin, David. "Cotton Mather's Misnamed Diary: Reserved Memorials of a Representative Christian." *American Literary History* 2, no. 2 (Summer 1990): 183–202. https://doi.org/10.1093/alh/2.2.183.

Levin, David, and the Massachusetts Historical Society. "Cotton Mather's letter to John Richards, May 31, 1692." Salem Witch Trials: Documentary Archive. Accessed May 13, 2023. https://salem.lib.virginia.edu/letters/to_richards1.html.

Lindrio, Patricia. "When Land Ownership Is in Doubt, Some Ugandans Face Witchcraft Accusations and Eviction by Mobs." *Global Press Journal*, December 10, 2019. https://globalpressjournal.com/africa/uganda/land-ownership-doubt-ugandans-face-witchcraft-accusations-eviction-mobs/.

Longfellow, Henry Wadsworth. "Giles Corey of the Salem Farms." In *The Complete Poetical Works of Henry Wadsworth Longfellow*, 607–636. Boston: Houghton, Mifflin and Company, 1902.

Luongo, Katherine. "The Wakamba Witch Trials." In *Witchcraft and Colonial Rule in Kenya, 1900–1955*, 98–128. Cambridge: Cambridge University Press, 2011. doi:10.1017/CBO9780511997914.005.

"Man Burnt Alive on Suspicion of Witchcraft in Visakhapatnam." *Times of India*, September 26, 2019. timesofindia.indiatimes.com/city/visakhapatnam/man-accused-of-using-black-magic-killed/articleshow/71300981.cms.

Mather, Cotton. *Diary of Cotton Mather*. New York: Frederick Ungar Publishing, 1957.

———. *Durable Riches: Two Brief Discourses*. Boston: John Allen, 1695.

———. *Magnalia Christi Americana: or, the Ecclesiastical History of New-England, from its First Planting, in the Year 1620, Unto the Year of Our Lord, 1698*. London: Printed for Thomas Parkhurst, 1702; Osher Map Library Rare Books. https://digitalcommons.usm.maine.edu/oml_rare_books /9/.

———. *Memorable Providences Relating to Witchcrafts and Possessions: A Faithful Account of Many Wonderful and Surprising Things That Have Befallen Several Bewitched and Possessed Person in New-England*. R. P., 1689; Ann Arbor, MI: Text Creation Partnership. http://name.umdl.umich.edu/A50139.0001 .001.

———. *A Midnight Cry: An Essay for Our Awakening Out of That Sinful Sleep*. Boston: John Allen, 1692; Early English Books Online Text Creation Partnership. Accessed May 13, 2023. http://name.umdl.umich.edu/N00498 .0001.001.

———. *A Town in its Truest Glory*. Boston: B. Green, 1712.

———. *On Witchcraft: Being the Wonders of the Invisible World, First Published at Boston in Octr. 1692 and Now Reprinted, with Additional Matter and Old Wood-Cuts*. New York: Bell Publishing, 1974.

Mather, Increase, and Deodat Lawson. *A Further Account of the Tryals of the New-England Witches: With the Observations of a Person Who Was upon the Place Several Days When the Suspected Witches Were First Taken into Examination: To Which Is Added, Cases of Conscience Concerning Witchcrafts and Evil Spirits Personating Men*. London: Printed for J. Dunton, 1693; Ann Arbor, MI: Text Creation Partnership, 2011. http://name.umdl.umich.edu/ A70086.0001.001.

Matica, Ann. "I Visited Salem and Toured a Haunted Airbnb, Got a Psychic Reading, and Met a Practicing Witch." *Business Insider*. October 26, 2022.

www.businessinsider.com/i-toured-salem-massachusetts-halloween
-visited-psychic-witch-haunted-airbnb-2022-10.

Matossian, Mary K. "Ergot and the Salem Witchcraft Affair." *American Scientist* 70, no. 4 (July–August 1982): 355–57.

McWilliams, John. "Indian John and the Northern Tawnies," *New England Quarterly* 69, no. 4 (December 1996): 580–604.

"Middlesex County, MA: Abstracts of Court Files, 1649–1675." American Ancestors. New England Historic Genealogical Society, 2003; Unpublished abstracts by Thomas Bellows Wyman. "Abstract of Middlesex Court Files from 1649." n.d. https://www.americanancestors .org/DB432/rd/12381/192/138357655.

Moore, George Henry. *Notes on the History of Witchcraft in Massachusetts; with Illustrative Documents. From Proceedings at the Annual Meeting of the American Antiquarian Society, October 21, 1882.* Worcester, MA: Charles Hamilton, 1883.

Navasky, Victor S. *Naming Names.* New York: Viking Press, 1980.

Nevins, Winfield S. *Witchcraft in Salem Village in 1692, Together with a Review of the Opinions of Modern Writers and Psychologists in Regard to Outbreak of the Evil in America.* Salem, MA: Salem Press, 1916.

New Frame. "Bloody Land-Grab Strategy Targets Older Kenyan Women." This Is Africa. May 30, 2022. https://thisisafrica.me/politics-and-society /bloody-land-grab-strategy-targets-older-kenyan-women/.

Newman, Caroline. "With UVA's Help, Salem Finally Discovers Where Its 'Witches' Were Executed." *UVA Today.* University of Virginia. January 19, 2016. news.virginia.edu/content/uvas-help-salem-finally-discovers -where-its-witches-were-executed.

"Nicaragua: Pastor, 4 Church Members Convicted of Young Woman's Exorcism Death." NBC News. May 10, 2017. https://www.nbcnews.com /news/latino/nicaragua-pastor-4-church-members-convicted-young -woman-s-exorcism-n757311.

Norton, Mary Beth. *In the Devil's Snare: The Salem Witchcraft Crisis of 1692*. United Kingdom: Knopf Doubleday Publishing, 2007.

Nwachukwu, John Owen. "Witch Group Rejoices over Sack of Cross River Forest Boss, Tawo." *Daily Post* (Nigeria), August 6, 2021. dailypost.ng /2021/08/06/witch-group-rejoices-over-sack-of-cross-river-forest-boss -tawo/.

Ogembo, Justus Mozart. "The Rise and Decline of Communal Violence: An Analysis of the 1992–94 Witch-Hunts in Gusii, Southwestern Kenya." PhD diss.: Harvard University, 1997.

Ongala, Maureen. "Kenya: Poverty Fuels Land Disputes, Killings in Kilifi." *AllAfrica*, July 13, 2021. https://allafrica.com/stories/202107130908.html.

Panko, Ben. "Last Person Executed as a Witch in Europe Gets a Museum." *Smithsonian*. August 29, 2017. www.smithsonianmag.com/smart-news /last-witch-executed-europe-gets-museum-180964633/.

"Papua New Guinea Minimum Wage Rate 2023." Minimum-Wage. Accessed June 20, 2023. www.minimum-wage.org/international /papua-new-guinea.

Parish, Jane. "From the Body to the Wallet: Conceptualizing Akan Witch-craft at Home and Abroad." *Journal of the Royal Anthropological Institute 6*, no. 3 (March 2003): 487–500. https://doi.org/10.1111/1467-9655.00028.

Parris, Samuel. *The Sermon Notebook of Samuel Parris, 1689–1694*. Edited by James F. Cooper and Kenneth P. Minkema. *Publications of the Colonial Society of Massachusetts*, vol. 66, 1993. Distributed by the University Press of Virginia. Accessed May 26, 2023. https://www.colonialsociety.org/node /1188#dlheads01.

Perley, Sidney. *The History of Salem, Massachusetts*. Vol 2. Bloomington, IN: Indiana University, 1924.

Price, David Wayne. "Cotton Mather's Cosmology and the 1692 Salem Witch Trials." PhD diss., University of North London, 2001.

Radford, Benjamin. "Facebook Post Leads to Witch Hunt, Tragedy in Brazil." Yahoo News. May 13, 2014. https://www.yahoo.com/news/facebook-post-leads-witch-hunt-tragedy-brazil-113332389.html.

Raj, Suhasini. "India Struggles to Eradicate an Old Scourge: Witch Hunting." *New York Times*, May 13, 2023. https://www.nytimes.com/2023/05/13/world/asia/india-witch-hunting.html.

Randolph, Edward, and Robert Noxon Toppan. *Edward Randolph: Including His Letters and Official Papers from the New England, Middle, and Southern Colonies in America, with Other Documents Relating Chiefly to the Vacating of the Royal Charter of the Colony of Massachusetts Bay, 1676–1703*. Boston: Prince Society, 1967.

Rasch, Juan Cruz López, and Lucio B. Mir. "Collective Rights and Enclosures in 13th-Century England: An Interpretative Approach around the Statute of Merton (1236)." *Merton Historical Society Bulletin* no. 176 (December 2010): 13–15.

Ray, Benjamin C. "The Geography of Witchcraft Accusations in 1692 Salem Village." *William and Mary Quarterly* 65, no. 3 (July 2008): 449–78. https://www.jstor.org/stable/25096807.

———. *Satan and Salem: The Witch-Hunt Crisis of 1692*. Charlottesville: University of Virginia Press, 2015.

Reed, Isaac. "Why Salem Made Sense: Culture, Gender, and the Puritan Persecution of Witchcraft." *Cultural Sociology* 1, no. 2 (2007): 209–234. https://doi.org/10.1177/1749975507078188.

Reis, Elizabeth. *Damned Women, Sinners and Witches in Puritan New England*. Ithaca, NY: Cornell University Press, 1997.

"Remote Nicaragua Village Backs Pastor in Fatal Exorcism." AFP. March 11, 2017. https://www.rfi.fr/en/contenu/20170311-remote-nicaragua-village-backs-pastor-fatal-exorcism.

Roach, Marilynne K. *The Salem Witch Trials: A Day-by-Day Chronicle of a Community under Siege*. Lanham, MD: Taylor Trade Publishing, 2004.

Rosenbaum, Betty B. "Sociological Basis of the Laws Relating to Women Sex Offenders in Massachusetts (1620–1860)," *Journal of Criminal Law and Criminology* 28, no. 6 (March–April 1938): 815.

Rosenthal, Bernard, Gretchen A. Adams, Margo Burns, Peter Grund, Risto Hiltunen, Leena Kahlals-Tarkka, Merja Kytö et al. *Records of the Salem Witch-Hunt*. Cambridge: Cambridge University Press, 2009.

Rumsey, Peter Lockwood. *Acts of God and the People, 1620–1730*. Ann Arbor, MI: UMI Research Press, 1986.

Ruxton, Dean. "The Story of the Last 'Witch' Burned Alive in Ireland." *Irish Times*. November 24, 2016. https://www.irishtimes.com/news/offbeat/the-story-of-the-last-witch-burned-alive-in-ireland-1.2880691.

Salem Witch Museum. "Martha and Thomas Carrier." Quoting the *New England Journal* from June 9, 1735. Accessed August 5, 2023. https://salemwitchmuseum.com/locations/martha-thomas-carrier-widow-allen-home-site-of/.

Schiff, Stacy. *The Witches: Suspicion, Betrayal, and Hysteria in 1692 Salem*. New York: Little, Brown, 2015.

Schmidt, Samantha. "'She Was Demonized': Nicaraguan Woman Dies after Being Thrown into Fire in Exorcism Ritual." *Washington Post*, March 1, 2017. https://www.washingtonpost.com/news/morning-mix/wp/2017/03/01/she-was-demonized-nicaraguan-woman-dies-after-being-thrown-into-fire-in-exorcism-ritual/.

Schwirtz, Michael. "Man Admits Killing 2 Women with Hammer, Officials Say." *New York Times*. January 29, 2014. www.nytimes.com/2014/01/30/nyregion/suspect-arrested-after-2-women-were-found-beaten-to-death-in-queens.html.

Sewall, Samuel. *The Diary of Samuel Sewall, 1674–1729*. Vol. 1. Edited by M. Halsey Thomes. New York: Farrar, Straus and Giroux, 1973.

Shmakov, Aleksandr, and Sergey Petrov. "Economic Origins of Witch Hunting." *Studies in Business and Economics* 13, no. 3 (December 2018): 214–29. https://doi.org/10.2478/sbe-2018-0044.

Sinha, Shashank. "Witch-Hunts, Adivasis, and the Uprising in Chhotanag-pur." *Economic and Political Weekly* 42, no. 19 (May 2007): 1672–76. www.jstor.org/stable/4419566.

Spanos, Nicholas P., and Jack Gottlieb. "Ergotism and the Salem Village Witch Trials." *Science* 194, no. 4272 (December 1976): 1390–94. https://doi.org/10.1126/science.795029.

Specter, Michael. "In Modern Russia, A Fatal Medieval Witch Hunt." *New York Times*, April 5, 1997. https://www.nytimes.com/1997/04/05/world/in-modern-russia-a-fatal-medieval-witch-hunt.html.

Starkey, Marion L. *The Devil in Massachusetts: A Modern Enquiry into the Salem Witch Trials.* New York: Anchor Books Editions, 1969.

Stoughton, William. *New England's True Interest Not to Lie.* Cambridge: Printed by S. G. and M. J., 1670; Ann Arbor, MI: Text Creation Partnership, 2011. https://quod.lib.umich.edu/e/eebo2/A61699.0001.001?view=toc.

Taylor, Charles. *A Secular Age.* Cambridge: Harvard University Press, 2009.

Thomas, Keith. *Religion and the Decline of Magic: Studies in Popular Beliefs in Sixteenth- and Seventeenth-Century England.* United Kingdom: Penguin, 1971.

UN General Assembly. Resolution 47/8. Elimination of Harmful Practices Related to Accusations of Witchcraft and Ritual Attacks. A/HRC/RES/47/8, 2. July 12, 2021.

United Nations Independent Expert on the Enjoyment of Human Rights by Persons with Albinism. "Concept Note & Preliminary Data: Elimination of Harmful Practices: Accusations of Witchcraft and Ritual Attacks." In collaboration with the Witchcraft and Human Rights Information Network and its member-networks: Under the Same Sun, National FGM Centre, UK, Doughty Street Chambers, UK, Australia National University, Divine Word University, Papua New Guinea, Lancaster University, Staffordshire University, the Centre for Human Rights of the University of Pretoria and the International Human Rights Program of the University of Toronto. March 2020. Available for download at www.ohchr.org/en

/documents/tools-and-resources/concept-note-elimination-harmful
-practices-related-witchcraft.

Upham, Charles W. *Salem Witchcraft*. Vol. 2. Boston: Wiggin and Lunt, 1867.

———. "Salem Witchcraft and Cotton Mather: A Reply." *The Historical Magazine*. Salem, MA: Henry B. Dawson, 1869; Project Gutenberg, 2008. https://www.gutenberg.org/files/26978/26978-h/26978-h.htm.

Waller, Richard D. "Witchcraft and Colonial Law in Kenya." *Past & Present*, no. 180 (August 2003): 241–75. https://www.jstor.org/stable/3600744.

Washburn, Emory. *Sketches of the Judicial History of Massachusetts from 1630 to the Revolution in 1775*. Boston: Charles C. Little and James Brown, 1840.

Wheeler, Ryan. "Cutshamache and Cochichawick." *Robert S. Peabody Institute of Archaeology* (blog). Phillips Academy Andover, May 13, 2021. https://peabody.andover.edu/2021/05/13/cutshamache-and-cochichawick/.

Whitney, Elspeth. "The Witch 'She'/The Historian 'He': Gender and the Historiography of the European Witch-Hunts." *Journal of Women's History* 7, no. 3 (Fall 1995): 77–101. https://doi.org/10.1353/jowh.2010.0511.

Wiesner, Merry E. *Working Women in Renaissance Germany*. New Brunswick, NJ: Rutgers University Press, 1952.

WikiTree. "Thomas Carrier (abt. 1626–1735)." Accessed February 17, 2023. https://www.wikitree.com/wiki/Carrier-2. Citing unavailable article by Pierre Comtois. "Billerica family's 323-Year Exile Ends." *Lowell Sun Newspaper*, March 16, 1999.

Winthrop, John. "A Model of Christian Charity." In *A Library of American Literature: Early Colonial Literature, 1607–1675*, edited by Edmund Clarence Stedman and Ellen Mackay Hutchinson. New York: C. L. Webster, 1888.

Wodu, Ada. "Suspected Mob Leader 'General Iron' Shot Dead in Cross River." *Punch Newspapers* (Nigeria), August 27, 2021. punchng.com/suspected-mob-leader-general-iron-shot-dead-in-cross-river/.

"Woman Burned Alive for 'Sorcery' in Papua New Guinea." BBC News. February 7, 2013. https://www.bbc.com/news/world-asia-21363894.

"Woman, 73, Tortured over Witchcraft Allegation." *Kathmandu Post,* November 18, 2018. kathmandupost.com/national/2018/11/19/woman-73-beaten-fed-feces-on-witchcraft-charges-in-dhading.

Yaa, Elias. "Kaya Godoma Marks 10th Year Hosting Elderly." *Star* (Kenya), January 20, 2020. https://www.the-star.co.ke/counties/coast/2020-01-20-kaya-godoma-marks-10th-year-hosting-elderly/.

About the Author

Alice Markham-Cantor is a writer and fact-checker from Brooklyn, New York. Her reported work has appeared in *New York Magazine*, *Scientific American*, *The Nation*, and elsewhere. She serves on the working committee of the International Network Against Accusations of Witchcraft and Associated Harmful Practices. This is her first book.

To Write to the Author

If you wish to contact the author or would like more information about this book, please write to the author in care of Llewellyn Worldwide Ltd. and we will forward your request. Both the author and publisher appreciate hearing from you and learning of your enjoyment of this book and how it has helped you. Llewellyn Worldwide Ltd. cannot guarantee that every letter written to the author can be answered, but all will be forwarded. Please write to:

Alice Markham-Cantor
℅ Llewellyn Worldwide
2143 Wooddale Drive
Woodbury, MN 55125-2989

Please enclose a self-addressed stamped envelope for reply,
or $1.00 to cover costs. If outside the U.S.A., enclose
an international postal reply coupon.

Many of Llewellyn's authors have websites with additional information and resources. For more information, please visit our website at http://www.llewellyn.com.